Reflections on Grief and Spiritual Growth

Edited by
Andrew J. Weaver
and
Howard W. Stone

ABINGDON PRESS
Nashville

REFLECTIONS ON GRIEF AND SPIRITUAL GROWTH

This book is printed on acid-free paper.

Library of Congress Cataloging-in-Publication Data

Reflections on grief and spiritual growth / Edited by Andrew J. Weaver and Howard W. Stone.
    p. cm.
    Includes bibliographical references.
    ISBN 0-687-06508-9 (pbk. : alk. paper)
    1. Grief—Religious aspects—Christianity.   2. Spiritual formation.   I. Weaver, Andrew J., 1947-   II. Stone, Howard W.

    BV4905.3.R44 2005
    248.8′6,—dc22

2004024647

05 06 07 08 09 10 11 12 13 14 – 10 9 8 7 6 5 4 3 2 1
MANUFACTURED IN THE UNITED STATES OF AMERICA

To Carolyn and Karen, with love

Contents

Acknowledgments

We are thankful to William H. Willimon, former Dean of the Chapel at Duke University and now United Methodist Bishop of the Birmingham Area for writing the foreword for this volume. A portion of the proceeds from this book will go to the United Methodist Committee on Relief for the AIDS Orphan Trust, a ministry in Africa.

We are also appreciative of the exceptional editing of the Reverend Carolyn L. Stapleton for her help in preparing the manuscript.

Foreword

William H. Willimon

We do "not grieve as others do who have no hope," says Paul (1 Thessalonians 4:13). Note that Christians *do* grieve. Discipleship does not grant us immunity from the pain of bereavement, the emptiness of loss, and all the pain that comes when a life of one whom we have loved is taken from us. In Christ we have a hope, but that hope does not negate grief. Rather, our hope in Christ helps put grief in its place.

Paul asks, "Where, O death, is your victory? Where, O death, is your sting?" (1 Corinthians 15:55). From where I sit just now, death seems mighty victorious. Nothing is more certain than the fact that you shall die. And if you will, then what about me? The church has told me that I have been made out of the earth and that every day, since my first day of life, I am being pulled inexorably back toward the earth from whence I came. That truth comes to me as something of a sting, no matter what Paul says. Here in my late fifties, I am getting perilously close to earth.

Then again, I am clergy, so I am in the business of death and dying. A research program was recently announced at Duke, at the gym, for "those with Type A personalities who had no previous exercise program." Of course my wife immediately enrolled me. This meant not only that for six months I had to get up in the morning and go sweat it out at the gym—lifting and pulling, huffing and puffing—but also that I was subjected, with the others, to lectures from a nutritionist who extolled the values of lentil casseroles and yogurt, wheat germ, and other nutritionally virtuous foods instead of red meat. The implication was that mortality is a premodern unpleasantness that enlightened, disciplined folk need not put up with.

Some mornings, as I am struggling on the treadmill or lifting weights and the nutritionist is bubbling excitedly about the glories of nonhydrogenated fat, I want to grab the microphone out of her hand and scream to my fellow exercisers, "Look, I'm clergy. I don't care what you eat or how much you work out, I'm going to get all of you in the end. You are all animals. Animals are created by God to grow up, grow old, and die! I, or somebody like me, will bury all of you!"

I am a preacher, the one who is periodically charged with standing up before a group of otherwise death-denying, lusting-for-immortality, fantasy-devising early twenty-first-century Americans and telling them, "By the way, all of this ends at the cemetery."

Yet that is not all I am charged with telling them. The challenge is to think about our dying, all of the big and little losses, all of the deaths along the way, in a specifically, peculiarly Christian way. The challenge is not only to grieve, but also to grieve as those who have a hope.

A while back, I read a study of persons who were suffering from "pathological grief," those who had lost someone they loved and who, months later, were having great difficulty functioning. Pathological grief was defined as grief that goes on without end.

I was surprised that the study said the one theme running through the stories of those suffering from pathological grief was this: in one way or another, nearly all of these people had missed the funeral of the person for whom they were grieving. For some it was because of an automobile accident, which left them laid up in the hospital recovering, and the decision was made to go ahead and have the funeral without them. For others, they were too far away to attend the service. Something happens at the funeral, said the commentator, that enables many people to go on. That "something" at the funeral, the researchers said, was the "confrontation with the reality of death." Death has a sting that must be felt, must be acknowledged, or the grief will get to you.

As somebody who presides at funerals, I think it is absolutely important for people to be at them and for funerals to be a time when we all confront the reality of death. But perhaps we could say that it is not only important to confront "the reality of death," but also crucial that we confront the reality of resurrection—God's great defeat of death in the resurrection of Jesus. Christians are those who make the wildly outrageous claim that God not only raised a crucified and dead Jesus, but also shall one day, somehow, some way, take us along toward life as well. We shall be raised.

The theological challenge is always, at the time of death, to keep cross and resurrection together, honesty and hope in tension. I do not know which side of the gospel equation is the more difficult—cross or resurrection. I once thought that it was the easiest thing in the world to preach on Good Friday. After all, nearly everyone knows that the good get it in the end, you "can't fight City Hall," injustice is stronger than justice, and death always wins; just pick up this morning's paper and you can believe in Good Friday.

I thought Easter was the greater challenge for the preacher. How, with so much accumulated evidence to the contrary, do we still sing that God triumphs, that life is stronger than death, that love conquers all, and that as Jesus was raised, so shall we be raised? That is a tough assignment for a sermon.

Yet now, at least today, I wonder if a greater challenge is to convince a group of pagans drunk on fantasies of their own immortality that their unavoidable, and final. How do you convince folk who think they may be gods unto themselves that if there is not a God who loves to raise the dead, then they are without hope?

I do not know.

The good news is that this book is full of those who do know how to preach cross and resurrection, teachers who are not numbed into silence in the face of even the worst of our dying, who when asked by the grieving and the dying, "Is there any word from God?" have a sure word of hope that manages to be both realistic and expectant at the same time.

I would say that preaching about death is just about the greatest homiletical challenge I know. As a young preacher in my little church, I was faced with the death of a four-year-old child who had been killed in an accident. I had to stand up two days later and say something on behalf of God to a church so filled with anger and hurt that you could hardly breathe. At that time, I wondered if I really wanted to be God's spokesperson or not.

Fortunately, as Paul says, we do not grieve as those who have no hope. In fact, our hope enables us to grieve as honestly as anybody. Yet our grief testifies to the reality of our hope. Andrew Weaver and Howard Stone have given us some wise, wonderful counselors in their collection of reflections on grief. I particularly like the way in which grief is presented here as an opportunity for spiritual growth. In the eyes of faith, even something so painful as grief may be seen as a kind of gift or an invitation to live life more deeply, to experience God's love more intensely than ever before.

The voices in this collection beckon us to look at and to think about something that most of us, even we clergy, spend much effort avoiding. These testimonies are proof that, when placed in the hands of a loving God, even something so fearful and painful as death can be a source of growth, a means of drawing us closer toward the heart of God.

William H. Willimon
Duke University Chapel
Holy Week, 2004

Contributors

Herbert Anderson is Professor Emeritus of Pastoral Theology at Catholic Theological Union, in Chicago, Illinois. Dr. Anderson is currently Director of Pastoral Care at St. Mark's Episcopal Cathedral in Seattle, Washington. He is a Lutheran pastor, husband, grandfather, and author of numerous articles and books on grief and the family, including: *Becoming Married* (Westminster John Knox Press, 1993), *Regarding Children: A New Respect for Childhood and Families* (Westminster John Knox Press, 1994), *Jacob's Shadow: Christian Perspectives on Masculinity* (Bridge Resources, 2002), and *All Our Losses, All Our Griefs* (Westminster John Knox Press, 1983), widely regarded as a classic in grief literature.

Paschal Baumstein is a Benedictine monk and Catholic priest at Belmont Abbey in Belmont, North Carolina. Working primarily in the field of Intellectual History, he has published about seven dozen essays and other texts, as well as over one hundred reviews. His recent projects include serving on the Advisory Board of the new *Encyclopedia of Monasticism,* as well as contributing several entries. At present, he is writing a study of the thought of Anselm of Canterbury (eleventh through twelfth centuries).

Duane R. Bidwell is director of the Pastoral Care and Training Center at Brite Divinity School, Texas Christian University, in Fort Worth. He is also the author of *Brief Spiritual Direction* (Fortress Press, 2004). In addition to teaching pastoral care and counseling, Duane is an ordained minister of the Presbyterian Church (USA) and serves as pastor of First Presbyterian Church, Bridgeport, Texas. He has worked as a pastoral counselor, spiritual director, and chaplain in a variety of settings. In the early 1990s, he served as executive director of an interfaith HIV/AIDS ministry, where he first engaged the relationships between spirituality and grief. He received a Ph.D. from Brite Divinity School and a licentiate in spiritual theology and spiritual direction from the Anglican School of Theology at the University of Dallas. Duane lives in Fort Worth with his wife and son.

Mary Louise Bringle is professor of philosophy and religion and chair of the Humanities Division at Brevard College in Brevard, North Carolina. She received her Ph.D. from the Graduate Division of Religion at Emory University, with a particular interest in practical and pastoral theology. Her scholarly publications focus on bridging the disciplines of theology and psychology in a contemporary approach to the seven deadly sins, including: *Despair: Sickness or Sin?* (Abingdon Press, 1990) and *The God of Thinness: Gluttony and Other Weighty Matters* (Abingdon Press, 1992). She has served as a consultant on eating disorders for the Office of Health Ministries of the Presbyterian Church (USA). She also was recognized by The Hymn Society in 2002 as "the emerging hymn text writer of the US and Canada," for her recent first single-author collection of hymns, *Joy and Wonder, Love and Longing* (GIA Publications, 2004).

Joseph R. Jeter, Jr. is the Granville and Erline Walker Professor of Homiletics and Director of the Ph.D. Program at Brite Divinity School, Texas Christian University in Fort Worth, Texas. He is also a traveling preacher, stamp collector, and rescuer of stray and abused cats. He holds degrees from Texas Christian University, Union Theological Seminary in New York, and Claremont Graduate School. Married to a school administrator, he is the father of one son, who is currently a seminary student. His recent books include: *Preaching Judges* (Chalice Press, 2003), *One Gospel, Many Ears* with Ronald Allen (Chalice Press, 2002), *Crisis Preaching: Personal and Public* (Abingdon Press, 1998), and *Re/Membering: Meditations and Sermons for the Table of Jesus Christ* (Chalice Press, 1996). His current research involves the history of preaching, especially the proclamation of women.

Charles Merrick has served over fifty years as a funeral director. He retired from Service Corporation International in 1999 after serving in various management capacities in Arizona, California, Hawaii, and Texas. After retirement, he started his own consulting service in the cemetery and funeral business. Chuck and his wife, Beatrice, have three children and six grandchildren.

Donald E. Messer serves as Henry White Warren Professor of Practical Theology and President Emeritus of The Iliff School of Theology, Denver, Colorado. He previously served as president of Iliff for nineteen years and president of Dakota Wesleyan University for ten years. In addition to teaching and writing, he directs the Iliff Center for Global Pastoral Ministry. A high priority of the Center is to engage the church constructively in the struggle against global HIV/AIDS. Speaking and leading workshops has taken him to more than thirty countries around the world. The most recent of his nine books include: *Contemporary Images of Christian Ministry, A Conspiracy of Goodness* (Abingdon Press, 1989), and *Caught in the Crossfire: Helping Christians Debate Homosexuality* with Sally B. Geis (Abingdon Press, 1994). His upcoming book, *Breaking the Conspiracy of Silence: Christian Churches and the Global AIDS Crisis* (Augsburg Fortress Press, 2004), will focus on the church and global AIDS.

Rebecca L. Miles is associate professor of ethics at Perkins School of Theology, Southern Methodist University. Her recent books include: *The Pastor as Moral Guide* (Fortress Press, 2000) and *Bonds of Freedom: Feminist Theology and Christian Realism* (Oxford University Press, 2001). Miles is one of seven scholars nationwide named as a Henry Luce III Fellow in Theology for 2003–2004. As a Luce Fellow, she is writing a book entitled *Good Kids, Good Society, Good God: Theological and Ethical Reflections on Raising Moral Children*. She is also currently finishing a book on work and vocation that explores the ways American workers balance the competing demands of work, home, and community. Her interest in balancing work in and outside of the home and on raising moral children emerges from her own experience as the mother of two preschool-age daughters. Miles, also a United Methodist clergywoman, was elected as a delegate to the United Methodist General Conference in 2004.

Bonnie J. Miller-McLemore is Professor of Pastoral Theology at Vanderbilt University in Nashville, Tennessee. After receiving her Ph.D. in Religion at the University of Chicago, she began teaching at Chicago Theological Seminary in 1986 and joined the faculty at Vanderbilt University Divinity School in 1995. Her books and articles addressing major cultural issues include: *Death, Sin, and the Moral Life: Contemporary Cultural Interpretations of Death* (American Academy of Religion, 1988) and *Also a Mother: Work and Family as Theological Dilemma* (Abingdon Press, 1994). A recipient of a distinguished Henry Luce III Fellow in Theology grant in 1999–2000, she recently completed another book entitled *Let the Children Come: Reimagining Childhood from a Christian Perspective* (Jossey-Bass, 2003) and is currently working on a related book, *Forming Family: Care of Children as a Religious Practice*. Ordained in the Christian Church (Disciples of Christ) in 1984, she has served in various capacities as associate pastor, chaplain, and pastoral counselor. Married for twenty-three years, she is proud of and perhaps most happily shaped by her three growing sons—now twelve, fourteen, and seventeen years old.

R. Esteban Montilla is an ordained minister, pastoral counselor, and educator known for his capacity to integrate Scripture and psychology at both theoretical and practical levels. Chaplain Montilla is a pioneer in creating and fostering pastoral care and counseling programs in several Latin American countries. He is a certified Clinical Pastoral Education Supervisor and Diplomate with the College of Pastoral Supervision and Psychotherapy. He is a professional member of the American Counseling Association and of the International Association of Marriage and Family Counselors. He is the author of *Viviendo la Tercera Edad*, a book on ministry with older adults that integrates biological, psychological, sociological, and theological aspects of aging. Chaplain Montilla served for five years as a chaplain for VistaCare Family Hospice and Harvest Senior Services. He is currently working as CPE Supervisor for Driscoll Children's Hospital in Corpus Christi, Texas, and the Ecumenical Center for Religion and Health in San Antonio, Texas.

M. Basil Pennington entered the Cistercian Order in 1951 after graduating from Cathedral College of the Immaculate Conception. After his ordination in 1957, he spent several years in Rome gaining a S.T.L. (Licentiate in Sacred Theology) and a J.C.L (Licentiate in Canon Law). He assisted at the Second Vatican Council as a *peritus* (advocate) and in the preparation of the new Code of Canon Law. He started Cistercian Publications in 1968 with Thomas Merton and founded the Institute of Cistercian Studies at Western Michigan University in 1973. He became known internationally through his efforts to help the Catholic Church rediscover its contemplative dimension through the Centering Prayer Movement. In 1983, in collaboration with leaders from other churches and the synagogue, he formed the Mastery Foundation to empower those whose lives are centered on sacred ministry. From 1986 to 1989 he served at Assumption Abbey in Missouri. Then, in 1991, he went to Lantao to help his Chinese brethren at Our Lady of Joy Monastery, where he served until 1998, while continuing his worldwide ministry in Centering Prayer. He has published over fifty books and almost one thousand articles in various languages. His most recent publications are *Lectio Divina: Renewing the Ancient Practice of Praying the Scriptures* (Crossroad Publishing, 1998) and *A Place Apart: Monastic Prayer and Practice for Everyone* (Ligouri, 1998).

Donna Schaper is the Senior Pastor of Coral Gables Congregational Church in Miami, Florida. She is the author of twenty-two volumes, and her most recent books are *Sacred Speech: A Practical Guide for Keeping Spirit in Your Speech* (SkyLight Paths, 2003) and *Mature Grief: When a Parent Dies* (Cowley Publications, 2002). Her avocational interests are gardening, humor, and writing. At her funeral, she hopes people will sing, "My Lord, What a Morning."

Donald J. Shelby retired in 1998 after forty-five years of active ministry in The United Methodist Church in Southern California. For the last twenty-five years of his ministry, he served as senior pastor of First United Methodist Church in

Santa Monica. He is the author of four books, including: *Meeting the Messiah* (Upper Room, 1980), *Bold Expectations of the Gospel* (Abingdon Press, 1983), *Forever Beginning: Exploration of the Faith for New Believers* (Upper Room, 1987), and *The Unsettling Season* (Upper Room, 1989). One missional objective of the Santa Monica congregation during his last decade of ministry resulted in the construction of affordable housing for seniors and homeless families in transition, built on the church's parking lots above an underground parking facility. He and his wife, Jean, now reside in Los Osos, California, which is located halfway between their two daughters, sons-in-law, and six grandchildren.

Karen Stone is an artist and art educator. She has shown her work in local, national, and international exhibitions and has artworks in over thirty private and public collections. She received her Master of Fine Arts degree from Arizona State University. At present, she is adjunct professor of art at the University of Texas at Arlington and art specialist for the Fort Worth schools. Her most recent book is *Image and Spirit: Finding Meaning in Visual Art* (Augsburg Books, 2003). She has presented workshops on the subject of art and spirituality in the United States, South America, Africa, and Great Britain. She lives with Howard, her husband of over forty years, and enjoys her daughter, son-in-law, and two granddaughters.

David K. Switzer is Emeritus Professor of Pastoral Care and Counseling at Perkins School of Theology, Southern Methodist University. His books include: *The Dynamics of Grief* (Abingdon Press, 1970), *The Minister as Crisis Counselor* (Abingdon Press, revised 1986), *Coming Out as Parents: Parents of Gays and Lesbians* (Westminster John Knox Press, revised 1996), *Pastoral Care of Gays, Lesbians, and Their Families* (Fortress Press, 2000), and *Pastoral Care Emergencies* (Fortress Press, 2001). He served as a pastor in two churches, a college chaplain, and Minister of Pastoral Care and Counseling at First Methodist Church in Pasadena, California, before finally retiring from Perkins in 1993 (first as Associate Dean for Academics, then as Professor of Pastoral Care and Counseling).

James M. Wall served from 1972 through 1999 as editor and publisher of the magazine *Christian Century,* a publication that deals with religion and society, based in Chicago, Illinois. He is now Senior Contributing Editor of *Christian Century,* where he writes a regular column and is an advisor to the editor. Wall, a United Methodist clergyman, is also president of ForChildren, a group that works with nonprofit organizations in developing countries to assist them in meeting United Nation standards for children in the areas of health, education, and welfare. His most recent book is *Hidden Treasures: Searching for God in Modern Culture*, published by Christian Century Foundation (1997).

Halbert Weidner is a priest of the Oratory of Saint Philip Neri. During his years of ministry, he has served as a parish priest, campus minister, and retreat guide in both South Carolina and Hawaii. He holds degrees from Catholic University, Graduate Theological Union, and Oxford University. He edited and introduced John Henry Newman's *The Via Media*, the first of the Anglican works to be published in Oxford University Press's uniform editions of Newman. His other work includes: *Praying with John Cardinal Newman* (St. Mary's Press, 1997), *Hidden Light: Paths to Meditation* (Ka'imi Pono Press, 2002), and *Island Affirmations: If These Islands Exist, What Else Is Possible?* (Ka'imi Pono Press, 2003). He has published essays and reviews in various Catholic and ecumenical journals. He is currently a pastor and is founding a house of the Oratory in Hawaii.

Susan J. White is the Harold L. and Alberta H. Lunger Professor of Spiritual Resources and Disciplines at Brite Divinity School, Texas Christian University. Her recent books include: *Spirit of Worship* (Orbis Press, 2000), *Christian Worship and Technological Change* (Abingdon Press, 1997), and *A Great Commission: Christian Hope and Religious Diversity* (Peter Lang, 2000).

William H. Willimon was Dean of the Chapel and Professor of Christian Ministry at Duke University in Durham, North Carolina, through August 2004. Dr. Willimon directed the programs of campus ministry at Duke and taught in the divinity and undergraduate schools. Since September 1, 2004, he is serving as the United Methodist Bishop of the Birmingham Area, which includes the North Alabama Conference. He has given lectures at colleges and universities throughout the United States, Europe, and Asia. He is the author of more than forty books. His most recent book is *Pastor: The Theology and Practice of Ordained Ministry*, published by Abingdon Press (2002). Bishop Willimon has earned degrees from Wofford College, Yale University, and Emory University. Six colleges and universities have awarded him honorary degrees.

Introduction: The Effects of Loss Linger

Andrew J. Weaver and Howard W. Stone

A friend tells of sitting in his living room, when he heard a loud thud at the window. He stood up to see what had happened. There on the deck below the window lay a female goldfinch on its side, breathing hard, one wing oddly extended and its head twisted. In a matter of moments it lay still.

Death flies into our lives. Usually it is not quiet or mild mannered; sometimes it crashes into us. Unlike the passing of a poor goldfinch, when a human dies, the effects linger. It cannot be swept away or tossed over the bank. It stays around.

The Scriptures tell us that loss and grief are universal human experiences, and the process of mourning is often prolonged, painful, and emotionally complex. The writer of Ecclesiastes reminds us that grief comes to all of us: there is "a time to weep, and a time to laugh; a time to mourn, and a time to dance" (Ecclesiastes 3:4). In the Letter to the Romans, we are instructed to "mourn with the mourners" (Romans 12:15 NEB). In Christ's parable of the prodigal, the father is grieved over his wayward son (Luke 15:24). Hannah suffered a deep and lasting sorrow because of her infertility (1 Samuel 1:15). John's Gospel speaks of Jesus grieving deeply over the loss of Lazarus. "Jesus wept," and those around him saw his tears as a clear sign that Jesus had lost a close friend: "See, how much he loved him" (John 11:35-36). But there were also emotions other than sorrow. In front of the tomb of Lazarus, Jesus was "deeply moved in spirit and troubled" (John 11:33, 38 RSV). The Greek word for "troubled" implies sadness, distress, and even anger.

Annually, over 2.4 million people die in the United States (U.S. Bureau of the Census, 2000). There are over 800,000 new widows and widowers each year. Other losses triggering grief include divorce, separation, retirement, miscarriage, sudden job loss, as well as a serious illness (such as Alzheimer's disease) that results in the loss of a *person* long before physical death occurs (Stone, 1994; Weaver, Flannelly, and Preston, 2003).

For every individual who dies or departs mentally, many are left behind to grieve. Millions of these sorrowing people seek spiritual guidance for dealing with their loss. Religious faith can help us deal with the death of a loved one. Several studies in diverse populations have shown a positive relationship between religious involvement and a successful coping to the loss of a family member or close friend. For example, in a study of 312 adults in Buffalo, New York, 77 percent said that their religious beliefs helped considerably in their response to death and in their grief (Frantz, Trolley, and Johll, 1996). Researchers in California (Davis, Nolen-Hocksema, and Larson, 1998) and Great Britain (Walsh et al., 2002) studied individuals grieving the death of a family member or very close friend. They discovered that there is a strong link between positive psychological adjustment to a death and one's ability to make sense of the loss through one's faith and religious practices. Religious faith helps those who are mourning make sense of the death and the experience of mourning.

For *Reflections on Grief and Spiritual Growth,* we invited various writers to reflect on the effect of loss on their lives and their faith. We asked them to consider these questions: How did death change you? What happened to you and your spiritual life when death visited you and your family? What lessons and wisdom can be shared about your personal experiences with grief? In what ways did these losses shape your life? What counsel does our Christian heritage offer as we grieve the loss of a parent, spouse, child, marriage, job, or health? How has mourning diminished or deepened your faith? Have spiritual resources been helpful in addressing the anger, guilt, and depression that is often a part of the grieving process? Have you experienced spiritual growth or transformation from these losses? How has faith been an asset as you face the increasing and cumulative losses of growing older?

You may have read these authors before. Their writings on such diverse topics as theology, ethics, art and spirituality, Scripture, worship, and pastoral care have already contributed greatly to the life of the Christian community. You may have read one of them debate the nuance of a Greek verb, discuss the ethics of genetic cloning, explore the value of prayer, analyze the design of a sermon, consider the theology of a contemporary topic, or write about one of the giants in the history of Christian spirituality.

Now you will see these writers in a different light. They are reflective and personal, wise, and full of passion and beauty. We got more than we asked for, and you are the benefactors. These authors offer original and insightful lessons about the changes and challenges of grieving. They have been very generous in sharing their experiences of grief and loss. The results are truly a blessing.

What is the effect of death—and its companion, grief—on your life? Whether it came quietly or stormed in, it surely made its presence known. You knew it had happened.

Each author has a different view of death or loss and its effect on his or her faith and life. You will have much to reflect upon as you consider what loss has meant for you and how grief has affected your own life. In fact, that is why we put together this book. We hope for a three-way conversation among your own experiences of loss and grief, your faith and relationship to God, and the experiences of these authors as they try to make sense of grief in the context of their faith.

References

Davis, C. G., Nolen-Hocksema, S., and Larson, J. (1998). Making sense of loss and benefiting from the experience: Two construals of meaning. *Journal of Personality and Social Psychology, 75(2),* 561-574.

Frantz, T. T., Trolley, B. C., and Johll, M. P. (1996). Religious aspects of bereavement. *Pastoral Psychology, 44(3),* 151-163.

Stone, H. W. (1994). *Crisis Counseling.* Minneapolis: Augsburg Fortress.

Walsh, K., King, M., Jones, L., Tookman, A., and Blizard, R. (2002). Spiritual beliefs may affect outcome of bereavement: Prospective study. *British Medical Journal, 324,* 1551-1554.

Weaver, A. J., Flannelly, L. T., and Preston, J. D. (2003). *Counseling Survivors of Traumatic Events: A Handbook for Pastors and Other Helping Professionals.* Nashville: Abingdon Press.

U.S. Bureau of the Census (2000). S*tatistical Abstract of the United States: 2000.* Washington, DC: U.S. Bureau of the Census.

Moments of Loss, Seasons of Grief

Herbert Anderson

When I was five, I had rheumatic fever and did not walk for six months. Although I have no memory of this life-threatening illness, it has shaped the way I live and what I believe. Until I graduated from high school, my parents kept the medication that they believed to have saved my life in the lower left corner of the refrigerator. For me, it was not a symbol of the gift of life, but rather a sign of human fragility and death. The fear of death became my constant companion, even though the rest of my life has been without tragic loss.

My parents died after a full life. The losses I have experienced have been only common disappointments. Some of those losses, however, have generated a deep, lingering sadness. I have learned from my ordinary, even predictable losses that: (1) it is impossible to live and love without loss, and (2) suffering because of a loss is always in the eyes of the beholder. Sometimes, for me, these ordinary losses are intensified by a persistent anxiety about death that is not diminished by the promises of God's care.

Both my paternal grandfather and my mother taught me lessons about grief that I had to unlearn. My father's mother died in 1905 shortly after her third child was born on the barren plains of North Dakota, leaving my grandfather to raise three children under the age of four. He never recovered from the loss of his wife, Emelia, and he never married again. His grief was compounded because Emelia's relatives in Sweden never forgave my grandfather for taking her away from her home to such a harsh land. For all the years I knew my grandfather, he was a gentle but sad man. Neither he nor my father ever spoke of their grief. I kept my early sadness to myself as well. It was a long time before I trusted people with my sadness or vulnerability. I was probably still learning the art of grieving when I began teaching about it in seminary. Learning to acknowledge my vulnerability turned out to be important preparation for the diagnosis of prostate cancer in 1999. Having prostate cancer was an experience of loss that challenged me to understand that power and vulnerability are not mutually exclusive in human life. I discovered what it means to be sustained by Christian communities of prayer and love.

Grief is more than an individual matter. Human systems, such as families, congregations, or even our nation as a whole, also grieve. Families that are unable to mourn their losses may develop patterns of denial or secret-keeping that last generations. In her family, my mother bore most of the grief for losses that were hidden and for shameful grief that was never expressed. The legacy of secrecy around loss I received from my mother's family made my early sadness about ordinary losses difficult to share. The extended family on my mother's side continues to suffer because of secret grief that is over a hundred years old. On the one hand, the inability to grieve our losses can negatively affect both individuals and human systems, like families, for generations. On the other hand, families that can grieve together are more likely to stay together and create communities in which both individual and common grief can be shared in ways that make healing possible.

In her book *Necessary Losses,* Judith Viorst makes a claim that I believe is true. The people we are, she says, and the ways we live are determined by our experiences of loss. The same could be said for our spirituality. What we believe about God or the character of human nature and how we live as people of faith is shaped not only by our experiences of loss, but also by the way we respond to those losses and live through them. In turn, how we respond to loss is influenced by a host of factors including religious formation, family experience of loss, gender, and dominant ethnic or cultural factors. With this in mind, I would reframe Viorst this way: the people we are and the ways we live are determined by our losses and by our beliefs which, in turn, *influence our interpretation of our losses.* For the remainder of this essay, I will examine some of the Christian beliefs that have sustained me through moments of loss and seasons of grief.

Human beings are relational creatures, attaching ourselves to people and things that are, at the same time, finite. This combination of attachment and finitude is the occasion for grief. Finitude is a shorthand way of speaking about the limitedness of everything. The fundamental human dilemma is that we are limited creatures who know that we will die. The fundamental human longing is that we might keep the unity we had before birth forever. Some years ago, my wife remembered the German word *ewigkeit* (forevermore) from the Lord's Prayer and used it to ask in her halting German if a wooden tray she wanted to buy had been treated to make it last. The German clerk replied rather brusquely, *"Nichts ewigkeit"* (nothing is forever). The clerk was right, of course. Only God is forever. *Finitude and death are part of the creation that God declared good.* But when our job, primary relationship, or vacation is pleasurable, we like to think it will never end. Therefore, it is not surprising that we struggle with being finite creatures. To be finite and limited temporally is no more problematic than to be finite and limited physically. And yet, when death occurs prematurely or when we are confronted with unexpected and inconvenient limits, it is difficult to acknowledge that finitude is generally a good thing. Even if we believe death is part of God's plan, we will rage at death when it is experienced as a thief that robs us of people we love. Jesus' acceptance of his death teaches us how to grieve loss, embrace others in our sorrow, and then accept God's love as the guarantor that death is not the final ending.

"Attachment" describes the inclination of all humans to form strong bonds of affection with people and things. Some people seek to limit their attachments because it is too painful to lose what they love. Some kinds of Christian spirituality support the conviction that we should limit our attachments because "this world is not our home." If, however, we limit our attachments in order to diminish our grief, we also may end up fleeing from the fullness of life to avoid the pain of loss. On the other side, there are people who seek to avoid grief by holding on to everything they love or value. Their lives are often diminished by the desire to preserve predictable life patterns and relationships or are immobilized by accumulated clutter and treasured relics. The human task is to love, knowing that we will eventually lose what we love. *Grief is an inevitable dimension of living because loss is an inescapable part of human life in its fullness. In loving, grieving begins.*

Understanding the pervasiveness of loss gives us opportunities for learning how to grieve and prepare for death from the beginning of life. In the process of writing the book *All Our Losses, All Our Griefs,* Kenneth Mitchell and I gathered more than a thousand vignettes about loss unrelated to the death of a person. From those stories, we developed a typology of loss that included the loss of material, the loss of role, the loss of physical functions, and the loss of dreams, as well as the loss of a beloved person. Our intent was to make loss a common dimension of living and to legitimate grief for losses other than death. *Understood this way, the human journey is an ongoing struggle with the perpetually perishing in life.* Therefore, the pains of grief are an inevitable part of finite living. The belief that suffering is a consequence of loving fully and living faithfully is embodied most clearly for me in the Christian symbol of the cross. If we hold on to life, we lose it: we find life by letting it go. Learning how to grieve is prelude to embracing this paradox at the center of Christian spirituality.

I am indebted to Ernest Becker for what he taught me about finitude. His book, *The Denial of Death,* challenged me to acknowledge finitude and then live creatively with the anxiety that comes from knowing that I will die. Becker's thought has also pressed me to think about the relationship between sin and death in a new way. As a slight variation on the Pauline perspective but in the spirit of Becker, I would articulate the relationship this way: "wages of death is sin." That is to say, we sin because we don't like limits and can't stand finitude. In order to deny my death, I am more likely to act in destructive ways that dominate or violate others. Whenever I have become aware of persisting patterns of negative behavior in my life, sooner or later I can connect it to a need to feel bigger than I am or less vulnerable to ordinary limits. It is therefore a moral mandate to live with the terror that death creates while celebrating the goodness of a finite creation.

Because we are finite creatures, we are vulnerable to suffering as well as to death. The courage to affirm and accept suffering as an element of finitude, in spite of the pain that accompanies it, is one mark of Christian spirituality. That is, of course, easier said than done. If we are intent on avoiding pain or discomfort, then finitude is always a problem and death is a permanent enemy. Living through grief takes courage because we are invited to bear the pain and intense sadness that accompanies significant loss. Consolation and comfort are to be found, Henri Nouwen observed in *A Letter of Consolation*, where our wounds hurt most. It takes courage to embrace suffering as an inevitable consequence of finitude. *The great danger is that we will flee from life and the risks of loving in order to avoid sorrow and grief.*

I believe finitude is a good thing despite the suffering it creates. Finitude makes judgment possible by rounding off a life or bringing an experience to an end. The boundary of death or any ending establishes the distinct shape and character of our lives. After the event is over, after an activity has ended, there is a kind of completeness that makes it possible for us to evaluate its meaning or significance. I sometimes wonder whether people may not fear incompleteness more than they fear death. If that is true, it is understandable that the judgment finitude makes possible strikes terror in the souls of those who feel they have failed to achieve what God or their family expected of them. For those who fear judgment, the awareness of finitude can be a gracious word. All of our achievements are limited, but so are our failures. If we could be perfect, even our perfection would be finite. We are therefore free to live and love in the confidence that God, who ordained finitude, will accept our limited completeness.

Listening to grieving people has challenged me to reexamine some of my core theological convictions. I had to rethink one of my favorite images of sin—*incurvatus in se* (turned in on oneself)—because, by definition, people who grieve are self-centered. *Grief is selfish. If selfishness is sin, then is grief sinful?* Grieving persons are preoccupied with their own loss, emotions, and survival. This response is necessary and appropriate. Grieving people are even possessive of their grief, especially when well-meaning friends and relatives want to take the pain from them prematurely. When we have lost someone or something we love, the grief we feel may be all we have left. Honoring the necessary selfishness of grief will make it possible for people to hold on to their grief, the closest connection they have to the lost person, until it is time to let go of the grief and hold on to a memory. When my mother died, I did not want to hear about others whose mothers had died. *My* mother had died. Efforts to diminish selfishness by generalizing very particular grief are not only theologically indefensible, but also psychologically hurtful.

Grief is immoderate or excessive. In his letters of spiritual counsel to a variety of people who were experiencing grief, Martin Luther was consistent: it is appropriate for us to grieve the loss of someone we love—but not too much. Because we are not made of stone, we will mourn for our losses. Otherwise it would appear that we had no love. But our grief, Luther insisted, must be moderate because it cannot be compared to the sufferings of Christ. Efforts to moderate grief, even for religious reasons, usually have negative consequences. Because if excess of grief is often disturbing, especially for people who have worked hard to be in control of their destiny, those who care for the bereaved need to be accepting of the excessive, irrational character of grief.

People also grieve differently because of ethnic traditions. An Italian wake is more excessive than a Norwegian Lutheran funeral. Some people fear the excessiveness of grief because they do not want to be out of control. The cultural pluralism in the United States presents us with a new challenge to honor radically different views of death and diverse modes of grieving.

The human creature is communal by nature. For that reason, when I lose someone or even something that I value, there is a hole in my soul. All loss is self-depleting. If the fullness of my self depended on the role that was lost or the relationship that ended, *grief would be self-depleting.* People will use words such as *emptiness* or *impoverishment* to describe this dimension of grief. If we are apprehensive about that emptiness in our grief, we may be tempted to fill it up quickly in hopes that the pain will go away. People in grief need to preserve the emptiness because it keeps the bond with the person whom they have lost, even at the cost of pain. Although God's promised presence sustains us through grief, it does not and should not fill the emptiness.

Our presence with those who mourn mirrors God's presence. If we isolate mourners, we intensify their personal impoverishment. In order to live with the pain of emptiness, grieving people need friends and caregivers who will stay close by but not try to fill the emptiness until healing covers it with enough scars to enable a person to hope again.

The *unpredictability of grief* is more psychologically unsettling than theologically challenging. It is unsettling because we cannot always anticipate when or where we will be surprised by tears or unexpected sadness. I was reminded of the unpredictability of grief years after my father's death. My wife and I celebrated our twenty-fifth wedding anniversary by going to a performance of *Les Miserables* in the elegant Chicago Theater. At the conclusion of the musical when the father, Jean Valjean, sings a blessing to his daughter, Cossette, and her lover, Mario, I began to sob uncontrollably. It did not take me long to connect my tears with hearing my father's voice for the first time in four years when we played a tape of our wedding at breakfast that morning. I was crying for my father. But even more, I was crying for a blessing I had never received. It was still a deep hole in my life. We may grieve at unexpected times and in surprising places. This unpredictability adds to the complexity of grief because we cannot always be sure that what we think we are grieving for is actually what we are grieving about.

Recent experiences of violent death have made us aware that how people grieve is determined not only by the intensity and complexity of the relationship to the lost person or object, *but also by the way the person died.* All death evokes a sense of helplessness. A violent death intensifies the feeling of being helpless. Even if we understand death as part of life and believe that death, however it occurs, cannot separate us from God, our ordered view of the world is shattered when someone dies a violent death. Healing the grief of violent death must include rehearsing the painful memory of the death in order to fashion a new, restorative narrative. When death is violent, we are also reminded in painful ways that we do not have life as a possession. If we believe that life is something we possess, then any death is a destructive rupture, a blow to faith, a thief in the night. Violent death challenges our presumptions of invulnerability and undermines our effort to possess life or control our destiny.

The work of grieving happens between remembering and hoping, between building a treasured memory and anticipating a new future. Grief often gets stuck when mourners are unable to explore those wounds that hurt the most. Hope for the future is stymied when we cannot unlock painful memories. It is the hard work of grieving that makes newness of hope possible. Without hope, we are slow to remember. The New Testament scholar, J. Christiaan Beker, helped me understand the close connection between grieving and hoping in a book called *Suffering and Hope.* If we divorce hope from grief and suffering, we may become victims of illusions that create images of false hope. If, however, we divorce suffering from hope, then we may succumb to cynicism and despair and relinquish hope completely. In order to find hope again that will heal hearts broken by tragic loss, we need to fashion a cherishable memory, practice ritual lament, and discover the promise of God that transcends death.

People need hope in order to grieve. Sometimes they may need to borrow hope for a while from a friend. The bereaved may also find hope in story and song, in the gentle touch of those who listen to our pain, in the empathic words that confirm our grief and validate our grieving. When we overlook the pains of grief or offer premature assurance that everything will be all right, the griever is not validated and hopes are dashed. C. S. Lewis was very clear about pious religious words in *A Grief Observed*. "Don't talk to me about the consolations of religion," he said, "or I shall suspect that you do not understand." The promise of life forever in the care of God may diminish our worries about the well-being of the person who has died, but we still grieve the loss of his or her presence. When we grieve, someone has to hear our words and respond in a way that confirms the story we need to tell and the feelings we want to express. In this sense, hope is not something we possess, but something we discover in the empathic listening of friends and family.

Finding hope again after suffering a tragic loss is an experience of mutuality rather than a solitary process. It comes from "hoping *with*" someone more than "hoping *for*" something. The mutuality of consolation transforms the dread of abandonment and the terror of isolation into communities of hope. Whenever we decide not to speak the truth to dying people so they "do not lose hope," we in fact diminish hope by limiting their possibility of "hoping with" those they love. It is that same kind of mutuality that helps those who grieve hope again as they fashion a cherishable memory.

We learn to hope again through *ritual lamentation*. We live in a time in which it is easy to become apathetic because we feel so powerless in the face of so much irrational suffering. When we say "nothing matters," we shut ourselves off from the world's suffering, or from our own, and "die" before we are dead. Because apathy is such a tempting alternative, learning how to grieve and lament is a necessary prelude to living today. We are not powerless in the face of suffering. We can lament. The recovery of the biblical tradition of lament is a necessary counter to the temptation of apathy and a resource for expressing the anguish of grief. The prophet Jeremiah urges the mourning women to raise a dirge and teach it to their daughters and neighbors (Jeremiah 9:20). Authentic rituals provide the occasion, the language, and the gestures that help people encounter realities and truths that most of us would otherwise avoid. Lament transforms mute pain into a story that can be shared. The *recovery of rituals of lament* that provide an environment in which the deepest pains of grief can find expression builds supportive communities for those who are suffering.

When I was a junior at Gustavus Adolphus College, Fr. Martin Jerret-Kerr, an Anglican monk from South Africa, was visiting professor of religion and literature. He had written a book that had a profound effect on me, entitled *When You're Dead, You're Dead*. It was the first challenge to my childhood convictions about the immortality of the soul. Since then, I have discovered that people believe tenaciously in the immortality of the soul in ways that defy reason. The human need for continuity is powerful. In 1972, Krister Stendahl gave a Nobel Lecture at that same college, entitled "Immortality of the Soul Is Too Much and Too Little." It is too much, Stendahl argued, because it promises more than we can know for certain about the mysteries of life with God after death. It is too little because it presumes that the life and death of Christ was for my individual salvation. Stendahl's argument presumes a communal view of humanity and encourages us to understand that the resurrection of Christ is an affirmation of God, rather than a testimony to the indestructibility of the human soul. The hope of the resurrection story is that God's love is stronger than death. When we die, I believe, we are kept in the love of God. That is enough for me to know. It is, I believe, all I can know. The rest is mystery.

Selected Bibliography

Attig, Thomas (1996). *How We Grieve: Relearning the World.* New York: Oxford University Press.

Becker, Ernest (1973). *The Denial of Death.* New York: The Free Press.

Beker, J. Christiaan (1994). *Suffering and Death: The Biblical Vision and the Human Predicament.* Grand Rapids: Wm. B. Eerdmans Publishing Company.

Billman, Kathryn, and Migliore, Daniel (1999). *Rachel's Cry: Prayer of Lament and Rebirth of Hope.* Cleveland: United Church Press.

Lewis, C. S. (1961). *A Grief Observed.* New York: Seabury Press.

Mitchell, Kenneth, and Anderson, Herbert (1983). *All Our Losses, All Our Griefs.* Philadelphia: Westminster Press.

Nouwen, Henri J. M. (1982). *A Letter of Consolation.* New York: Harper & Row.

Stendahl, Krister (1973). "Immortality Is Too Much and Too Little," in John D. Roslansky (ed.), *The End of Life: A Discussion at the Nobel Conference* (pp. 73-83). Amsterdam: North-Holland Publishing Co.

Viorst, Judith (1986). *Necessary Losses.* New York: Simon and Schuster.

Walsh, Froma, and McGoldrick, Monica (eds.). (1991). *Living Beyond Loss: Death in the Family.* New York: W. W. Norton.

To Mourn Beyond the Grief

Paschal Baumstein

Grieve for an hour, perhaps, then mourn a year.[1]

In my parents' house, Thelma was the only maid ever allowed to double as the children's nanny. Of course she only supplied this service when the need arose, but that gave her more than enough opportunity to earn my special affection. Because I was so young during her years with us, I have retained only select scenes and general impressions of Thelma. I recall that at naptime she would escort rather than send me to bed. I still know the sound of her laugh but cannot summon an image of her face. I loved Thelma and remember how at her death, because that was only my fourth year, I was prohibited from attending her funeral. Only after I threatened to go there "on the tramp" did my parents compromise by allowing me to accompany them to her home for their condolence call.

That night, Thelma's family received us in their front parlor. I had thought that our visit would be all about Thelma, but as I followed my parents' conversation that evening, I found that our purposes were far more complex. Although people kept saying things such as "She'll be happier now," or "She's gone someplace better," they seemed to be talking less about Thelma than about themselves. Everything was filtered through their loss. It was a dynamic—and a dichotomy—that I simply could not grasp. We were there *because* of Thelma, but we were there *for* those who survived her.

In the Beatitudes found in Matthew's Gospel, Jesus commends the comfort lent to mourners (Matthew 5:4). This does not, however, suggest that mourning is meritorious in itself. Although the Beatitudes do cite some people of virtue (for example, peacemakers), they also include those afflicted with suffering (for example, the hungry and the persecuted). Mourning, presumably, is of this latter group. The factor that links these *beatitudes* as summarized at the list's end is the character of their endeavor: Those who experience suffering and mourning are blessed because they endure for God's sake (cf. Matthew 5:11). But how does one cede to faith, and thus to God, that predominance in life?

We monks have a colloquialism that reflects the beginnings of such an approach. When an abbot dies, we say of his abbey, "The widow mourns." That might sound like nothing more than a medieval conceit, but it is a statement of perspective. Its reference, of course, proceeds from the abbot's service as father in his monastic home.[2] By that connection, reasonably, his monks mourn his passing as family. The point, however, is that the monastic *community* mourns. Grief is experienced individually, of course; it is a pain in each person's own heart, but not something solitary. It is not just *my* pain: rather *we* mourn.

Saint Benedict left his monks a number of prescriptions that provide for this approach. He installs a perspective that addresses the individual, but places him in a broader context. For example, Benedict counsels the infirm,[3] being careful to situate them in the context of Christ.[4] But he also gives instruction to those who minister to the sick, thereby ensuring that even an individual's suffering is positioned in the environs of community.[5] Even personal pain has a societal and providential context.[6]

Like so many of Benedict's proposals, this dictum is imminently applicable outside the cloister, too. The context Benedict invokes is Christ: the Lord should give hue to all elements of life. That, of course, is a standard that is not exclusive to monastic environs. According to Benedict's vision, this perspective requires continual application. He follows Ecclesiastes' assertion that what God intends is meant to stand enduringly (Ecclesiastes 3:15). In the cloister, the perseverance demanded thereby is regarded as a moral imperative.[7] Benedictines even vow stability. Saint Benedict's path does not provide escapes; he prefers that his followers confront difficulties, deal with them, accept them, and persevere in the course of the greatest rectitude. Thus, for example, in preparing the monks to face death, he is unyieldingly intent: Benedict would have mortality pondered daily *(mortem cotidie ante oculos suspectam habere).*[8] He integrates death and makes it quotidian, ordinary to daily life, and thus much more readily confronted and addressed.

This wisdom of Benedict's standard conditions a person to the fact that both the living and the dying participate in the same providential schema. Death is not an aberration; it is an ordinary constituent in human existence. That is important because it disallows that modern polemic whereby human life is postulated as reality's highest valuation.[9] The flaw in such a premise is that, of course, God is the supreme greatness *(summa magnitudo).* The sanctity and inviolability of human life are derived through the divine origins of humanity. That is why life is rightly God's alone to claim.[10] By identifying life's value as a derivative of its link to divinity, one places death in perspective, highlighting its role in providential design.

Christianity already possesses an exemplum for this revaluation of life: martyrdom. Were human life the supreme value, martyrs—knowing that death will be the result of their conscientious stand—would be accounted suicides. The testimony of the martyrs, however, from the protomartyr Stephen (Acts 6:5–7) to the witness of modern figures such as Franz Jägerstätter,[11] contributes a vital clarification in our understanding of a Christian's life and a Christian's death. As Saint Anselm, an eleventh-century Benedictine, explains: even the threat of death cannot compel the will to abjure, for example, truth.[12] Christ himself notes that it is the person's motivated gift (not the preservation) of her life that reflects the fullness of love (John 15:13). Still, it must be emphasized that none of this devalues life. It provides perspective, not redefinition. The designation "Supreme Life" *(summa vita)*[13] is borne only by Christ who is the way, truth, and life (cf. John 14:6). So, human life is not rightly interrupted outside of God's divine design and will; nonetheless, providence envelops both life and death, whether rightly realized or flawed.

Anselm supplies a helpful reference concerning how one enlists faith in effecting and living life with this orientation and commitment. He believed that a Christian's way, life, and truth are not rightly or profitably separated, but should instead be integrated. By that standard, one ought always to will conformity with the way of Christ, with divine truth, through a life by Christ's measure.[14] That is the rectitude of the martyrs and the daily life of Christians.

For those of us with relatively mundane lives, the martyrs' course might not seem very pertinent. Martyrdom's relevance, however, lies not in the fact that life was taken, but in the martyrs who:

(1) readied their lives for return to God, then
(2) did not resist that return when the time came.

Anselm's articulation of this standard holds that one must be ready to let one's blood be taken or spared according to the will of God (whatever that will might prove to be and regardless of what one confronts), while remaining unfailing and uncompromising in uprightness.[15] Perhaps the individual person will never understand the divine wisdom whereby every death (like every life) has a place and purpose in the unfolding of providence. But because faith is denotative of the being of God—who is as, and who is all, that we believe God to be[16]—the Christian recognizes and accepts that there is nothing, including death, so vile that God cannot turn it to good.[17] Death, after all, is not capacitated by, for example, the blade that beheaded Jägerstätter or the stones that assailed Stephen. Death is defined by the character wherewith it is addressed by a Christian.

The better one prepares for death, faces it, prepares to embrace it for Christ—whatever its cause or timing—then the better he or she will be able to meet death when it happens to someone else. Grief places demands upon the faith of the *survivor*. Indeed, faith is rudimentary to giving bereavement the right character and for approaching prosperously the mysteries of life and death. Faith serves as a necessary prelude to understanding. In fact, according to Anselm, a person can understand only because she does believe.[18] He argues that it is one's faith that seeks understanding.[19]

Benedict and Anselm insisted that the engagement of faith is neither extraordinary nor occasional. Benedict argued that all things should daily point toward God.[20] Similarly, Anselm said that a person owes God a debt so absolute that it entails all that one is and does.[21] Both Benedict and Anselm invoke Deuteronomy 6, "You shall love the Lord your God with all your heart, and with all your soul, and with all your might."[22] Conceivably, however, grief could compromise a person's attainment of such an absolute focus upon divinity. As the psalmist warns, "For in death there is no remembrance of [the Lord]" (Psalm 6:5*a*). Yet, Benedict and Anselm's confidence in the practicability of turning all things to God's glory stands without modification.

Dealing with death is a process, not a static level of attainment. It is to be faced continually. In Anselm's estimation, such constancy of effort is the hallmark of the Benedictine vision.[23] Such application also explains why Benedict regards one's daily mindfulness of death as a means rather than an end. It is for him an "instrument" or "tool" *(instrumenta bonorum operum and instrumenta artis spiritualis)*[24] that affects how one approaches life, death, and bereavement; and emphasizes their placement within the embrace of divine purposes.[25] In the midst of one's grief, it is important not to lose sight of this. Not only does death have a role in God's purposes, so too does the survivor's response to that loss: providence is unfailingly inclusive.

There are colors that transition grief to mourning, ensuring that it is more than a distinction in terminology: this move transforms the issues. Think of its service as comparable to the shift that modern schools effect in their graduation ceremonies. Graduation denotes an ending. So, seeking to redefine both ceremony and event, they graduate in a rite reconfigured and termed a "commencement," a beginning. Thereby, schools demarcate and refine function and purpose, not just the language. Similarly, whereas in grief one bears the wounds of parting and concentrates on loss, in mourning—whether or not one understands mortality itself—one enrolls in providence. She esteems and embraces that course of life, of death, and of divine design, whereby one's own path is united to God's will and wisdom. Mourning is an agency of trust. It refocuses. It opens the door for the shift that Alexander Pope describes, saying, "Grieve for an hour, perhaps, then mourn a year."[26]

My father provided me with an early insight into mourning. When I was still a schoolboy, I was allowed to accompany my father to my uncle Max's funeral. We had an exhausting journey, employing automobile, then air, and finally rail, only to debark to the news that Max's widow, Aunt Rebecca, had also died. It was to be a double funeral.

By the time our trek ended at the cemetery, we were numb with grief and fatigue. It surprised me, therefore, that as the caskets were being lowered, there was nothing but peace on my father's face. Then I realized that he was not really watching the burial. Following his line of vision, I found that just a few steps away stood the ossuary of his first wife, Sara. Father had purchased that site at her death two decades earlier, along with an adjacent plot reserved for his own interment.

Father was holding my hand, but I withdrew it briefly to claim a small stone I had spied at the edge of the cemetery's path. Offering it to father for Sara's grave, I was surprised to find him unresponsive, replying by neither expression nor word. Then, surfacing from this interval of silence, he knelt down to me, hugged me, looked me in the eye, and said in Hebrew, "The glory of the Lord is greater than the blessings we can pay him." This made his point immediately.

Whereas my secular schools favored memory and information, the yeshiva was geared to invigorate reason, sedulously alerting a boy to plumb texts for their wisdom. Our preceptors were intent upon seasoning a youthful mind, preparing it to seek and penetrate, and the soul to savor and take a very real pleasure in the mingling of grace and intellect. My father, confident in the education I had begun, replied to this training by choosing his text wisely. The lesson of his aphorism was: do not multiply good(s); after all, even a bounty of blessings would stretch no closer to Divinity than will a single perfect, pure blessing. Specifically, on that day in that cemetery, this meant that to mourn an additional person would not add to the glory of God. Instead, one should do the present good, well and rightly.

I kept that stone. I put it in my pocket that day, then took it home. A decade and a half later, by then a Christian, I left it at my father's grave.

"The glory of the Lord is greater than the blessings we can pay him" is a line from *Kaddish,* a Jewish prayer offered at times of mourning.[27] That is important: *Kaddish* is very precisely a prayer of mourning, not of grief. It had been among the first religious texts I ever committed to memory. Its mystery intrigued me as much as its theology, especially since only mourners recited it. Because of this select clientele, at Sabbath services I remained seated while *Kaddish* was voiced. Only the men who mourned would stand, leaving me to watch at what seemed a very great distance. As was their protocol, the men stood and rocked at their places, communicating thereby the eloquently pulsed Hebrew chant as it engaged a heart and mind stretching out to the divine Lord.

Wanting to be prepared for when it would fall to me to offer *Kaddish,* I had learned it for myself. When recited *sotto voce,* I found *Kaddish* timed perfectly to the walk from my room to our piano bench. Since I practiced music before school each morning, *Kaddish* fit readily as a preface to my daily ritual.

Consequently, at the cemetery that day with my father, I could recognize his citation.

Part of the profundity of *Kaddish* is that it makes no mention of the deceased. Rather than bemoaning death, *Kaddish* confronts it with faith, posing a bold assertion of the wisdom and benevolence of providence. This particular line, "The glory of the Lord is greater than the blessing we can pay him," suggests that the mourner clings to God, turning to God at times of death as well as in celebration of life; and we still praise and trust God. *Kaddish* eloquently and wisely reaffirms in the face of loss, of death, of this abandonment inflicted upon us, that it is good to be part of this providence, to live in this sacred design that is God's wise ordering of existence.

Providence, it must be remembered, embraces both the deceased and the survivor. That understanding is pivotal in the move from grief to mourning, in shifting perspective from "my" pain to "our" place in God's plan. An astute application of this approach has been left by the sixteenth-century saint Aloysius Gonzaga. In his last days, Gonzaga wrote a letter advising his mother not to lament his death. Noting the excellence of their love for each other in this life, Aloysius urged his mother to consider how much greater that love would be once he attained heaven. For, he said, at God's side, "love is perfected."[28] Aloysius's observation is that, whether in life or death, the closer one grows to God—to the One who is love (cf. John 4:8*b*)—the greater will be that person's love. This might not seem the most comforting deathbed message a young man might offer his disconsolate mother, but amid this studied flexing of his faith, there stands a penetrating truth. The endowment Aloysius leaves to his mother is faith. Death, he knows, can neither dim their faith nor lessen their love.

There is another lesson to be drawn from this letter. It resides in the precise warning Aloysius gives his mother.[29] In English language editions of the Roman *Breviary* (the daily prayer of Catholic clergy), Aloysius's concern is translated as a proscription of inapt *mourning*[30]; whereas C. C. Martindale, in his biography of Saint Gonzaga, quotes this passage as an admonition against *grief*.[31] Actually, however, if we dare trust Aloysius's own statement, the caution he conveys to his mother is that she should not *weep* unduly.[32] Perhaps these translators have missed a profound distinction. Aloysius does not seek to inhibit either grief or mourning. It is, after all, healthy that his mother should grieve his loss and respectful of providence that she should mourn. His injunction pertains instead to the character of bereavement. In bidding his mother not to weep, Aloysius calls upon her faith. Tears would be an imperfect response because she ought not regret his passing: she should not bemoan that his life had found its meaning in the love that is perfected in eternity.

Aloysius recognized, as had Anselm, that faith precedes understanding and that we can move toward real understanding only because we have faith. Must this faith expose death's reason or purpose? Must the survivor understand the workings of providence? No, because the imperative of faith is not that one comprehend, but that she embrace. Only once embosomed in faith will grief yield to the movement of eternity.

Endnotes

1. Alexander Pope, "Elegy to the Memory of an Unfortunate Lady," line 56.

2. The Benedictine monastery works on a familial model. The abbot, as the word suggests, is father to the monks, who are brothers to one another. Several other Catholic religious orders work on a community model. In a religious community, as in the civil form, members come together according to the wisdom of providence, of course, but with shared "active" ambitions and purposes (for example, defense, order, media of life). They are members of a larger "family" (for example, civilly a nation, vocationally the Order [for example, Jesuits]) and thus might be transferred to another local community as circumstances recommend. In the familial model, however, there is restricted, permanent attachment as in a family. The Benedictine monk, for example, even vows stability to his one monastic family (in other words, to his particular abbey).

3. Benedict warns the sick not to use their illness to win special advantage or indulgence. Benedict of Nursia, *Regula Benedict (RB)*, 36:4.

4. Benedict, *RB*, 36:4. Matthew 25:36, 40.

5. Benedict prepares the nursing brothers by saying how necessary patience will be. Benedict, *RB*, 36:5.

6. Those who minister in the infirmary are guided to respond with compassion and solicitude to their brothers' needs. Benedict, *RB*, 36:7.

7. Saint Anselm (ca. 1033–1109), a Benedictine at the close of the eleventh century, argued that whatever God initiates is meant to be perpetuated. Cf. Anselm of Canterbury, letter [#347] to Queen Matilda (of England), ca.1104/5.

8. Benedict, *RB*, 4:47.

9. One hears this argument raised in various "life" issues, for example abortion, capital punishment, and war/violence. Despite the worthiness of the cause(s), that particular argument is specious. A more appropriate contention would be that life is inviolable because it is a gift of God's and thus is God's alone to claim. Benedict argues (as will Anselm later) that a person should not claim even his body as his own possession. Cf. Benedict, *RB*, 58:25.

10. Were one's life being claimed outside of the divine will (for example, murder), then that person should take instruction from the beatitudes, offering it for Christ's sake. Cf. Matthew 5:11*b*.

11. Franz Jägerstätter (1907–1943) was martyred in a witness reminiscent of that of Saint Maximilian of Carthage in the third century. Jägerstätter, an Austrian Catholic, when conscripted by the Nazis, refused military induction. In response, he was beheaded. Cf. Gordon C. Zahn, *In Solitary Witness: The Life and Death of Franz Jägerstätter* (Springfield, Ill.: Templegate Publishers, [1964] 1986).

12. Anselm of Canterbury, *De Libertate Arbitrii*, chap. 9.

13. Saint Anselm includes "summa vita" in his list of divine attributes. Cf. Anselm of Canterbury, *Monologion*, chap. 16.

14. In weighing such measures, Anselm did not allow for culpability in cases of secondary causality. Thus, for example, when he willed truth (even though it might have resulted in his death), so long as he had willed this truth for its own sake, he considered that he had not willed (not even indirectly) whatever secondary effects followed thereupon. Thus he believed that he was not culpable for secondary effects. Similarly, were that secondary consequence an assault upon his way of life (for example, imprisonment, or exile), Anselm held that the person would still be responsible (or culpable) only for what he actually willed (for example, truth), not for any resultant disruption of his vocation.

15. Cf. for example, Anselm of Canterbury, letter [#311] to Ernulf of Canterbury, ca. 1104.

16. Substantiation of this is one of the objectives of Anselm's famous argument on divine being. Cf. his statement(s)-of-purpose in Anselm of Canterbury, *Proslogion, prooemium*, and chap. 2.

17. Anselm of Canterbury, *Cur Deus Homo*, I:15.

18. Anselm of Canterbury, *Proslogion, prooemium*.

19. Ibid. He makes the point explicitly: *"Fides quaerens intellectum."*

20. Benedict believes that God can be glorified in all things. Cf. Benedict, *RB*, 57:9.

21. References to this appear variously throughout the Anselmian corpus. In his so-called second prayer to Saint John the Evangelist, for example, Anselm proposes that it is not even possible to love God too much or too soon. Cf. Anselm of Canterbury, *Oratio alia pro Impetranda Dilectione Dei et Proximi* (sometimes listed as a second *Oratio ad Sanctum Iohannem Evangelistam*).

22. Deuteronomy 6:4-9; Benedict, *RB*, 4:1. Anselm of Canterbury, *Monologion*, chap. 74; *Proslogion*, chap. 25; *et al.* Luke 10:27.

23. In his *Oratio ad Sanctum Benedictum*, Anselm characterizes the Benedictine ethos according to its incessant application *(conversatio)* to the Lord and his purposes.

24. Cf. Benedict, *RB*, 4:75.

25. It is interesting to note its placement within *Regula Benedict*'s sequence of good works. Cf. Benedict, *RB*, 4:44-49.

26. Cf. n. 1, *supra*. This poem was included in the earliest published collection of Pope's verse (1717). He does not develop a full treatment of bereavement; indeed the "Unfortunate Lady" remains relatively undefined. This line's context is cynical, citing "the mockery of woe . . . and the public show" (lines 57-58).

27. *Kaddish* is said during *Shiva* (the seven days of intense mourning), in *Sheloshim* (the thirty days of remembrance), and daily through the first eleven months after the death (in honor of the deceased); it is repeated, then, at *Yahrzeit* (the anniversary of death) and in *Yizkor* (the memorial service that is part of certain holy days, most notably *Yom Kippur*).

28. Luigi Gonzaga, letter (10 June 1591) to Donna Marta Gonzaga, *Lettere e Scritti*, ed. Gualberto Giachi (Roma: Città Nuova Editrice, 1990), 194. A complete transcription of the letter (with annotations) appears on pp. 193-195 of that volume. Aloysius was born 9 March 1568, and died on the night of 20 or 21 June 1591. At the time of this particular letter, his mother, Donna Marta, was Dowager Marchesa of Castiglione.

29. I am indebted to Dom John Oetgen, a Benedictine of Belmont Abbey, whose counsel and proficiency in languages contributed to this analysis.

30. This letter can be found in any post-Counciliar edition of the Roman *Breviary* in the propers for 21 June. Perhaps some of the vernacular renderings of this letter are translations of the Latin rather than the Italian original.

31. Cf. C. C. Martindale, *The Vocation of Aloysius Gonzaga* (New York: Sheed and Ward, 1927), 225-227. This passage is found on p. 226.

32. Cf. Giachi edition, 194. Cf. n. 28, *supra*.

We Will Be Changed: Resurrection and Grief

Duane R. Bidwell

For years, as a pastoral caregiver I would nod and smile—benignly, I hope—when a grieving husband or distraught lover started talking about heaven. It's a little embarrassing to admit, but there it is: while the man or woman or child in front of me talked about streets of gold or a new body free of pain or a joyful heavenly reunion in some timeless future or eternity with God, I would think, "Wow, cool, groovy; how nice that you've found a metaphor that works for you."

For most of my life, that's what heaven and resurrection were for me: metaphors, constructs, temporary ways of making sense of death—effective, perhaps, in the moment, but probably not capable of withstanding the storm of "real grief," a hurricane of loss that would sweep away a person's theological balance beam and leave her paddling in midair like the coyote walking off a cliff on some Saturday morning cartoon. Sooner or later, I thought, the grieving person would find something else to cling to, and when she did, life would go on. That was necessary, in my understanding, for "normal" life to begin again: let go of the old, grab hold of the new, and stop looking back.

Grief as a process of "letting go" is carved deeply into North American consciousness, etched there by the hydraulic force of attachment theory, a psychological perspective that churns steadily (and in some ways invisibly) through our culture. Broadly stated, attachment theory holds that "successful" grieving requires people to let go of the deceased, to end their attachments to the dead person in order to redirect energy to new relationships. From this perspective, maintaining a bond with the deceased—even a bond rooted in the hope of heaven or the doctrine of resurrection—can be at best unhealthy and at worst pathological.[1]

This view can present a dilemma for a minister, especially one who is Christian. The hope of resurrection is central to our faith, and we want to represent that hope authentically. But we also want to facilitate healthy grieving. For me, this meant taking pains not to pathologize talk of heaven or to reject the possibility of an afterlife; but it also meant not encouraging people to dwell on heaven or new life as a part of their grieving. This approach worked for me in part because the concept of resurrection had not taken root in my imagination;

instead I had interiorized the counsel of my Buddhist teacher: "Maybe there is a heaven; maybe there is not a heaven. Knowing for certain will not end suffering in this world. Heaven cannot help you achieve enlightenment."

I like to imagine, of course, that none of this made me ineffective as a pastor, trauma chaplain, pastoral counselor, or AIDS professional. Heaven or not, I'd stick by you through disease, death, and the long, black tunnel of grief; I'd listen at length to what you thought death would bring or what your traditions taught would happen once death wiped the dark mirror clean; and I would speak words of hope out of my own Christian faith and pray in the name of Jesus. I affirmed the church's position on eternal life; I never forced my personal theology on others; and my disregard for what can only be considered a central—if not *the* central—doctrine of my faith never caused a problem for me, personally or professionally. But I didn't much question my assumptions, either, and I did not engage the question of life after death at more than an intellectual level.

Then Kent died. More specifically, he was murdered.

* * * * *

Kent was a tall, attractive gay man who was also HIV positive and a massage therapist with strong and healing hands. On the surface he was so unlike me— a nerdy intellectual, married to a woman—that it is difficult to comprehend why Kent and I were friends. Yet, I cannot imagine being who I am without his presence in my life. Much of this chapter, in fact, was written in a newly opened gallery and coffee bar located across the street from the bar where Kent most loved to dance. Each day that I wrote, I began by looking out on a street on which I knew Kent had often walked, speaking directly to him through the keyboard. I wrote:

You would love this place, Kent: the silver chandelier festooned with Christmas bulbs and Mardi Gras beads; a hulking transvestite in a blond wig and blue sundress, cackling through the eBay auctions; nervous, preppy, pretty boys on their first date, trying to act normal being so out in public. I think of you every so often when I'm here—when Michael offers a smile as he sets a latte next to my laptop; or Viktor bounces up like an eager Labrador retriever, asking for a hug; or Rita and Beverly and Susan settle in for late-night tea, shuffling the baby back and forth between them. There's no place else in this city where I'm surrounded by so many people who knew you; and when I see them and think how much you would love this place and then remember you're gone, a fresh awareness of loss slices through my chest—not grief, exactly, or

*sadness, but an awareness that my life is supposed to include you and you're
not here.*

Kent died on a January-cold suburban street, run down by an SUV driven by
a man who had stalked him and his partner for months. The circumstances of his
death created the conditions for traumatic grief,[2] a reaction to sudden or violent
death that can lead bereaved persons to question lifelong beliefs about self, people, the world, and God.[3] My grief for Kent, however, was not primarily traumatic. I was not angry at God, nor did I wrestle with the existence of the evil;
and in many ways his death confirmed rather than shattered my assumptions
about the world. Long pastoral and personal experience with suffering served
me well when Kent died; I had reached a truce with questions of theodicy years
earlier, and neither Kent's suffering with AIDS nor his sudden and violent death
sent me into existential or theological crisis.

More troubling for my grief was the nature of our relationship. Kent was not my
parent or sibling or grandparent or child or spouse—those relationships whose
losses our culture perceives as most devastating and for which it most willingly
tolerates passionate expressions of grief. Kent was, for lack of a better description,
"only a friend," someone with whom I had (and have) a deep and abiding spiritual connection. But no English word or phrase captures this bond; and in the days
after his death, I was continually frustrated by my inability to offer a relational
term that succinctly explained to others why his death was so significant for me or
that signaled the profundity of my loss. North American culture fails, for the most
part, to recognize the depth of grief that can be associated with the loss of a close
friend,[4] a failure that is becoming pastorally problematic as increasing numbers of
people say friends are more important than family in their daily lives.[5]

Thus, Kent's death was, for me, a textbook example of *disenfranchised
grief*—loss not recognized or validated by the dominant culture.[6] But more than
the inability to name our relationship contributed to this sense of illicit grieving.
The loss was complicated by the facts that Kent was gay, that he had AIDS, that
he was murdered, and that his murder had overtones of domestic violence. In
death as in life, Kent's illness, sexual orientation, and interpersonal relationships
gave others an excuse to marginalize him; in turn, my relationship to him was
also marginalized. In fact, the places where I most needed support when he
died—at my work and church communities—were the places where others
seemed most confused by, and uncomfortable with, the depth of my grief and
the circumstances of Kent's death. Church and work provided little confirmation
of the grief I felt; only with my spouse and closest friends, and in the AIDS community, did my loss feel real and valid. As a result, I began to draw false boundaries around my grief, discounting it to others and to myself.

* * * * *

If I am honest, I will admit that I had grieved Kent's death for years before he died. His AIDS diagnosis meant death was always present between us. Death, in fact, had brought us together; just after his diagnosis, Kent became a client of the HIV ministry of which I was director. At the time he said he did not expect to live more than five years. In fact, he lived for eight more years, and together we spent long hours and years dancing with his illness, mourning mutual friends, and facing our own anxieties about death, dying, grief, leaving, and being left behind. I find it impossible to articulate the intimacy that comes when death brings two people together and they commit not to ignore this invisible third partner in their relationship. My wife, Karee, said recently, "One of the reasons time with Kent was so special to me is that we always knew he would die. He knew it; I knew it. It was always there. That's hard to explain to people who haven't experienced it."

Weeks after our introduction, Kent asked me to deliver the eulogy at his funeral. "I talk to you about things I don't talk about with other people," he explained. Thus began our collection of memories, lyrics, poetry, images, and stories for his memorial service. I attended to our friendship and to his experiences with HIV with a writer's eye for detail and a preacher's ear for anecdote. Nothing escaped my observation: subtle emotional shifts, physical changes, the synergism of our spiritual energies, the heightened awareness of meaning that freighted each touch and glance and word and moment because it might be the last. I dutifully recorded his T-cell count after each doctor's visit, as if the information would somehow help me understand him or make sense of his illness.

We were a family, and we took care of each other. During one hospitalization, when HIV medications had compromised Kent's liver functions so severely that no one thought he would leave the hospital, Karee and I spent hours each night massaging his body to break up toxins and ease his pain. I accompanied him to the emergency room when a stroke temporarily robbed him of the ability to speak. During the dark days when he lay dying at his mother's home, we cleaned up urine and saliva and tried to decipher a monologue born of dementia and medicine-induced hallucinations. Always, we made sure nothing remained unsaid; each parting was the last, and we said deathbed good-byes three times. But somehow, Kent always managed to improve.

And then, amazingly, he got better, no longer oscillating between infections, but steadily reclaiming his life from HIV. A newly approved cocktail of retroviral drugs caused his T-cell count to soar; his viral load dropped. He returned to school and then to work; he fell in love with Blaise, a classical musician; they bought a house and began a comfortable, if secretive, domestic routine. The four of us cooked dinner together each week, and one night we learned Blaise's ex-lover was stalking them—tracing phone calls, threatening Kent's mother, defacing their property, and slashing their tires. The police could not or would not intervene. Kent and Blaise were frightened. Kent bought a gun.

On a dark night after Christmas, Kent surprised an intruder outside their home. He chased the man for two blocks, a shot was fired, and the SUV ran over him. Six months later, the perpetrator was convicted of criminally negligent homicide and sentenced to five years probation and mandatory substance-abuse treatment.

* * * * *

After Kent's death my life became constant crisis intervention. I am a *masculine griever*[7]—someone who expresses loss through action rather than through reflection—so I attended to funeral arrangements, negotiated with Kent's family, met with police, tried to protect and comfort Blaise, and spoke to reporters. Karee and I cried together, gathered with Kent's coworkers, and let our friends feed us. I juggled calls from both AIDS activists and Kent's family, whose agendas for the media and the courts differed significantly.

I know Kent believed in life after death. He never called it "heaven" or "resurrection," but at his sickest he admitted to an intense curiosity about, and even a longing for, life "on the other side." He never voiced to me what he imagined or hoped would happen after death. He would only say that he was certain life did not end, that his energy—and our shared energy—would continue. These conversations almost always happened during massages, one of us on the table and the other kneading muscle. When he said these things, I would feel the current of *élan vital* course between us and say, "I hope you're right. I hope you're right."

* * * * *

Days after Kent's eulogy, late one night, I sat at my desk reading Mark's Gospel. Jesus was scolding the disciples: "Do you still not perceive or understand? Are your hearts hardened? Do you have eyes, and fail to see? Do you have ears, and fail to hear? And do you not remember?" (Mark 8:17*b*-18*b*). After the tongue-lashing, Mark and the disciples arrived at Bethsaida. "Some people brought a blind man to him and begged him to touch him. . . . Jesus laid his hands on his eyes again; and he looked intently and his sight was restored, and he saw everything clearly" (Mark 8:22, 25).

The reference to touch reminded me instantly of Kent; and in my gut I realized that his hands would never again touch me, and my hands would never touch him. The enormousness of that realization ripped a sob from my throat; tears burned my cheeks, and I hung my head to cry. Above me on the rolltop desk stood an icon of the Syrian Christ—dark haired and dark eyed like Kent, with strong hands raised in blessing, palms facing outward like a masseur about to begin *effleurage*. But I did not see the icon; I was unaware of anything but my loss.

Then I felt gentle energy on my shoulders. There was no corporeal pressure, no entity or presence; the sensation was not like being touched. I simply felt the tingle of energy resting on my body. I raised my head, and my eyes locked at once with the eyes of Christ peering out from the icon. He looked into a part of me that had never been seen; and staring into the eyes of Christ, I felt energy stream from his raised hands to my aching soul, binding us together.[8] In an instant, I knew wholly that the healing[9] touch I had experienced with Kent for so many years had been Christ's touch all along. It had not disappeared with Kent; it was present in all things, flowing with abandon through creation just as it was now flowing through the icon. What happened was simply this: my eyes were opened, and I recognized Christ—and Kent—in a new way.

* * * * *

Describing that moment in writing makes it sound more intense than it seemed. Nothing dramatic happened; no soundtrack swelled, no smell of roses filled the room. The moment was absolutely ordinary and absolutely unreal. I am at a loss to explain the experience—the bodily sensation of energy, the real spiritual presence and compassion of Christ, a new and intuitive understanding of what is real. Would it be accurate to say I encountered Kent's energy, alive in death? Did he reach across a boundary of time and space to touch me a final time? Did resurrected life pierce temporal existence as it "never yet always" has? Did I see for the first time the source and goal of the love we shared, a vision of the full ocean wave when before I had seen only the foam on the surface?

These are good questions. I cannot answer them. I can only say that the moment forever changed my perception of resurrection and, with it, my understanding of grief. Life beyond death is real, and in grief it is no longer necessary or desirable to break my attachments. Rather, authentic Christian grieving requires me to maintain a bond with the deceased, a connection that does not belong to us at all but comes from another source altogether, entrusted to our care for a few brief years. That bond is real! It exists in, but reaches beyond, space and time; and the transfusion of living energy I felt with Kent and after Kent had nothing to do with him or with me. It belongs to someone or something greater, One in and with whom we continue to participate.

The dual effect of my encounter—a new understanding of my relationship with Kent and a new awareness of a different order of reality—corresponds with psychological descriptions of spiritual experience, including spiritual change related to bereavement.[10] In addition, recent psychological models of grief have increasingly recognized both the prevalence and benefit of maintaining *continued bonds* with the deceased.[11] Many clinicians now affirm that a dynamic, ongoing relationship with someone who has died—sensing or seeing the deceased, hearing the person's voice, communicating with deceased persons, seeking their advice, treating the dead as an audience for one's personal narratives[12]—is not only normal, but also healthy.

This "new" understanding of grief and the research that supports it are remarkably congruent with New Testament accounts of resurrection. In the Gospels, the risen Christ is at once familiar and unrecognizable, sustained by broiled fish, but able to come and go from locked rooms; present in both Emmaus and Jerusalem at the same time; communicating through human speech but revealing a reality not normally perceptible to human eyes. The Pauline writings of the New Testament affirm resurrected existence as a mystery, both like and unlike physical life.

It seems to me that in recognizing, affirming, and normalizing continued bonds with the deceased, psychology is finally confirming what Christian tradition has long maintained. For what is Christian affirmation of resurrection—indeed, what is Christian faith—but the knowledge and practice of continued bonds with the deceased, particularly with the deceased man Jesus? Our faith tradition is rooted in the reality of presence in absence, of abiding with and being nourished by that which both participates in and transcends worldly existence. Pastoral theologian S. Bruce Vaughan defines grief as *"essentially love under the condition of absence."* He says, "To ignore the absence of our beloved is to deny death and all that makes grief grievous.... *We experience grief as an absence that is simultaneously a presence, and a presence that is simultaneously an absence."*[13]

For me, the presence-in-absence I know through Kent's death has changed me in several ways. First, I no longer smile benignly when a grieving person talks about heaven or resurrection, but engage the subject with respect and curiosity. Second, I no longer view such talk as a pragmatic tool for pastoral care, but as a Christian responsibility. Finally, I am no longer comfortable waiting for the bereaved person to introduce the topic, but instead actively inquire about people's experiences of continued bonds. When I do, people usually pause—to see if I am serious—and then qualify what they are about to share by saying, "You're going to think I'm crazy...." But no one has ever denied at least one experience of presence or interaction with someone who has died.

Continued bonds with the deceased are far more common than our funeral liturgies or pastoral care literature recognize. As people who live at the Celtic "thin places," where the slightest membrane separates sacred from mundane, providers of pastoral and spiritual care must speak about and normalize experiences of life in death. Resurrection encounters are not limited to New Testament stories; the light of Christ shining through every death has the potential to validate and mediate the truth of the risen life God intends for all creation, just as an icon once awakened me to the truth of resurrection.

Paul wrote to the church at Corinth that in death we will be changed. Kent's death taught me that there are times in life when the fragrance of that transformed existence draws near through the presence of those who have gone before.

Endnotes

1. See David E. Balk, "Attachment and the Reactions of Bereaved College Students: A Longitudinal Study," in *Continuing Bonds: New Understandings of Grief*, ed. Dennis Klass, Phyllis R. Silverman, and Steven L. Nickman (Washington, DC: Taylor and Francis, 1996), 311; Dennis Klass and Tony Walter, "Processes of Grieving: How Bonds Are Continued," in *Handbook of Bereavement Research: Consequences, Coping, and Care*, ed. Margaret S. Stroebe, Robert O. Hansson, Wolfgang Stroebe, and Henk Shut (Washington, DC: American Psychological Association, 2001), 432; Samuel J. Marwit and Dennis Klass, "Grief and the Role of the Inner Representation of the Deceased," in *Continuing Bonds*, 297; Robert A. Neimeyer, Luis Botella, Olga Herrero, Meritxell Pacheco, Sara Figueras, and Luis Alberto Werner-Wildner, "The Meaning of Your Absence: Traumatic Loss and Narrative Reconstruction," in *Loss of the Assumptive World: A Theory of Traumatic Loss*, ed. Jeffrey Kauffman. The Series in Trauma and Loss, ed. Charles R. Figley and Therese A. Rando (New York: Brunner-Routledge, 2002), 37; Phyllis R. Silverman and Dennis Klass, "Introduction: What's the Problem?" in *Continuing Bonds*, 3-4; Margaret Stroebe, Mary M. Gergen, Kenneth J. Gergen, and Wolfgang Stroebe, "Broken Hearts or Broken Bonds: Love and Death in Historical Perspective," *American Psychologist, 47:10* (1992): 1206-1207; Margaret Stroebe, Mary Gergen, Kenneth Gergen, and Wolfgang Stroebe, "Broken Hearts or Broken Bonds?" in *Continuing Bonds*, 32-35; Camille B. Wortman and Roxane Cohen Silver, "The Myths of Coping with Loss Revisited," in *Handbook of Bereavement Research*, 406.

2. See John H. Harvey, *Give Sorrow Words: Perspectives on Loss and Trauma* (Philadelphia: Brunner/Mazel, 2000); John H. Harvey and Eric D. Miller, eds., *Loss and Trauma: General and Close Relationship Perspectives* (Philadelphia: Brunner-Routledge, 2000); and Kauffman, *Loss of the Assumptive World.*

3. Kenneth Doka, "How Could God? Loss and the Spiritual Assumptive World," in *Loss of the Assumptive World*, 49-54; Harvey, *Give Sorrow Words*, 22-26; and Jeffrey Kauffman, "Introduction," in *Loss of the Assumptive World*, 1-3.

4. Edith S. Deck and Jeannette R. Folta, "The Friend-Griever," in *Disenfranchised Grief: Recognizing Hidden Sorrow*, ed. Kenneth J. Doka (New York: Lexington Books, 1989), 77-89; Harold I. Smith, *Grieving the Death of a Friend* (Minneapolis: Augsburg Press, 1996).

5. Deck and Folta, "The Friend-Giver," 78; Smith, *Grieving the Death of a Friend*, 14.

6. See Doka, *Disenfranchised Grief*.

7. Kenneth J. Doka, "Theological and Biblical Interpretations of Current Movements and Emerging Paradigms Within Bereavement Studies," *Pastoral Psychology, 46:6* (2000): 470-471.

8. In many ways, this incident illuminates the theology (and experience) of icons in the Orthodox churches. Among the Orthodox, icons are understood as windows into the sacred, a "concise means of remembering" (John Damascus). As revelation, they are granted equal status with scripture and incarnation; icons awaken divine knowledge in the creature through the personal presence of the image they represent. See Constantine Cavarnos, *Orthodox Iconography* (Belmont, MA.: Institute for Byzantine and Modern Greek Studies, 1977); Jim Forest, *Praying with Icons* (Maryknoll, NY: Orbis Books, 1997); Leonid Ouspensky and Vladimir Lossky, *The Meaning of Icons* (Crestwood, NY: St. Vladimir's Seminary Press, 1983); and Michel Quenot, *The Resurrection and the Icon* (Crestwood, NY: St. Vladimir's Seminary Press, 1997).

9. Here I use *healing* in the New Testament sense of the Greek *sodzo:* being made whole, brought to completion, restored to balance, established in health.

10. See David E. Balk, "Bereavement and Spiritual Change," *Death Studies, 23* (1999): 485-493; Richard Golsworthy and Adrian Coyle, "Practitioners' Accounts of Religious and Spiritual Dimensions in Bereavement Therapy," *Counseling Psychology Quarterly, 14:3* (2001): 183-202; Robert Marrone, "Dying, Mourning, and Spirituality: A Psychological Perspective," *Death Studies, 23* (1999): 495-519; and T. Anne Richards, "Spiritual Resources Following a Partner's Death from AIDS," in *Meaning Reconstruction and the Experience of Loss*, ed. Robert A. Neimeyer (Washington, DC: American Psychological Association, 2001), 173-190.

11. See Dennis Klass and Robert Goss, "Spiritual Bonds to the Dead in Cross-Cultural and Historical Perspective: Comparative Religion and Modern Grief," *Death Studies, 23* (1999): 547-567; Klass and Walter, "Processes of Grieving," 431, 435-436; Marwit and Klass, "Inner Representation of the Deceased," 305;

Paul C. Rosenblatt, "A Social Constructionist Perspective on Cultural Differences in Grief," in *Handbook of Bereavement Research*, 290; and Klass, "Introduction: What's the Problem?" 18; Stephen R. Shuchter and Sidney Zisook, "The Course of Normal Grief," in *Handbook of Bereavement: Theory, Research, and Intervention*, ed. Margaret Stroebe, Wolfgang Stroebe, and Robert O. Hansson (New York: Cambridge University Press, 1993), 23-43; and Stroebe, Gergen, Gergen, and Stroebe, "Broken Hearts or Broken Bonds," 1209-1210.

12. Robert A. Niemeyer, "The Language of Loss: Grief Therapy as a Process of Meaning Reconstruction," in *Meaning Reconstruction and the Experience of Loss*, ed. Robert A. Niemeyer (Washington, DC: American Psychological Association, 2001), 261-292.

13. S. Bruce Vaughn, "Recovering Grief in the Age of Grief Recovery," *Journal of Pastoral Theology, 13:1* (2003): 40.

References

Attig, T. (1996). *How We Grieve: Relearning the World*. New York: Oxford University Press.

———. (2001). Relearning the world: Making and finding meanings. In R. A. Neimeyer (ed.), *Meaning, Reconstruction, and the Experience of Loss* (pp. 33-53). Washington, DC: American Psychological Association.

Balk, D. E. (1996). Attachment and the reactions of bereaved college students: A longitudinal study. In D. Klass, P. R. Silverman, and S. L. Nickman (eds.), *Continuing Bonds: New Understandings of Grief* (pp. 311-328). Washington, DC: Taylor and Francis.

———. (1999). Bereavement and spiritual change. *Death Studies, 23,* 485-93.

Cavarnos, C. (1977). *Orthodox Iconography*. Belmont, MA: Institute for Byzantine and Modern Greek Studies.

Deck, E. S., and Folta, J. R. (1989). The friend-griever. In K. J. Doka (ed.), *Disenfranchised Grief: Recognizing Hidden Sorrow* (pp. 77-89). New York: Lexington Books.

Doka, K. J. (ed.) (1989). *Disenfranchised Grief: Recognizing Hidden Sorrow*. New York: Lexington Books.

Doka, K. (2002). How could God? Loss and the spiritual assumptive world. In J. Kauffman (ed.), *Loss of the Assumptive World: A Theory of Traumatic Loss* (pp. 49-54). New York: Brunner-Routledge.

Forest, J. (1997). *Praying with Icons*. Maryknoll, NY: Orbis Books.

Golsworthy, R., and Coyle, A. (2001). Practitioners' accounts of religious and spiritual dimensions in bereavement therapy. *Counseling Psychology Quarterly, 14(3),* 183-202.

Harvey, J. H. (2000). *Give Sorrow Words: Perspectives on Loss and Trauma.* Philadelphia: Brunner/Mazel.

Harvey, J. H., and Miller, E. D. (eds.). (2000). *Loss and Trauma: General and Close Relationship Perspectives.* Philadelphia: Brunner-Routledge.

Kauffman, J. (ed.). (2002a). *Loss of the Assumptive World: A Theory of Traumatic Loss.* New York: Brunner-Routledge.

Kauffman, J. (2002b). Introduction. In J. Kauffman (ed.), *Loss of the Assumptive World: A Theory of Traumatic Loss* (pp. 1-9). New York: Brunner-Routledge.

Klass, D., and Walter, T. (2001). Processes of grieving: How bonds are continued. In M. S. Stroebe, R. O. Hansson, W. Stroebe, and H. Shut (eds.), *Handbook of Bereavement Research: Consequences, Coping, and Care* (pp. 431-448). Washington, DC: American Psychological Association.

Marrone, R. (1999). Dying, mourning, and spirituality: A psychological perspective. *Death Studies, 23,* 495-519.

Marwit, S. J., and Klass, D. (1996). Grief and the role of the inner representation of the deceased. In D. Klass, P. R. Silverman, and S. L. Nickman (eds.), *Continuing Bonds: New Understandings of Grief* (pp. 297-309). Washington, DC: Taylor and Francis.

Massey, D. L. (2000). Theological and biblical interpretations of current movements and emerging paradigms within bereavement studies. *Pastoral Psychology, 46(6),* 469-486.

Neimeyer, R. A., Botella, L., Herrero, O., Pacheco, M., Figueras, S., and Werner-Wildner, L. A. (2002). The meaning of your absence: Traumatic loss and narrative reconstruction. In J. Kauffman (ed.), *Loss of the Assumptive World: A Theory of Traumatic Loss* (pp. 31-47). New York: Brunner-Routledge.

Ouspensky, L., and Lossky, V. (1983). *The Meaning of Icons.* Crestwood, NY: St. Vladimir's Seminary Press.

Quenot, M. (1997). *The Resurrection and the Icon.* Crestwood, NY: St. Vladimir's Seminary Press.

Richards, T. A. (2001). Spiritual resources following a partner's death from AIDS. In R.A. Neimeyer (ed.), *Meaning Reconstruction and the Experience of Loss* (pp. 173-190). Washington, DC: American Psychological Association.

Rosenblatt, P. C. (1996). Grief that does not end. In D. Klass, P. R. Silverman, and S. L. Nickman (eds.), *Continuing Bonds: New Understandings of Grief* (pp. 45-58). Washington, DC: Taylor and Francis.

Silverman, P. R., and Klass, D. (1996). Introduction: What's the problem? In D. Klass, P. R. Silverman, and S. L. Nickman (eds.), *Continuing Bonds: New Understandings of Grief* (pp. 3-27). Washington, DC: Taylor and Francis.

Smith, H. I. (1996). *Grieving the Death of a Friend.* Minneapolis: Augsburg Press.

Stroebe, M., Gergen, M. M., Gergen, K. J., and Stroebe, W. (1992). Broken hearts or broken bonds: Love and death in historical perspective. *American Psychologist, 47(10),* 1205-1212.

Stroebe, M., Gergen, M., Gergen, K., and Stroebe, W. (1996). Broken hearts or broken bonds? In D. Klass, P. R. Silverman, and S. L. Nickman (eds.), *Continuing Bonds: New Understandings of Grief* (pp. 31-44). Washington, DC: Taylor and Francis.

Stroebe, M., Stroebe, W., and Hansson, R. O. (eds.). (1993). *Handbook of Bereavement: Theory, Research, and Intervention.* New York: Cambridge University Press.

Wortman, C. B., and Silver, R. C. (2001). The myths of coping with loss revisited. In M. S. Stroebe, R. O. Hansson, W. Stroebe, and H. Shut (eds.), *Handbook of Bereavement Research: Consequences, Coping, and Care* (pp. 405-429). Washington, DC: American Psychological Association.

Why Are You Cast Down, O My Soul? Grief and Indeterminate Loss

Mary Louise Bringle

Friday (2:45 A.M.)

It is either very early or very late. I am wide-awake from nerves: wired, tense. It would take but the slightest shift in the emotional wind for me to be in torrents of tears. But I don't have the energy, don't have the trust that I could navigate through such storms—so I am keeping myself forcibly becalmed. It is exhausting. My head aches constantly. I am eating about it—eating a huge bowl of cereal even now because I long for that thick layer of carbohydrate comfort around my jangling brain. My eyes are sore and craving sleep, but my mind is racing.

Sunday (7:10 P.M.)

I am still weary. Tears tremble just at the edges of my eyes. I have wept several times today already and could weep again with no provocation. The only thing keeping me from it is the fear that once I get started I won't be able to stop—that and the fear of descending into the pain. I do not like pain; I am cowardly. So I pay the price of avoidance: a constant headache (it has been with me since Wednesday), a *sub-rosa* anxiety that might even diminish if it could be faced. But I just can't face it alone, and I am too timid to call those people whom I might dare trust to face it with me. In fact, the people closest to me are the ones I am most reluctant to talk to, for fear they would feel somehow implicated. This is not anyone's *fault*, for pity's sake. It is not even *my* fault. It simply hurts, and I don't know why.

I am sobbing now and can't seem to avoid it any longer. I don't know how I am going to make it through this reasonless anguish. (*Why are you cast down, O my soul? Why??*) I feel raw and small. My mouth is open in a silent, straining scream, so stretched back that my jaw muscles are beginning to ache. I can't breathe through my nose. My head is pounding—no longer the dull throb of earlier in the week, but a fierce stabbing directly above my eyes. My ears are ring-ing, my breath is labored, and my chest feels imploded. Just when I think a moment of calm has descended, a new wave of pain washes through me, contorting my face, sending new tears and new screams—like waves of nausea churning up and up. . . . But with nausea, at least, one eventually does clean oneself out. I don't know about tears. I don't know about my heart. I wish I could vomit it out and be empty, but be at peace.

This hurts. I stop typing for a moment and hold my face in my hands for comfort—the feel of touch, cool palms on my overheated cheeks and forehead. Pain does stop; I know that intellectually. But right now it feels unremitting, constant, inevitable. I do not see any way out. I do not see any escape.

Exercise would do me good, but I cannot get myself to move. My whole body feels like lead. (Didn't I *used* to be an energetic person? What has happened to me??) Sleep would do me good, but when I lie down, the pain becomes even more frightening. At least here at the computer, words serve as a buffer, a distraction. Naming the pain does not make it disappear but does push it to a slightly more bearable distance.

(7:50 P.M.)

Now, for the moment, I am quieted. I have sat here, holding my head, stroking my own hair, for several minutes. My breathing has returned to normal; my tears are flowing softly, but with no accompanying tremors or sobs. They are simply spilling over, quietly building and spilling over. I can breathe without shaking. My head feels aflame, as though it were filled with layers of cotton wadding soaked in some highly volatile liquid, stuffed tightly inside my skull in a band across my eyebrows, stretching to the tops of my ears. I am quieted, and yet: if someone were to light a match in this room, I would explode.

The Story of Loss

Depression has dogged me for much of my life—sometimes watching from a distance with wary, yellow eyes; sometimes creeping forward to snarl around my ankles and lunge for my throat. The earliest episode I remember occurred in high school, when a protracted case of mononucleosis left me wondering if I would ever *not* feel tired—physically tired, emotionally tired—again. I recovered, of course, from the sore throat and swollen glands. The emotional lassitude lingered. Still, it could easily be chalked up to residual effects of the illness, to having fallen so far behind at school, to suffering the throes of general adolescent moodiness.

In college, though, bleak moods continued to snarl and snap, with somewhat more intensity and persistence. A cherished mentor once suggested that therapy might be helpful for me. As an obsessive A student, I heard his suggestion as a grade of F on my personal life. I felt devastated—and resolved *not* to "get help," but rather to work more conscientiously at keeping my gray spells out of sight.

But I could not keep them out of mind. In graduate school, I discovered Søren Kierkegaard as a kindred spirit, and proposed a dissertation on the topic of despair as treated in *The Sickness unto Death* and various other works of the Christian tradition. Another mentor, Don Saliers—who was keenly insightful—asked if I were not afraid that treating such a topic would raise problems of "underdistance" from the material. Well: yes. But still, I had to try to understand.

All of the understanding in the world, though, would not prevail against a problem whose roots were more chemical than conceptual. One might as well try to "understand" appendicitis away. I wrote the dissertation on despair. I revised it into a book on despair. I continued to live, off and on, in despair: in a grief-stricken sense of lost hope, lost confidence, lost resilience, and lost enthusiasm and zest for living. The paragraphs with which I opened this essay come from a journal I kept about a year prior to the time that depression finally seized me by the throat: when I could no longer even write about it, but simply wandered about doing my job (I was still proficient at concealment), thinking all the while about hoses and duct tape and abandoned garages along highway 501.

Grief and Indeterminate Loss

Now, depression is not grief *per se*. Yet there are powerful affinities between the two, between *feeling bereft* and *being bereaved*. Both carry an emotional tone of bleakness, ranging from dull ache to piercing anguish. Both share physical symptoms: disturbance of sleep cycles, energy levels, and appetites. Both live with the internal story line: "Something terrible has happened. I have lost something/someone vitally important to my well-being." But in grief, one can normally identify what has been lost: a loved one, a love relationship, a job, or a home. In depression, what has been "lost" is more indeterminate and encompassing. (*Why are you cast down, O my soul?* Why??)

In the chronicle of his own depression, author William Styron makes the point about "lostness" well:

> Loss in all its manifestations is the touchstone of depression.... The loss of self-esteem is a celebrated symptom.... [Thereafter] one dreads the loss of all things, all people close and dear. There is an acute fear of abandonment.... As one nears the penultimate depths of depression ... the acute sense of loss is connected with a knowledge of life slipping away at accelerated speed.[1]

54

At its lowest point, as Styron indicates, depression sinks into anticipatory grief, mourning over all that will be lost with one's suicide, but unable to see any other way of escaping the pain.[2]

The Story of Recovery

Blessedly, though, there *are* other ways of escaping the pain. As I sat at lunch in a restaurant with a friend one day twelve years ago, unable to lift a fork to my mouth, unable to speak, unable to do anything but weep silently, he said simply, "You need help." He neither asked nor advised. He simply paid the bill and took us back to campus. He got on the phone and called a psychiatrist. He made me an appointment. Another friend drove me there. After due consultation, I started on a course of SSRIs (selective serotonin reuptake inhibitors).

Not immediately, but bit by bit (and with that long-deferred therapy to supplement the medication), the fog lifted. One morning, in the midst of teaching a class, I realized that I felt as if lead weights had been taken off my wrists and ankles, as if a gray-yellow film had been peeled from my eyes. Was this how "normal" people experienced life all the time? I sensed a new spring to my movements, a renewed vibrancy to my outlook. *Hello, brightness, my old friend. How sweet to dwell in you again!*

Learnings from Loss and Recovery

I have no doubt that I am a better theologian, teacher, counselor, writer, and friend because of my times of passage through the heaviness and the shadows. I say this, I hasten to add, from the far side of the valley. In the thick of the pain, it would be small consolation at best—and a crude mockery at worst—to proclaim, "This is making me [or, heaven forbid, you] a better person." From my current vantage point, however, I can reflect more clear-sightedly on what I have learned, using the rubrics of five key moments from the broader Christian journey.

Incarnation

A great wisdom of the Hebraic and Christian traditions teaches us that *bodies matter*. We learn this truth from the creation narrative, in which God lovingly molds a *human* being out of the *humus* and enlivens that creature with God's own breath. We find the point dramatically reinforced in the Gospels when God chooses to become flesh and to dwell among us. Yet, many of us seem inclined to overlook the significance of our own fleshliness as part of our spiritual journeys. We act as if the number of times we pray or take communion bears significance, but not the number of times we jog or eat junk food. Yet, being brought to my knees (both literally and figuratively) by a kink in my brain chemistry has taught me the inextricable interweaving of soma with psyche. Now I must be careful to engage in regular physical exercise, both aerobic and anaerobic (both pulse-elevating and weight-bearing). I must watch how much sleep I get and how much caffeine or alcohol and how many fat grams I consume. In their very *corporeality*, such disciplines constitute fit acts of stewardship, tending the embodied spirit and spirited body that are God's gift to me for the living of my days.

Crucifixion

Not only does God choose to become flesh among us; God also chooses to endure suffering alongside us and for our sake. To be honest, I must admit there are times when this doctrine seems cold comfort: when a Celestial Superhero who magically *fixes* things would seem a far better "divine action figure" than a Suffering Servant who descends into whatever hell we find ourselves occupying and sits with us there. And yet, I have to acknowledge that I have learned things through the grief of depression that I might not have learned so readily in other ways. At least on my better days, I am a less arrogant, more humble person, a little more adept at confessing my own neediness and frailty. On my better days, I am more sensitive to the griefs of other people; more able to let them *be* in their hurting, more equipped to be *present* with them without insisting that they "cheer up" so that I or someone else will feel less uncomfortable. Although I do not profess to understand it intellectually, I nonetheless feel viscerally the wisdom of what the author to the letter of Colossians has written: in our own flesh, we complete what is lacking in Christ's afflictions (1:24), for the sake of a world whose full redemption is won through the crosses of passion and compassion.

Resurrection

God's role in our lives is not to serve as some bionic Mister (or Miss) Fixit. Nevertheless, our faith proclaims that beyond meeting us in the Good Fridays of our suffering, God also works to bring forth Easter victories. I have learned to be suspicious, though, of people who jump too quickly to the "happy endings" of triumph, wanting their faith served up in praise choruses and Alleluias without any hint of a miserere or a minor key. It may be true that, as the gospel song proclaims, "There's no disappointment in heaven."[3] Nevertheless, this side of the unimaginable beyond, genuine hope must live with the tension of hurts and unsatisfied longings. Moreover, when grace does "Easter up" out of the shadows, it can do so in quite subtle ways: no "angel visitant or opening skies,"[4] but a morning when tears feel soothing rather than searing; a song on the radio that conjures up unambiguously happy memories; a friend who says, "You need help," and goes unpretentiously about making it happen.

Church

As C. S. Lewis has written, "When pain is to be borne, a little courage helps more than much knowledge, [and] a little human sympathy more than much courage."[5] As the whole creation groans beneath its weight of determinate and indeterminate losses, Christ continues to be made incarnate wherever we minister sympathetically to the needs of one another. My times of passage through the valley of the shadow have taught me this: when I cannot act, the Body of Christ makes bold to move into action. When I cannot pray, the Body of Christ persists in praying for me; when I cannot sing, the Body of Christ keeps on offering its songs. When I am able, by the grace of God, I will and do return the favor.

The songs of the church, indeed, have constituted one of its greatest spiritual resources in assisting me through my own times of shadowed passage. The psalmist's question offers the comfort of fellow-suffering in perplexity: *Why are you cast down, O my soul?* (42:11). Likewise, so too have the words and melodies of other important predecessors in the life of faith provided comfort. Beyond these, I have also found myself called to the vocation of crafting new hymns of both lament and hope, for myself and for my sisters and brothers in the family of God. In so doing, I am taking part in that fifth moment of the Christian journey that sums up my learnings from loss and recovery.

Songs of New Creation

In the beginning, God created us in the divine image—which is to say, in the very image of One who creates. Thus, it is both our birthright and our bounden duty to become creative artists ourselves, to the extent of our God-given abilities. Moreover, since God is perennially doing a "new thing" en route to bringing a wholly new heaven and new earth into being, we as God's people are perennially charged to "sing a new song." For me, the crafting of such "new songs" fulfills not only a theological, but also a therapeutic, end.

For many years, I have sought solace in the healing power of words. In countless journals—including the one from which I cited at the opening of this

57

essay—I have struggled to *name* both the pains and joys of daily living. I suspect that such naming serves, in its own small way, to draw cosmos out of chaos, to give order and meaning to otherwise potentially overwhelming experiences. Sometimes, journal entries evolve into prayers; sometimes, they become grist for theological reflection. More recently, they have provided raw material for the crafting of metric, musical verse. They have given rise to hymn texts such as: "Peace, Be Not Anxious," written during the emotional upheaval of leaving a home and community of seventeen years to move to a new city and new job; "When Memory Fades," written for a friend whose mother was in the late stages of Alzheimer's disease and whose father, as the primary caregiver, was growing increasingly frail; "When Terror Streaks through Morning Skies" and "We Seek You Here, as Well, O God," written in response to the national and international outpouring of grief surrounding the events of September 11, 2001.

I know that I am not alone in turning to hymns as a resource for healing in my spiritual journey. Among my cherished mentors in this therapeutic practice I count John Henry Newman, who wrote "Lead, Kindly Light" (1833) on an occasion of physical sickness and emotional despair; Elizabeth Payson Prentiss, who cried out "More Love to Thee, O Christ" (1869) at a time when she was feeling, in the words of her own journal, "empty hands, a worn-out, exhausted body, and unutterable longings to flee from a world that has so many sharp experiences"; and George Matheson, whose poignant "O Love that Wilt Not Let Me Go" (1882) emerged from a period of "severe mental suffering" (the authors' personal disclosures are cited by Kenneth Osbeck in *101 Hymn Stories and 101 More Hymn Stories* [Grand Rapids: Kregel, 1982 and 1985], 53-55, 68-69, and 102-103).

Of course, we need not all write our own texts for hymns to help us through the shadows of our grief toward the ultimate dawn of God's new creation. A published hymn collection makes a wonderful bedside table book, an ever-ready source of devotional reading. Indeed, more than for reading alone, hymns are written to be *sung*, whether the voices singing them are cultivated or raw, whether the sounds emerging are cries of sorrow or sighs of consolation. For those of us who grew up in religious traditions, the simple melodies of hymn tunes root as deeply in our memory as fragrances and are just as capable of conjuring rich associations. Not surprising, people who work with Alzheimer's patients and stroke sufferers note that hymns remain familiar long after other memories grow confusing. In fact, because of this very familiarity, a physical hymnbook may prove unnecessary. When we feel arid and "unable to pray as we ought," when we are aching for words of comfort and courage, a long-loved hymn can arise spontaneously out of memory to keep us company—like an old friend, easing us past the rough places until we can stand on our own again.

For each of us, the hymns that fill these functions of spiritual companionship will be different. The ones that work best for me convey a tension of poignant sorrow and persistent conviction. "O Love that Wilt Not Let Me Go," mentioned before, is a personal favorite, despite—or perhaps even because of—its mildly Victorian language: "O joy, that seekest me through pain, I cannot close my heart to thee." In words like these, we hear the healing "nevertheless" of Christian faith: although the anguish of crucifixion is real, nevertheless we believe in the victory of resurrection; although this creation is groaning in travail, nevertheless God's new creation *will* come.

Coda

Of course, no artist has captured this tension of pain and confidence better than the ancient hymnwriter of the Hebrew tradition. Thus, it seems a fitting conclusion to listen afresh to the psalmist's version of the great "nevertheless," as it sings out a spiritual passage through the shadows of indeterminate grief toward the light of inextinguishable trusting:

> Why are you cast down, O my soul,
>   and why are you disquieted within me?
> Hope in God, for I shall again praise [the Holy One],
>   my help and my God. (Psalm 42:11)

So, by grace, shall we all.

Endnotes

1. William Styron, *Darkness Visible* (New York: Random House, 1990).

2. In like manner, grief can also sink into depression. Feelings of sadness are highly appropriate following a traumatic loss. When those feelings endure for months on end, however, coupled with feelings of guilt, hopelessness, worthlessness, flattened affect, and thoughts of suicide, depression may be setting in and calling for medical attention.

3. Words and music by Frederick Lehman (1868–1953):

> There's no disappointment in heaven,
> No weariness, sorrow or pain;
> No hearts that are bleeding and broken,
> No song with a minor refrain.

The text and tune can be found in Kenneth W. Osbeck, *Beyond the Sunset: 25 Hymn Stories Celebrating the Hope of Heaven* (Grand Rapids: Kregel Publications, 2001), 68-69.

4. From George Croly's 1854 hymn, "Spirit of God, Descend Upon My Heart":

> I ask no dream, no prophet ecstasies,
> no sudden rending of the veil of clay,
> no angel visitant, no opening skies;
> but take the dimness of my soul away.

Numerous denominational hymnals contain Croly's text, although the 1990 edition of the Presbyterian hymnal unfortunately omits this verse. The United Methodist 1989 hymnal includes it.

5. C. S. Lewis, *The Problem of Pain* (New York: Macmillan, 1955), viii.

Grief by Another Name

Joseph R. Jeter, Jr.

I cannot say that my parents and I were especially close during the first half-century of my life. We were quite different. I had heard the adage that the acorn does not fall far from the tree but just assumed that mine had hit a rock and bounced away. Joseph Roscoe Jeter was born in 1914, the child of a hard, gruff father and a fanatically religious mother. It is probably no surprise that he grew up quiet and shy with a disdain for religion. He was small of stature, his growth having been stunted by a childhood illness. My father was intelligent, the first person in our family line with a college education. He was an excellent optometrist. He was also socially inept, a lousy businessman, and a mostly functional alcoholic. When I was a teenager, I was embarrassed by him and avoided bringing friends to our house for fear he might be drunk.

Helen Virginia Reams Jeter was born in 1917, the child of a gorgeous hairdresser and a handsome rake and rounder. Her mother died in suspicious circumstances when my mother was eight. Her father being unable (or disinclined) to care for her, my mother and her younger siblings were passed from relative to relative and raised as virtual orphans. She did not graduate from high school and was always embarrassed by her lack of education. When she was old enough to work, her father reclaimed her and had her drop out of school to get a job. He waited for her on Friday evenings, took her paycheck, gave her a couple of dollars to feed her siblings, and took the rest to spend on his lady friends.

I never knew any of this while growing up. I just knew my mother as a beautiful woman who wore stylish hats to church. She was also what one might call a nervous and flighty person, one who had lots of dreams that never came true.

My parents used to argue a lot, generally about money and alcohol. Sometimes I would get caught in the middle and hated that. Early on my parents and I basically agreed to leave each other alone. From about the age of fifteen, I was left to make my own decisions, and by eighteen, I was on my own financially. Our relationship after that was proper, cordial at best, and generally distant. Rarely did I live within a thousand miles of them.

Fast forward now, some thirty years. I got a phone call that Mama had fallen into a diabetic coma and was not expected to live the night. I dropped everything and went to be with Dad. My mother did not die that night or the next. Eventually she was able to go home, but the experience had done two things.

First, it proved to be the trigger that transformed her growing forgetfulness into full-blown Alzheimer's disease. Second, without any medical insurance apart from Medicare, the family's finances were exhausted by her illness.

Dad agreed to move near me in Fort Worth to a little house we found nearby, and he took care of Mama for three years. I would care for her one day a week to give him a caregiver's day out. But the day finally came when he could no longer pick her up from the floor when she had fallen. I took her to a nursing home where she lived the last sixteen months of her life. Dad went every day and spent most of the day with her, tending her and helping staff with other patients. Her mental and physical disintegration were hard on the two of us. Watching the lights in her eyes blink out one by one was tough. Harder still was watching this woman, from whom I had never heard an untoward word, suddenly break into streams of profanity. Before she fell into silence, she would curse and hit me until I gently hugged her and lullabied her into peacefulness.

Out of that horrible experience, two marvelous things occurred. First was the transformation of my father from what the world would have seen as an alcoholic loser into a veritable saint. His new life was built around caring for her and others. As hard as her disintegration was, he approached it quietly, almost—dare I say it?—spiritually. Sometimes I would walk up behind them when they were sitting in a little glider and just watch as they slowly moved back and forth, silent, holding hands. I cannot speak the magnitude of my admiration and respect for him in those days.

Throughout this whole painful five-year process, there was one magic moment that became more than a blessed memory, and almost a mantra. I told the story in a sermon and recount it here:

> After my mother had been in the nursing home for a while, she lost her ability to speak, and it was difficult to know what, if anything, she was thinking. On what would be her last Thanksgiving my father wondered if we might bring Mama to our house for Thanksgiving dinner. I was nervous about it, and the doctor recommended against it, saying that Alzheimer's patients tend not to do well outside their familiar environment. But after thinking about it, I said "Let's do it."
>
> Dad took Mother's best clothes over to the nursing home and, with the help of the staff, got her dressed. I went to another town to pick up my Uncle Jack, Mama's brother, who also had Alzheimer's. We knew it would be the last time they would see each other in this world, but we didn't know if they would recognize each other. We walked in. Mama and Jack walked toward each other. They met in front of the fireplace and hugged each other for a long time. Then they looked at each other, and in a moment of perfect clarity, Jack said, "Oh,

we had some times, didn't we, kid?" And Mama smiled and said, "We sure did."

There was much pain and suffering in my mother's life. But I will never forget the brief interlude of grace that came that day in front of the fireplace, when good memories of the past reached forward to redeem the present.

Before the next Thanksgiving could come, my mother died. I wrote these words the week after her death:

My mother, Helen Virginia Reams Jeter, died on Wednesday, November 17, 1993, at 12:25 P.M. Death is significant. And yet the rush of numbing activities that attend death in our culture leave little time to feel and reflect on that significance. During a talk with a friend about some of my unfocused feelings, she suggested that I write them down. And so I am.

I love my mother. She not only gave me life, she gave me home and spirit. She was a good and caring person, someone genuinely to be missed. So I am surprised that my reaction to her death is not what I expected, not what I have seen as a pastor in so many other people. Shocked by her death? No. It had been expected for a long time. Saddened by her death? No. At least not for her. She had wanted, begged to die for a long time. The main feeling that I am aware of now, apart from my concern for my father, is anger. Anger that this good person had to go through five years of hell in order to die. Anger at those talented and conscientious doctors who time and again, over the past five years, pulled her back from the brink and would not let her go. Anger at God? Oh, I suppose not. I've been around the theological block too many times for that. I know that doesn't work. But I do agree with Carlyle Marney. Once, when someone said that we all have things we must answer for before the throne of grace, Marney replied, "So does God." I don't blame God for my mother's suffering, but I'm not real happy with God either.

In times of great mystery like that of death, we often turn to the poets. Sometimes they help us understand, sometimes they help us frame problems we cannot understand, and sometimes they are just wrong. I have heard many times and admired Shakespeare's line from *Julius Caesar,* "Cowards die many times before their deaths; the valiant never taste of death but once." But it never occurred to me till this week how untrue that line has become. In his time, perhaps, you got killed once or you got sick and died once. But now our technology allows even the valiant to die time and time again, until body, mind and spirit finally say "enough."

Who is correct? Dylan Thomas, who urged his father: "Do not go gentle into that good night; rage, rage against the dying of the light"? Or William Cullen Bryant, who said, "Approach thy grave like one who wraps the drapery of his couch about him, and lies down to pleasant dreams"? The answer, of course, is "it depends." We are not off the hook on this one. But neither are we alone. Whether death comes as enemy or friend, our faith is that death does not have the final word.

After the death of my mother, we asked my father to live with us, but he declined. We cleaned up the house from the after-death activities. I asked Dad if he wanted help sending Mother's clothes to Goodwill. He declined that too. He wanted to keep Mother's things. Some days later I noticed that Mother's toiletries had been set back out in orderly fashion in the bathroom: hairbrush, face cream, and so forth. I also noticed that a black marker had completely obliterated November 17 on the calendar. The next week, Dad proudly showed me his new wedding ring, which had cost over $1300 and wiped out his savings. His original ring had been stolen when he took it off in the nursing home to help wash Mother. Now he had "it" back. At that point I knew we would have to finance the rest of Dad's life. But I had no idea how short that time would be.

On January 22, 1994, sixty-six days after Mother's death, Dad got out of his chair to stoke up the fire in the fireplace. He was struck with an aneurysm in his brain and fell over backward. I happened to call a while later and got no answer, called again to no response, and went over to the house and found him on the floor. The ambulance took him to the hospital where they did surgery to relieve the pressure, but he died the next day. I had the great honor of holding his hand as he died.

I struggled with guilt about not being there to help him when he was struck, but his doctor told me that if I had been standing next to him it would not have made any difference, and I suppose he was right. I was saddened that he had not had that "new life" I wanted for him, that reward for those years of caring for Mama. But I realized in time that this was what I wanted, not what he wanted. His reward was in the caring, and his actions after her death demonstrated that caring for her was his reason for living. He had done his duty and now his work was done. His death certificate reads brain aneurysm. It might have better read, "His work was finished."

At last, I get to my assignment in this essay. How about me? How did I handle my parents' deaths? In some ways, I did it like everybody else—kept a stiff upper lip and carried on. As I hope the foregoing indicates, I was closer to both my parents in the last few years of their lives than I ever was before. The downside of this is that I really was not around during many of their best years, and my memories of them were warped by their end-time experiences. I looked at pictures of Mother as a young woman and marveled, but the pictures that lingered in my head, even after a decade, were those of that physical remnant of her after her mind had left. Dad I still saw lying on the floor.

After Mother's death, I was not particularly sad or sorry, but I was angry. When the call came, I rushed to Mama's room to find her body dead and naked and alone on the bed, without even the dignity of a cobwebbed sheet. "Please cover her," I said and left the room. My father died with his hair shaved off and a pointless surgical invasion tracking his head. My parents deserved better than they got—in life and in death. People remarked at Mama's funeral how, at age seventy-six, she had not one gray hair on her head. Well, there was that. We covered Dad's head with one of his smart 1930s hats. Dapper even in death. There was that. I was still angry. But when I could find no reason to be angry at God, the anger faded, since there was no one else with whom to be angry. Anger without an object cannot long endure.

For a while after my parents' deaths, I was beset with a profound loneliness. Since I had been on my own for most of my life, I did not expect it. I recently expressed my feelings in an e-mail to a friend after the death of his mother:

> Got your message about the death of your mom and have appreciated the words of our friends. The only thing I know to add is that a death is a death. Whether it's easy or hard, good or bad, at 23 or 93, if it's someone we love, it's still a loss and a permanent change in our own lives. Secondly, among all the roles our parents have is the one of serving as a buffer between us and that great unknown. And, if your experience is anything like mine, when your last parent dies, there's a feeling not only of loss and loneliness but also of abandonment. We are really on our own in a way we've never been before. All linebackers now and no blockers. We do the best we can and then we lateral to our kids and block for them as long as we can. Peace to you and those you love.

A friend in the e-mail circle, who is fighting cancer, wrote back:

> Good analogy. We all relate to the buffer business. All our blockers are gone. My offensive line stunk. Dad gone at 70, Mom at 46. No wonder some SOB linebacker nailed me 1.5 years ago. But here is the good news. Once you've been drilled (and survive), you are a lot tougher buck, yourself. There are things in the unknown that aren't so hard to face after you get decked once.

Grief came to me then in the form of anger and abandonment. But I thought I had made it past my grief in good shape. Then it came again, like a thief in the night. I am a preacher and teacher. This requires me to be on my feet before groups of people, quick-witted and sure-footed. Suddenly, after years of confident speaking, I began to lose names, to find words slipping away from me. After years of watching my mother struggle to speak and make sense, I suddenly lost my rhythm and stood there while my tongue tied itself in knots. And I would say to myself, "Here it comes." I began to be nervous in front of groups. When people would want to thank me or honor me for something, I could only stand there and look down at the floor. My mother's loss of speech, my father's discomfort in front of people, were born again in me. Their pain, their frustration, and their weakness had been transferred to me. Grief by another name. The acorn had not fallen so far away after all. Physicians assured me that this was normal for someone of my age, but that has been very hard to accept.

What have I done? Four things, really. I have more to learn, but this is a beginning. First, I have learned to live with these feelings. I do not do interviews. I make sure I am well prepared when I stand up before a class or a congregation. Maybe these feelings of fear or failure or silence or loneliness will go away, but if they do not, I plan to live through them as creatively and faithfully as I can.

Second, I have written this piece. Whether or not the editors choose to use it, writing these thoughts and feelings and memories has helped me immensely. It has helped me name my grief. I have written elsewhere that naming the crises "we face can be a touchstone to understanding [them] and having power to overcome [them]. This is sometimes called "the Rumpelstiltskin effect" by modern psychologists. Find the monster's name and its threat is lessened."[1] I would further suggest that writing these things down can be useful as well.

Third, I have put two beautiful pictures of my parents on my wall. Now, when the negative thoughts and pictures of my parents come, I can gently replace them with the lovely pictures and sense my parents alive and well. Sometimes words come to and from the three of us, in what might be called a "kything"[2] experience. This has been very helpful. I have accepted their deaths. But what this has helped me do is to accept their lives. I have remembered and learned and told stories about them—about Mother's magic cedar chest and how she held a family together, and about Dad's early sensitivity to others' hurts.

For example, after my father's death, it fell to me to call family and the few old friends of his that were still living. One of his friends still lived in the little country town of Cooper, Texas, where they both grew up three-fourths of a century ago. I identified myself, and he said, "Oh, yes, you're Roscoe's boy." I told him Dad was gone, and then I just let him talk. He told me how he met my father in September of 1919. It was his first day of first grade at the old East Ward School in Cooper, and he was lonesome and afraid. At lunch he took his sack and went over to sit under a tree by himself where no one would see him cry. A few minutes later he became aware of someone standing there; and he looked up and it was my father, towheaded and barefoot. Dad's first words to him were, "Don't be afraid. It'll be all right." They ate their lunches together that day and were friends for seventy-five years. But Dad's friend never forgot those two little sentences. And I am as grateful for him telling me that as I am that my father spoke them.

You see, I had thought my father was not an articulate man. But reflecting on his friend's story and on so many occasions in my life, I realized that he said just the right thing that needed to be said. My mother was wise beyond her education—a splendid mediator and a genuinely kind person. Few helped her. She helped many. And at the end, I think she was content.

Finally, then, God does not only use people at the peak of their abilities. God needs us both early and late. God was there early for my mother, my father, and me. I am confident that God will be around for a good long time to come. Perhaps the pivotal grace in dealing with grief is the same grace that has brought us "safe thus far": "Don't be afraid. It'll be all right."

Some Thoughts That Helped Me

When I think of death, and of late the idea has come with alarming frequency, I seem at peace with the idea that a day will dawn when I will no longer be among those living in this valley of strange humors. I can accept the idea of my own demise, but I am unable to accept the death of anyone else. I find it impossible to let a friend or relative go into that country of no return. Disbelief becomes my close companion, and anger follows in its wake.

I answer the heroic question "Death, where is thy sting?" with "It is here in my heart and mind and memories."[3]

* * * * *

No one ever told me that grief felt so like fear. I am not afraid, but the sensation is like being afraid. The same fluttering in the stomach, the same restlessness, the yawning. I keep on swallowing.

At other times it feels like being mildly drunk, or concussed. There is a sort of invisible blanket between the world and me. I find it hard to take in what anyone says. Or perhaps, hard to want to take it in. It is so uninteresting. Yet I want the others to be about me. I dread the moments when the house is empty. If only they would talk to one another and not to me.[4]

* * * * *

It was late at night when I returned home, but I assembled the family. I remember only what I said first and last. "Our Eric is gone," I said. And at the end, that we now must learn to live as faithfully and authentically with Eric gone as we had tried to do with Eric present.

How do we do that? And what does it mean? It will take a long time to learn.

It means not forgetting him. It means speaking of him. It means remembering him. *Remembering:* one of the profoundest features of the Christian and Jewish way of being-in-the-world and being-in-history is remembering. "Remember," "do not forget," "do this as a remembrance." We are to hold the past in remembrance and not let it slide away. For in history we find God.[5]

* * * * *

When we are young, heaven is a vague and nebulous and shadowy place. But as our friends gather there, more and more it gains body and vividness and homeliness. And when our dearest have passed yonder, how real and evident it grows, how near it is, how often we steal yonder. For, as the Master put it: where our treasure is, there will our heart be also. Never again will I give out that stupid lie, "There is a happy land, far, far away." It is not far. They are quite near. And the communion of saints is a tremendous and most blessed fact.[6]

Endnotes

1. See Joseph R. Jeter Jr., *Crisis Preaching: Personal and Public* (Nashville: Abingdon Press, 1998), 79-80.

2. *Kything* is defined as "spirit moving without regard to matter."

3. Maya Angelou, *Wouldn't Take Nothing for My Journey Now* (New York: Random House, 1993), 47.

4. C. S. Lewis, *A Grief Observed* (San Francisco: Harper & Row, 2001), 15.

5. Nicholas Wolterstorff, *Lament for a Son* (Grand Rapids: Eerdmans, 1987), 28.

6. Arthur John Gossip, sermon, "But When Life Tumbles in, What Then?"

I Would Do It All Again

Charles Merrick

It has been fifty years since I called my mother to tell her that I had decided to become an undertaker. There was a moment's pause, maybe two moments, and then she said, "That's nice."

No one in my family had ever been in the funeral business, so they could not understand my reasons for making death my life's work. Whenever someone asked me, "What are your plans for the future?" and I answered, "I am going to be an undertaker," the conversation would drift off in another direction.

My decision did not come out of the blue. Where I grew up, whenever someone died, the funeral directors would post a notice on the town bulletin board at 8:00 A.M. the next morning. By 8:15, everyone in town knew who had passed away. I used to ride my bicycle downtown to be there when the undertaker drove up in his black Cadillac, posted the notice, and drove away. I really liked that car. By high school, I had decided that I was going to go into the funeral business.

As it turned out, being a funeral director was not exactly what I had envisioned. The first Christmas Eve in my career, I missed being home because I was called to a small bar in Phoenix. A man had sat at the bar most of the night, then went to his car, pulled out a shotgun from the backseat, leaned on the fender, put the gun in his mouth, and pulled the trigger. I had never seen anything like this in my life, let alone during my short career as an undertaker. For the next two hours, we cleaned up small pieces of tissue that were scattered all over the parking lot. It was my first lesson that the funeral business was not going to be easy and that sometimes it would be extremely difficult.

In the five decades since that inauspicious beginning, I have seen significant changes in the way death is dealt with (or not dealt with) in America. I never dreamed that some of these changes would occur.

When I started out in the 1950s, everyone who died had a funeral. We only had to ask two questions at the time of the arrangements: "Where is the funeral to be held?" and "What cemetery will be used for the burial?" Cremation was rare—there was only one crematory in Phoenix. I was working at the Catholic funeral home; the family always had a rosary the night before the funeral mass, and the mass was still said in Latin. The burial usually took place in the Catholic cemetery. Friends served as pallbearers. At the cemetery, as the casket was lowered into the grave, everyone present knew that the separation between life and death was final. There were no grief counselors in the yellow pages, and, until the end of the decade, little if anything had been written for the general public about death, dying, and grief.

Today we seldom do things just because they are expected. People have ideas about their own funerals and the services for their family members. Some of their ideas are the result of thoughtful reflection and take into account the needs of their loved ones. Others are of the knee-jerk variety, disregarding the possibility that some of the survivors might need some sort of ceremony to help them with their grieving. Some people want no funeral at all—but rather a party, maybe, or someone to "just dispose of the body."

At the beginning, I had very little knowledge of the business I was getting into. I knew how to embalm bodies, go to funerals, wash cars, clean the mortuary, and dust the caskets; but I had little information about grief and the aftereffects of a death in the family. When we received a call, we would pick up the body, embalm and prepare it, make arrangements with the family, hold the funeral and the burial, and get ready for the next funeral. In those early days, there was no consideration for what would happen to the family afterward. Death happens, and life must go on.

My first personal lesson in grief came in the summer of 1961. My neighbor Ray was an Air Force pilot. On a training flight over Colorado, his plane exploded in the air. He and his crew chief were both killed. The base notified Ray's wife, Joan, that his plane was overdue. They had lost contact with him and would continue to keep her informed. Early the next morning, two blue sedans stopped in front of her house. The base commander and the chaplain informed her of the accident that had claimed her husband's life. The chaplain offered a prayer, the commanding officer told her that he and the Air Force were sorry for her loss, and then they were gone. The funeral took place a few days later in the small Midwestern town where Ray had been born and raised, and afterward Joan and her children were back in Tucson, getting on with life.

Several months later I went over to see how Joan was doing. I found her on the floor, sobbing. I helped her to a chair and asked her what the matter was. "The matter," she said, "is that every time I hear a car coming up the street I think, 'Oh, good, he's home!' I still have trouble believing he is dead. I never saw him after he died. I wanted to see him, but they told me that I couldn't. If I could have seen him dead, then I would know he is dead."

I had no advice for Joan. (I suspect there was little left of her husband—the Air Force had sealed the casket so that it could not be opened.) I only knew that grieving people viewed bodies because it was expected. Most had a visitation with the body present and the casket open. I had not thought about the reasons for it; I did not know that seeing a person in the trappings of death, in the casket, surrounded by flowers and other things that symbolize death in our culture, confirms for the survivors that death has really occurred.

In that regard, the decade of the 1960s was a learning time for all of us who try to help families survive a death. More was written in the sixties and seventies about death, dying, and grief than ever before. Edgar Jackson published *Understanding Grief* in 1957, after his small son had died as a result of an accident at home, but this classic book did not become popular until the sixties. Jackson, along with writers such as Earl Grollman, Elisabeth Kübler-Ross, Robert Fulton, William Lamers, C. S. Lewis, and many more opened the doors to information about death and dying.

Even so, in much of society death remained taboo, an off-limits subject in polite conversation. My first boss advised me, "If someone asks you where you work, just say Downtown. When Elisabeth Kübler-Ross tried to get permission to interview dying patients for her research, the patients themselves were more than willing to talk with her—but their attending physicians had all sorts of reasons not to allow it.

In 1963, Jessica Mitford wrote *The American Way of Death*. This best-selling, watershed book looked at the way we in the United States bury our dead. It especially focused on the role of the undertaker. Until this time, no one had really questioned the funeral business or the value of the funeral. Mitford alleged that American funerals were too expensive and funeral directors too greedy. Her little book had a big effect on the funeral business. It changed a lot of things that had been taken for granted. There was much press and television coverage about the cost of death. Every day, it seemed, there were more articles, books, and news stories about death and dying and the funeral business. Memorial societies sprang up as low-cost alternatives to conventional funeral arrangements.

Another important author during this period was Rabbi Earl Grollman. He wrote extensively about the death of a child. In 1984, 250 people gathered to hear him speak at Mercy Hospital in San Diego. But Rabbi Grollman did not do most of the talking. In the audience were many parents who had lost children, and they had a lot to say. Sitting there that night and listening to parents whose children (and stillborn babies) had died, I recalled a day I now regret.

A young Mexican American couple—married for less than a year when their twin boys were born dead—sat with me making funeral arrangements. I asked them if they had named the children. They had not. "That's all right," I said, "we can call them baby boy A and baby boy B."

How could I have said such a thing? Why would anyone deny parents the time or the opportunity to name their dead children? At that time (the 1950s), Arizona had the nation's highest rate of infants stillborn or deceased within twenty-four

71

hours of birth. Because we handled these funerals without charge to the parents, we saw a great many of them. It was all too easy for us to think of them as cases, something we did every day. But those of us who have chosen to work with grieving people have their fragile emotions in our hands. We must never let them become routine; if that happens, it is time to change ourselves or change our jobs. That evening in San Diego, I changed myself. I learned the terrible effects of the death of a child on the parents.

That effect lasts a lifetime. In the summer of 1984, as I walked through a large mausoleum in San Diego, I encountered an elderly woman and asked her if she was visiting a relative. She told me that she always tried to make daily visits to her daughter's crypt: "I am eighty-two now, and sometimes it is hard for me to come every day." We walked together down the long corridor. When we reached her daughter's crypt, I discovered that her daughter had died forty-five years before, at the age of eight. Every day for forty-five years—that's over 16,000 visits—this mother had visited her daughter. Sometimes it seems that life never dies, or maybe it is death that never dies.

"Do you know death personally?" The year was 1975. My wife and I were sitting with a group of colleagues at dinner following a seminar on death and dying, and this question made the rounds of our table. That night only two could answer that they had personally encountered the death of someone close. Our seminar leader followed up with a second question: "How can you be helpful to the people you serve if you don't know what they are going through?"

At the time I did not know death personally—my parents were living, my children were healthy, and my friends were young and hale. But I know it now. My wife and I have lost our parents, her brother, numerous friends, and our eldest son.

When my father died, we decided to have the funeral and burial in Nebraska, where he was born and lived until coming to Arizona to retire. A good friend of mine, Monsignor Robert Donohoe, went with us to Nebraska to take part in the funeral. We asked the United Methodist church in that small town to allow something that had never happened before: a Catholic priest conducting a funeral in a United Methodist church in the middle of the middle of the United States. But the pastor was more than helpful. He and Robert worked out the funeral plan together. For several years afterward, whenever we visited Nebraska, friends would always mention my father's funeral because of the Catholic priest who came from Phoenix and spoke in a United Methodist church. It wasn't traditional, but the uniqueness of the event helped mark the day for my dad's old neighbors and friends.

After we buried my father, we lingered in the cemetery, walking among all the other family graves. The history of our family is in that cemetery. We had a keen

sense of our transitory nature, walking among the graves of those ˈ
and who were once like us. I gazed at my father's marker, and it ˈ___ ___ ____
were the next generation—that my brother, my sister, and I would probably be
the next people in the family to die.

After a certain age, "personal experiences with death" seem to increase and
multiply. Throughout many years of arranging funerals, I had day-to-day expo-
sure to the many ways people die. I dealt with the deaths of many young people
and knew there was a chance that one day a child of my own might suffer the
same fate. It seemed so commonplace—how could we assume we would escape
such an everyday tragedy? In my mind I knew it was possible, and I thought I
was prepared for the worst. I was wrong.

When our eldest son, Mark, died in an accident three years ago, Bea and I were
utterly and completely unprepared. Mark was killed while crossing a very dark
street not far from our home. As we rushed to the hospital, the police would not
let us through the street, and we had to go several miles out of our way. (At the
time, we did not know that this was the accident scene where he was struck down.)

Mark was forty-two when he died—a grown man, but still our son. Children
are not supposed to die before their parents. Of course there is no guarantee of
this, nothing in writing—it's just not supposed to happen. His death was so sudden; there was no time to prepare for it, no opportunity to say good-bye. I cannot even remember leaving the hospital and driving home.

We had a viewing and a funeral for Mark. Our family and friends gathered
around us and gave us the support that is so needed when a death occurs. Mark's
funeral gave us an opportunity to say good-bye, and it brought us closer together as a family.

Of course we are not the only parents who have lost a grown child. Years ago
the sixteen-year-old son of our very close friends died from a fall while climbing in nearby mountains. In spite of their reluctance, the parents sat with their
son's body for a time. When we left the mortuary that afternoon, his mother told
me that she was so glad she had come to see him. "Now," she said, "I know
where he is, and I know he's safe; even though he's dead, he is safe."

When Mark died, I fully understood, at last, what she had meant. Our son is
buried in a cemetery near our home, where we can go and spend time with his
memory. Sometimes we even talk to him. We know where he is and that he is
safe.

We've been told that we need to have closure, but I am not sure that is possible. Grief dulls over time, but then something will come up—you'll hear a
phrase or see a picture or a scene in a movie—and there it will be again.

Our grief seems to come like the tide. Sometimes it is in and sometimes it is
out. Birthdays, Christmas, and special days in Mark's life always bring tears of

remembrance. Closure, for us, will come only with our own deaths. Other losses hover about us as well. Sometimes at night, I wake up thinking that I have not called my mother lately. She has been dead for eighteen years.

Traditional ceremonies such as viewing, the funeral service, and the burial had great meaning for us (as well as for our family and friends) in times of immense loss. They helped us grasp that our loved one was truly dead. They gave opportunities to say good-bye and occasions for others to gather around to love and support us. But many people in America have other ideas about the traditional rites. Over a quarter of people who die are cremated, and by 2010 it will be about 40 percent. In some cases a visitation is held before cremation, but more and more families are opting for a memorial service at a later date with no viewing of the body. A much-loved teacher in Texas who took ten years to die of ovarian cancer specified no services at all; instead, she wanted her family and friends to have a huge party in her memory (and party they did). A growing number of people choose to have no service and request that the cremated remains be scattered in a designated place by people other than family members.

I went out on a boat from San Diego to scatter cremated remains one day a number of years ago—my first and last trip. It was a typical San Diego day, a little hazy but perfect by most standards. There were eighty-four containers of cremated remains loaded in the boat, along with sandwiches, drinks, sunblock, and towels. We left the bay and headed out to the kelp beds about three miles out. This was not a big boat, and I was not all that happy about being on the ocean in the first place. Soon we stopped, and my friend, who was licensed by the state of California to dispose of cremated remains, announced that we were at the right place.

We began to shake out those eighty-four containers. Sometimes, a breeze would blow the dust of the remains back into the boat. I kept thinking that just a few weeks before all of the ashes in these containers were living, breathing people. After all of the boxes were emptied, we ate our lunch, caught some rays, and went back to the harbor. I found it hard to believe that families could leave the disposition of their family members' remains to complete strangers. It was so unceremonious—no words, just "out you go," and on with the afternoon.

Occasionally, perhaps not often, a traditional practice will strike the wrong note. A friend told me about her six-year-old student who died of a brain tumor. Chloe was a petite, dark-eyed beauty with remarkable artistic skills and a generous spirit. Finally her kidneys failed and her little body puffed up beyond recognition. At the viewing, parents of her classmates stood in line and gawked at her swollen body. Little children cried, "Who is that? That's not Chloe!" Some of them laughed. Her mother and father, who wanted and needed a viewing to help them come to grips with their loss, could not have predicted that it would become a spectacle. They were heartbroken. If they had known, they would have held a private viewing and closed the casket for the funeral.

Perhaps the inappropriate responses at Chloe's visitation have to do with changes in the way we treat death in our society. Many times a day we encounter virtual death on television and in movies and video games. In light of that it seems a little contradictory that so many people want no formal or even informal public recognition that a death has occurred. Society is changing, and changing fast. Obviously, if funerals have any value, they will change to meet people's evolving needs. Will funerals become more or less church centered? Will they be more personalized?

Already, many dying persons as well as their families are personalizing end-of-life rituals that bear little resemblance to the staid, formal funerals of the 1950s when I started my career. Loved ones, like those of the art teacher in Texas, have joyful parties celebrating the life of the deceased. People stand up in church and tell stories (some of them very funny) about the one who has died. Families write their own words for the ceremonies. They show video presentations of their loved ones' lives. Survivors gather for memorial services in unusual and sometimes odd places.

Often, now, the body is not present. How important is having the body? In the September 11, 2001, disaster, nearly 2900 people were killed, but fewer than ten intact bodies were found. I have read, and also have heard from colleagues who worked at the scene, that the family members waited weeks and months in the hopes of claiming whatever was left of their dead. When a body cannot be found, the grief is almost beyond help. If I still wake up at night thinking I must call my mother who died a natural death and had a traditional viewing and funeral, how much more must these survivors (of the not only dead, but also missing, eradicated, blotted out) struggle to accept the reality that these cherished persons are no more?

With or without the body present, it seems certain that people in our society will continue to do something—some rite or celebration—to mark the passing of those they love. Every culture in the world—from the most primitive to the most advanced—has done so. The question is not will they, but how will they? How will we guide and support them in their task?

When I talk with other funeral directors across the country about the future of caring for the dead and their survivors, most agree that funerals need more personalization. Funeral directors need to spend more time with the family making preparations that will honor the life lived in a way that is meaningful for those who are left behind. A lot of people think they have to hurry to bury their dead, but in fact there is no hurry. If we spend more time in the planning, with more participation from the family and their pastor, the services are bound to have a more evocative and significant purpose. Funeral directors are going to have to become more caregivers than merchants.

Clergy also need to decide how much importance they will assign to the care of the dying and their survivors. I have sat through thousands of funerals and listened to thousands of homilies. Many are very good and many are not so good. One minister who was not so good had typed up a script that he used for every funeral. At appropriate places in the script there was a blank line and the words, "Give the person's name." At least once that I know of, he read that line instead of giving the name of the deceased. That is not personalization of the funeral.

Here's one of the very good. I was involved in the funeral of a seventeen-year-old who was the first Vietnam casualty from this particular Catholic parish. The pastor spent a lot of time with the family. At the service, he proclaimed that this young man would be carried out of his church as an American hero. He told the family that they could be proud of his life and proud of his death as a soldier in an unpopular war that was not going well. I met with the boy's parents some months later. They told me that, though their pain had diminished little, they found hope in their sorrow because of their faith, their church, and the care of their pastor.

Perhaps some clergy underestimate how important they are when a member of their church dies. Just being there means so much to the family. Edgar Jackson, who has written about grief, tells about a close friend, a United Methodist minister from another church, who visited him after his son died. For an hour they just sat together, holding hands. Jackson said that this was the most meaningful moment during the time surrounding his child's death.

Of course it is not easy or fun to give care in times of death. Several years ago, someone asked me, "Don't you ever weary of being in the middle of death all the time?" My answer is yes, but I know that what I do is important to those I serve, and their responses compensate for the really bad times. However, I cannot dismiss the question too lightly. Sometimes death is so horrific that even longtime veterans of the funeral business cannot deal with it. You think to yourself, "I can't go on doing this."

The crash of Pacific Southwest Airlines Flight 182 in the middle of San Diego on Monday, September 25, 1978, was one such time.

A student pilot in a single-engine Cessna failed a runway approach as the airliner descended on its final approach to Lindbergh Field. The Cessna climbed into the airliner's right wing, out of view of the cockpit, sending the PSA plane nose down into a residential neighborhood. The deaths totaled 135 on the airliner, two in the Cessna, and seven on the ground. The impact was so great that bodies were propelled through the houses.

In its aftermath, the disaster took a toll on almost everyone who worked at the scene or behind the scenes. A number of employees of the medical examiner's office quit their jobs. Two pilots from PSA were sent by their company to help identify the crew; both died within a year of the crash (one by suicide). Many police officers and firefighters felt the impact of the tragedy to the degree that they left their line of work. Some of our mortuary employees had to work two shifts in order to prepare and make arrangements for the bodies to be returned to their families. Several of them left the funeral business for good, saying simply, "I just can't do this anymore."

How could I keep on doing it? I do not have a definitive answer, but another story may shed light on the reason. My first encounter with mass casualty came on December 16, 1956. We received an emergency call from a man who said he saw a train hit a car on the Southern Pacific tracks at 36th Avenue and Buckeye Road. When we arrived at the scene, nothing was there, no train, no car, no police—just the man who called and insisted that he had seen a car hit by the Golden State passenger train.

We walked down the tracks. From the weeds that grew on the banks alongside the rails, I heard a whimper. I followed the cry and found a baby girl in a blood-soaked dress, cushioned by the tall grass. It was amazing to me that she could cry since she seemed so badly hurt. I lifted her with great care and stepped through the weeds toward the ambulance. In the darkness I tripped over a body. When I landed in the dirt, with the baby in my arms, I found myself next to another body.

First things first. We rushed the little girl to the hospital, entrusted her to the emergency room doctors, and went back to the scene. If this had happened today, the police would have arrived with bright lights to aid our search. That night was black and cold and there were no lights. No lights, and no more survivors.

At dawn the next morning we were back on the scene. We gathered up the rest of the dead and picked up over 200 pounds of human tissue. At the time it was the worst car-train accident in American history. The baby girl was one of 13 passengers in a 1937 sedan. She survived and was taken to California to live with relatives. The train's engineer knew nothing of the accident until he walked around the train at the Phoenix station and found parts of a car affixed to the engine.

Twenty-one years later, I was sitting at the front desk of the mortuary when a man and a woman came in and asked for me. I identified myself. The young lady introduced herself and her uncle and said that she just wanted to come by and thank me for saving her life. She was the baby we had found that very dark and cold night by the side of the tracks. Meeting and talking with her, and then taking her to the cemetery to view the graves of her parents and other relatives, was one of the great gifts I have received. How could there not be a God?

When I first became an undertaker, I was of the opinion that death was a numbers game; when your number was called, no matter where you were or what you were doing, it was over. You were dead. Since then I have been with families who cursed God for the death of a child or a husband or wife, and others who thank God for taking a terminally ill person who has been dying for a long time.

It is not a numbers game. We die because of poor judgment, accidents, crime, illness, and old age. Death can contribute meaning to our lives when it brings families closer together and when it opens a door to help others. Such was the case when two families met after the deaths of their sons and out of their grief created the Compassionate Friends Society to care for others in times of loss. Parents of children killed in drunk-driving accidents formed Mothers Against Drunk Driving. In cities all over the country, widowed men and women meet to support one another. Loved ones of AIDS victims have brought about greater understanding and improved treatment for HIV sufferers. Bereaved people contribute to medical research and campaign for causes their loved ones believed in. Even sudden, untimely death can bring good out of the loss.

If I had to do it all over again, would I choose funeral service as a life career? Yes, without a doubt. I have made many friends from the families I have served. I consider my friends in the funeral business as some of the finest people I know. The compensation of helping families far outweighs the difficult times, and it has enriched me beyond any monetary rewards I could dream of.

Lately, people have started asking me if I have made my own funeral plans. No, I have not. But I do have some thoughts about it. First, I want to be buried next to our son; our graves are already reserved. The music has to be Sinatra: "Nancy with a Smiling Face," "My Funny Valentine," and maybe a couple more. I would hope that my family and friends participate. I would like the minister to shed some light on why we die and what is beyond. I hope there will be more laughter than tears and that someone will bring up all the good times we have had and no mention of the bad. I hope that my wife and children and grandchildren can all be there. And when everyone leaves, they will all agree that it was a darn good funeral and were glad they came.

Patches of Godlight

Donald E. Messer

It is ironic that as I began to write this chapter, I was surrounded by sorrow, struggling with family and friends who were facing painful experiences of heartbreak and angst. Let me share my reflections, not theories, on grief and spiritual growth, in light of these current concerns.

My sister's husband entered hospice care, and our family began to resign ourselves to reality. "Mutsch's" heart literally was worn out, and medical care had reached its limits. He decided that he wanted the doctor to disconnect the defibrillator that previously had shocked him back into life. Lazarus came back only once; but thanks to modern medicine, my brother-in-law had been revived several times.

My wife and I shared memories with a couple of close friends on the anniversary of their son's death and remembered Michael's life and love. For parents, the death of a child is truly like a period at the beginning of a sentence. The order of the universe seems reversed.

A friend's routine cataract surgery had unexpected consequences, as infection developed and loss of sight in one eye seemed probable. The trauma of growing older and the uncertainty of the future compelled Sally to seek the best medical care and her friends around the world to lift their fervent prayers for healing.

A visit to see Ila, a cherished friend suffering from Parkinson's disease, was a vivid reminder of the cruelty of untamed illnesses, such as Alzheimer's disease, AIDS, Lou Gehrig's disease, advanced melanoma cancer, and so many others. Robbed of her ability to communicate clearly, and experiencing so many physical problems, this friend reminded me of the finiteness and preciousness of life.

My niece's health situation took another turn for the worse yesterday. Karen has been struggling for health and life after a heart transplant operation six months ago. The transplant was successful, but she has remained hospitalized, suffering incalculable pain from multiple infections and other problems. The miracle of modern medicine keeps people alive, but tied up in tubes and costly procedures. How do persons cope with grief in such prolonged circumstances?

My son-in-law's beloved grandmother has entered the final stages of dying. She spent her lifetime in political activism for social justice, so it has been shocking to see her health decline so quickly. Did the years of caregiving that she provided for her ailing husband speed up her own ill health?

Even as I typed the above words, the phone rang and a pastor informed me that a longtime friend of mine had just died at age ninety-four. Many years ago, Bob asked me to preach his funeral because he said that I would remember him in the prime of life and in the good he sought to do.

Yes, with my family and friends, I seem surrounded by sorrow and grief and struggle to find spiritual meaning and hope.

These experiences of life and death deeply touch my soul, as they are the stories and struggles of my own beloved family and friends. They are very personal and profound as they tug on my heart and bring tears to my eyes.

I know, however, that they are neither unusual nor even the most catastrophic experiences that people face. Many individuals reading these words are themselves coping with awesome losses of love and health in their own lives. Their grief is immeasurable. But when it comes to coping with loss and facing grief, it is futile and foolish to suggest "my cross is heavier than your cross" or "my cross is lighter than others." Heartaches cannot be compared. The imprint of grief is too deep and too personal. Never triage the sorrow of others. The grief and loss of every person deserves attention. There is truth in the adage to "treat kindly every person you meet today, for they are having a hard time."

Living in a Constant Context of Loss and Grief

At this moment, an intensity of personal grief and sorrow permeates my life and thought, but in reality I recognize we always live in the context of loss and mourning. This is the flip side of the coin of life. The unfairness of life, the mystery of why the good suffer and the evil seem to prosper, the excessiveness of the pain and sorrow inflicted on some persons, and other such questions make life precarious and faith problematic.

However, what often escapes the radar of our feelings is the massive suffering of large groups of people. With the recitation of sizable numbers, our minds grow fuzzy and statistics lose their emotional effect and meaning.

For example, talking about the global HIV/AIDS pandemic and the 42 million people currently infected and the 22 million who have already died leaves most persons emotionally inert and spiritually inactive. This may be the worst heath crisis facing humanity for seven hundred years, but basically it is business as usual for most persons and congregations in the United States.

It has been said that to speak of a million deaths is to utter a statistic, but to tell the story of one death is to share a tragedy. We identify with individuals and their dilemmas. We only come to grasp the unspeakable, unfolding tragedy of the global AIDS crisis when we focus our heads and hearts not on:

- The fact that 30 million persons lack needed modern anti-retroviral treatment, but rather on a young abandoned woman in an Indian hospital holding a Bible in her hands who has not received the necessary dollar-a-day for treatment.

- 14.1 million AIDS-related orphans, but rather on a single child dying in an African orphanage hospice.
- Talk of homophobia or the church's prejudice against gays and lesbians, but rather on the young man recently diagnosed with HIV who received a letter from his parents containing his birth certificate ripped in two.
- News that the government is cutting $1 billion in AIDS appropriations, but rather on becoming acquainted with a person dying in excruciating pain in Thailand where there are no painkillers available in the Buddhist temple transformed into an AIDS hospice.
- The nearly universal stigmatization and discrimination expressed toward persons living with HIV/AIDS, but rather on the anguish of a mother in Kansas attending the funeral of a stranger to express her disenfranchised grief at the death of her only son. (Her husband had insisted he be buried secretly without a Christian funeral.)

Talk of "genocide by indifference in Africa" escapes us until we get up close and personal with human suffering and grief. When I recently visited South Africa, I was overwhelmed by my conversations with pastors and priests. I knew that some six hundred to one thousand persons reportedly were dying daily in South Africa, but I had not computed in my mind what that really meant in terms of human suffering and funerals. Clergy, for example, reported they were conducting ten to twenty funerals every week. How does one deal with assembly-line funerals? How does one even begin to cope with this type of tragedy? How does one minister to this magnitude of grief and sorrow?

Kahlil Gibran expressed the paradox of joy and sorrow when he wrote, "When you are sorrowful look again in your heart, and you shall see that in truth you are weeping for that which has been your delight."[1] But often such a similitude of spirituality escapes us; and we are simply overwhelmed, mystified, angered, stunned, frightened, or paralyzed by the tragedies of this world. Seeking answers and meaning, we cry with the Hebrew psalmist of old:

All this has come upon us,
    though we have not forgotten thee,
    or been false to thy covenant.
Our heart has not turned back,
    nor have our steps departed from thy way ...
... for thy sake we are slain ...
    Why dost thou hide thy face? (Psalm 44:17-18; 22*a*, 24*a* RSV)

We seek answers where there are no answers. We drink from the bitter waters of despair and eat the dry bread of depression. We hurt in places where no medicine can permeate. Our tears become clogged in the hidden spots of our soul. With Archibald MacLeish in *J.B.* we want to shout: "If God is God He is not good. If God is good He is not God."[2] Sometimes it is simply "too much, too much," and we are more than tempted to blame God for life's miseries. Joyce Rupp says we mumble, "Why isn't God fair? Isn't God the one who is ultimately to blame for this pain? Couldn't this God, who can do all things, have stopped it in an instant?"[3]

"Patches of Godlight"

Faced with such theological questions of theodicy, both in terms of personal grief and social injustice, I am reminded of C. S. Lewis's experiences of tramping through thickly forested woods. He notes how patches of bright sunlight occasionally break the dark coolness of the environment. Rays suddenly break through the branches and strike the hiker with feelings of warmth and life. He suggests an analogy with spiritual "patches of Godlight" that we spontaneously experience as we walk in the shadowy woods of life and death.[4] No matter how dark the night or how deep the grief, regardless of how painful the heartaches and headaches, there are special moments when as Christians we affirm the presence of God's grace amid our pain and perplexities. Our tears dry and our loneliness subsides as we are warmed from beyond by "patches of Godlight." What follows is my attempt to share some of those beams of divinity that have influenced my reflections on grief and spirituality.

First, I am reminded that how we imagine God makes a major difference as we walk through the valleys of death and grief. Joyce Rupp tells us that if we picture God as on our side, rather than against us or as responsible for our pain, we not only are closer to the biblical portrait, but also find spiritual strength to face each day. God does love us, even when we do not trust God or when we despair that God is absent. Rupp offers some practical theological suggestions as we grieve our loss:

> It helps to deliberately pray our pain, to cry out to God, to express our anger. Writing a letter to God, telling God how we feel, can help us to experience being "heard" by God. We can also write a letter from God to us, noting what God would want to say to us at this time of loss.[5]

Also, at such moments, I turn to the words and wisdom of Abraham Heschel, who draws a portrait of a God of pathos who is "never neutral, never beyond good and evil ... [and] always partial to justice."[6] Ours is a God who cares and grieves, a God who "does not stand outside the range of human suffering and sorrow," but is "personally involved in, even stirred by, the conduct and fate" of human beings.[7]

The God of Jesus Christ is a suffering God, who is wounded by our tragedies and hurting because of our sorrow: a God who lost an only son on a cross, thanks to human cruelty and injustice; a God who does not punish us for our sins by sending sickness; a God who Jesus tells us does not control every detail of life—accidents happen and towers fall on both the good and the bad—a God who cares and cries.

Second, I believe that we need to find ways of embracing life, even when the world seems to be tumbling down around us. In the musical *Zorba the Greek*, Zorba declares, as he breaks into dance, that the "only death is the death we die every day by not living." The greatest spiritual temptation for me is to give up, but the most triumphant among us always find ways of living—even when tortured by painful arthritis; or struck by sudden loss of sight and mobility; or faced with crushing losses in their work, family, or love life. All of us know remarkable people who seem to sparkle even when all the lights seem to have been turned off. They are "patches of Godlight," witnesses who provide help and hope to the rest of us in our struggles.

The events of September 11 shocked Americans into realizing that we are a part of a larger global community. We had fallen under the illusion that we were somehow immune from world terrorism and violence, that wars would always be fought on somebody else's soil, that we could be safe regardless of how much injustice, poverty, and inequality existed between the rich and the impoverished in this world.

We might sing the old lyrics from "No Man Is an Island," which say that "each man's joy is joy to me; each man's grief is my own"; but we really have not experienced the connectedness of being human. We have not shared the pain of orphans in Africa or the hunger of the starving in North Korea or the agony of the thirty million untreated persons with HIV and AIDS or the bloodshed of war-torn civilians of Sierra Leone, Liberia, or the Middle East. In reality, September 11, 2001, was the first day of a new millennium for most Americans: on that day we learned that there is no escape from the threat of grief and loss.

Third, I would emphasize the imperative of companionship as we struggle with issues of loss and grief. It is nearly impossible to cope alone; we need partners who will walk with us "through the valleys of the shadow of death."

Gail Sheehy suggests that the movement of grief is spiral, not linear. We do not just move from stage to stage—from denial to rage to bargaining to depression to acceptance. A person, she says, "may seem to be moving until a

83

memory or a sensory detail or another trauma piles on." Then "the person loops back down into despair, and it's necessary to thrust forward, to complete the loop and continue to move forward again."[8]

The dirtiest word in the lexicon of grief, says Sheehy, is *closure*. There is no such thing as final closure since memories persist and pain flares up anew. In her studies of families affected directly by the attacks of September 11 in New York City and by the Oklahoma City bombing, she contends that the second anniversary of a loss is an especially traumatic time. By that date, other people are anxious to move on and to put the past behind them and are tired of listening to the grief of others. But some wounds never quite close, and the spiritually sensitive person understands that human condition. What helps persons most are companions. In Sheehy's words:

> People in grief need someone to walk with them without judging them. Whether that's a minister or a rabbi or a friend. . . . Or whether it's a mental health professional or the members of a support group. It's that companioning through the spiral that seems to provide the greatest benefit for both the companions and the wounded.[9]

In my own life journey, I remember those companions as being critical. I do not particularly remember their words, but I can never forget their presence. I recall the nameless Roman Catholic nuns who walked with me from the hospital room all the way to my car in a distant parking lot after a family member's death. I recollect my wife's understanding companionship, when night after night I cried myself to sleep after my father's death. I still feel the hugs and prayers of hope that friends and family have shared with me at other critical moments of loss and grief. And over and over again, I have found the words of Jesus unbelievably supportive: "Lo, I am with you always" (Matthew 28:20 RSV).

Everyone, including children, needs understanding and companionship. Little Claire was only four months old when her father had his first seizure from brain cancer. For almost two years, she grew up in a home in which every day was a struggle to care for her father in the most difficult of circumstances. Unlike that of most children, her speech did not develop properly, and her use of words was limited. Surrounded by loving care, her father died after a lengthy illness. But she absorbed levels of grief and pain that no one could fully comprehend, and her silence was frightening. Then, suddenly, at age two years and four months, she asked her mommy, "Why did Daddy die?" Her mother answered as best she could, and Claire listened. Then she responded, "We took good care of Daddy." Obviously, her mother's loving companionship, both to her husband and to her children, had helped precious Claire navigate successfully through "the valleys of the shadow of death."

Fourth, though grief and loss are part of the constant context of our living and dying, I do not think any of us should yield too quickly to their powers. Yes, death is inevitable, but not necessarily right now.

Life, health, and relationships are precious; and we should do everything possible to preserve them. Just because someone's age is advancing is no reason not to seek the best medical care within reason. The will to live and to love are strong spiritual impulses for survival and strength.

In the face of the great human tragedies of this world, I am unwilling, for example, to give up hope that the HIV/AIDS pandemic can be controlled. It is a preventable disease; we can have a world without AIDS. Therefore, I resist, with the words of the British poet Dylan Thomas: "Do not go gentle into that good night. . . . Rage, rage against the dying of the light."[10]

There is nothing inevitable about the deaths of millions around the world who are currently suffering with AIDS. People can be saved if persons raise their voices in rage to governments, churches, and other agencies and demand that financial resources be allocated for prevention and treatment and that health care be considered a right for all persons. Hope exists, but passiveness in the light of the world's great holocaust cannot persist.

What William Sloane Coffin said, as he publicly reflected on the tragic accidental death of his son, needs to be underscored:

> What are we to say when someone dies too soon—in an accident, of cancer, of AIDS? One thing we must never say is that it is the will of God. No one knows that for sure, so let no one pretend that he or she does. . . . What we can say are Paul's words, "Love never ends," because as Paul also says, "I am persuaded that neither death nor life . . . can separate us from the love of God." In other words, the abyss of love is deeper than the abyss of death.[11]

A fifth "patch of Godlight" for me has been the gift of tears and the blessing of crying. Tears, I think, are God's way of letting us release some of our heartache and heartbreak.

Twenty-five years have now passed since my father died after a short illness. Though the intensity of grief's pain has long ceased, I trust there will never be "final closure." I cling to those words of an unknown poet who said "memories are like roses in December."

Occasionally when I remember something about my dad or my beloved late father-in-law, I have to stop and brush away a few tears. Everyone grieves on a different timetable, but I suspect at some point the emotional floodgates must be released, so that God's grace and healing can flow.

One is never too old or too sophisticated to weep. Following Dad's death, I learned for the first time that sometimes you are totally unable to control the waves of tears that engulf you. At unexpected moments and places, tears would flow and my body would tremble with feelings of unspeakable loss. When a parent or a loved one dies, a precious tie is broken and there can be unfathomable pain. To cry is to experience the mercy of God. Theologically, tears are a "means of grace."

Sixth, the hope of the resurrection remains fundamental to my faith and the "patch of Godlight" that helps me see beyond the present pain, grief, and tragedy. The resurrection of Jesus Christ demonstrates the Christian conviction that death and defeat are not final. I do not pretend to understand what precisely happened in Jerusalem a few days after the crucifixion, but I know it was an event in history that transformed the disciples' despair into hope and moved them beyond grief into life and sacrificial service.

In 1991, the noted composer Natalie Sleeth shared with me a copy of a little book, *Parable*, she had just written for her grandchildren to explain to them her approaching death. She wanted them to affirm both the goodness of her living and the goodness of her dying. In her book, Natalie expressed her belief that God wanted people to live as long as they could, "but not forever because then the world would be too full with no room for anybody."[12]

Composer of much church music, including the popular "Hymn of Promise," Natalie also expressed her vision of the resurrection and life after death. In words designed for children, but in language that touches my heart, she described a "heaven where there is no pain or sickness or sadness or anything bad." She shared that she had already begun her journey to heaven and that daily she "drew nearer to God" and "could see light and hear music and feel happiness [she] had never known before."

That is my prayer, not only for myself, but also for all God's family everywhere.

Endnotes

1. Kahlil Gibran, "On Joy and Sorrow," *The Prophet* (New York: Alfred A. Knopf, 1965), 29.

2. Archibald MacLeish, *J.B.: A Play in Verse* (Boston: Houghton Mifflin Co., 1956), 11.

3. Joyce Rupp, *Praying Our Goodbyes* (Notre Dame, IN: Ave Maria Press, 1988), 35.

4. See C. S. Lewis, *Letters to Malcolm* (New York: Harcourt, Brace & World, 1964).

5. Joyce Rupp, "Walking with God Through Grief and Loss," *CareNotes* (St. Meinrad, IN: Abbey Press, 1990).

6. Abraham Heschel, *The Prophets* (New York: Harper & Row, 1962), 231.

7. Ibid., 224.

8. Citations form Gail Sheehy are from "Gail Sheehy on America's Passage," Beliefnet, http://www.beliefnet.com/story/131/story_13177.html. See also Gail Sheehy, *Middletown, America: One Town's Passage from Trauma to Hope* (New York: Random House, 2003).

9. Sheehy, "America's Passage."

10. Dylan Thomas, "Do Not Go Gentle into that Good Night," from *The Poems of Dylan Thomas* (Cambridge, MA: New Directions Publishing Company, 1952).

11. William Sloane Coffin, "Eulogy for Alex." Sermon at Riverside Church, New York City (June 1968).

12. Natalie Sleeth, *Parable,* unpublished, 1991.

We Have This Treasure in Earthen Vessels

Rebecca L. Miles

All my life, people in my family have been talking about death and telling deathbed stories. My great-grandfather Miles, knowing he was near death, grabbed the hand of his oldest child and spoke his last words, "Son, don't y'all grieve. I have a 'house not made with hands, eternal in the heavens.'" In her final days, grandmother Ridgway sang hymns until she could sing no more; and then the family, gathering around the bed, sang for her. The only thing I know about my great-grandmother Cordelia Ridgway is what she said as she lay hemorrhaging on her deathbed in rural Arkansas. Knowing that she would not last much longer, she cradled her newborn son, my grandfather, and began to touch each part of his body. When at last she reached his feet and had touched each toe, she closed her eyes and said, "O, how I'll miss these precious little feet."

Death stories are common not only in my own Methodist family, but also in the larger family of Methodism. In his last two decades, John Wesley collected Methodist deathbed stories, publishing them in his *Arminian Magazine*. The story of Caster Garret is typical. Gathered around his deathbed, friends watched as "Satan made his last effort." Finally, Garret, "giving a stamp with his foot," cried out, "Satan! I stamp thee under my feet. O my dear friends and neighbors, praise, praise the Lord with me! For he is come in mercy to my soul! The terror is gone! . . . Blessed be Jesus who hath given me the victory! O I feel his love in my heart, 'Praise God from whom all blessings flow.'" Soon after, as friends were singing hymns, Garret said, "'I am happy!' and then he fell asleep in the arms of Jesus."[1]

Early Methodists told these stories not only to mark the great faithfulness of the dying, but, more important, to encourage greater faithfulness in the living. The deathbed was often a means of grace for the person dying, for the witnesses, and for those who would later hear the stories. After several years, the stories sent to Wesley for publication became formulaic. The dying person, surrounded by Christian witnesses, would often go through a series of temptations (to doubt or despair, for example), overcome the temptations with the help of God, offer praise to God and encouragement and counsel to those gathered around the bed, and then die, often with verses of Scripture or hymns on their lips. Little was said in these stories about the medical details, the work of the physician, or the ongoing struggles of family after the final moments of death. One scholar suggests that those who wrote down the death stories began, over time, to organize and write them following a particular formula that had become popular in *Arminian Magazine*.[2] It seems just as likely that these popular stories began to train Methodists how to die and how to witness death, shaping both their expectations and behavior.

When I ask people today about the deaths of their loved ones, I often hear not a narrative of spiritual struggle and growth, but one of medical diagnoses and procedures. We have been trained to pay attention to medical details and to tell medical narratives. At the same time, people are also shaped by the death stories from their religious and family traditions. These stories often provide a model that is more complex than the medical narrative. What stories do we tell about death in our families and our religious communities? And how, through these stories, are we being trained and training others to die and to witness death? The only way I know to respond to these questions is to tell a story.

Late one summer afternoon in 1913, when my grandmother was seven years old, she tiptoed past the bed of her older brother, Henry, who was sick with typhoid fever. Their parents and the older children were still working in the fields, as eleven-year-old Henry would have been had he not taken ill. Henry opened his eyes and saw his little sister Dora as she tried to slip by. Many years later she wrote, "When he opened his eyes and saw me, he asked me to fan away the flies from him. This I did until he closed his eyes again. Then childlike, I left my post and went merrily on my way." That evening, her brother died. Sixty years later, grandmother would tell this story with deep grief and regret. She wrote, "[That] summer a shadow, a deep shadow entered our home.... If I have a conflict with the thought of death, it began here. I did not recognize it then, but a feeling of guilt was being born in me because I had left my sick brother to the merciless flies and heat only a few hours before he left us forever. I was a very sad little tot. Ever after that death and burial experiences, caves, dark basements, or any place without air and sunlight bring out a morbid feeling in me."

Grandmother's "conflict with the thought of death" was not hidden from her family. She feared death and serious illness until a few days before her own death. As my grandmother's closest sisters lay dying—one in 1984 and another in 1986—my grandfather Mel would drive her every few days from their home in eastern Arkansas, past rice and cotton fields and across the Arkansas River to a hospital in Memphis. I drove them once and saw how pale she grew as we neared the hospital. When her sister Laura was dying in the summer of 1984, she kept a journal, writing only a few lines each day. "Laura is worse each time we see her. We all bear much grief." "Our precious Laura died today. Oh, what grief we bear!" The final entry for the year was a few days later. "Laura was buried today, her birthday.... Oh, God comfort me, *please! I am deeply grieved!*" Grandmother carried deep grief and regret that she was not with her sisters when they died and that she could not do more for them in their last days. The "feeling of guilt" that was "being born" in the girl of seven, was still with her after those many years.

The death trips to Memphis began long before the 1980s. On a Thursday afternoon in April 1951, Grandmother and her sister Prudie took the bus to Memphis to sit vigil with Laura at the bedside of their mother who had had a stroke. By Saturday morning, their mother was unconscious, and by suppertime, she was dead. They buried her the next day in their childhood home of Cotton Plant. I have few details about their mother's last days or funeral, but I do know that her grave was covered with pink and white gladiolas, red roses, and white lilies; and that the Vickery family gathered after the burial to eat ham, chicken, a variety of bean dishes, two casseroles of macaroni and cheese, two cakes, and three pies—including one mincemeat brought by Mrs. Carter.

I know these details because the sisters kept lists describing the flowers and food so that they could write thank-you notes. One sister also saved their letters to each other following their mother's death. Two days after the funeral, my grandmother was back teaching her fifth-grade class. From her school desk, she wrote, "My head hurts and my back is sore. I'm low in spirit and absentminded. I'm not really fit to teach." The following week, my grandmother wrote, "Sunday [a week after the funeral] was hard on me too; and when late afternoon and early evening came, I could hardly stand it.... I became more melancholy and Mel asked me if I would like to walk for a while. We walked for forty-five minutes I guess. I think it won't be so bad this Sunday, maybe." Over the next three weeks, Grandmother worked through her grief in a rush of activity. She remodeled her kitchen, put up twenty-seven pints of strawberry jam, dug up some sweet williams in the woods to plant in her backyard, dug up small dogwood trees to plant in her sisters' yards, welcomed several groups of overnight guests, and cooked—among other things—White River catfish, mustard greens, and quite a few pies.

Because I only have the letters that were written to Aunt Laura and not the ones that she wrote to others, I do not know how she described her own grief. Even so, the letters from her friends reveal her struggles. Her friends reassured her that she had nothing to feel guilty about and that she did all she could for her mother. An old school friend closed her letter of sympathy, "And remember ... no regrets at all."

In February 1990, my mother called one night to say that my grandmother was dying. As I drove from our home in Chicago down to Arkansas to witness her death, I watched the seasons change. Snow was still deep in Chicago, but the freeze had broken in Arkansas, and the first blooms were on the japonica bushes. Grandmother had hoped to see the flowers bloom in her yard one last time, so I stopped by her house and cut a branch of japonica blossoms. In past years, she had filled her springtime letters with exclamation points accenting a procession of flowers—Japonica! Crocus! Daffodils!! Iris!! Dogwoods!! Beautiful!!! Amazing!!! One by one, in each letter, she called out the roll of springtime flowers. When I arrived at the hospital in Little Rock, my mother set those few japonica blossoms on her mother's pillow. Grandmother was just conscious enough to squeeze my hand and smile at her first japonica blossoms of the season.

We had worried about Grandmother's last days because we knew how frightened she was of death and lingering illness. She had always talked openly about her fears and often told us how she hoped to die: "I want to be killed instantly in an automobile accident with Mel right there, going with me. Along will come another car, and WHAM! that'll be it." (She would shout and clap her hands.) My grandfather, never looking up from his reading, would always respond, "Dora, speak for yourself." (I should add that not all the Vickery women withdrew from the thought of death. When her dear friend moved to California, Aunt Prudie was distressed that her friend was going to miss her funeral someday and would never see how nice she looked in her casket. So she and a friend took a camera to the funeral home and while nobody was looking, Aunt Prudie climbed into a casket, folded her hands over her chest, closed her eyes, and waited for her friend to snap a picture for herself and anyone else who might miss her funeral.)

It was not just death and lingering illness that Grandmother feared. In her eighty-four years, she never spent a night alone and swore she never would. She refused to fly; and on the one occasion when she was forced to board an airplane to get to a funeral, she trembled. In preparation for this essay, I asked family members to write an account of Grandmother's death. All four accounts, each written independently in four Southern states, described my grandmother as a scaredy-cat.

We were all surprised, then, that she was not fearful when it came time to die. Grandmother was throwing clots, and the doctor insisted that her only hope was leg amputation and quadruple bypass surgery. Grandmother refused surgery, telling the doctor, "Young man, you are not listening to me. I am not going to have surgery. Every time you cut on me, it makes things worse." "You'll die without surgery," he said. "I know that," she said. She asked for pain medication and a private room where her family could gather around her and told her family that she was "ready to go."

Within a few hours, family members were traveling to Little Rock to witness her death. In the days before, when she still had strength, she had sung her favorite hymns. My husband's parents came to visit and found her with a wash-cloth over her eyes, unaware of their presence, singing "What a Friend We Have in Jesus." When she was too weak to sing, we sang for her. We told stories and prayed. We rubbed her feet and hands and then her legs and arms as they began to stiffen and grow cold. She was dying inch by inch. My mother told us that Grandmother's sisters and mother had died like this. They threw clots, and their extremities bore the first clear signs of death. That night in the hospital, we blamed it all on hog fat; the Vickery women put away washtubs of bacon grease. They all died skinny, but their arteries must have been saturated with fat. My grandmother's cornbread muffins were legendary; her secret was two table-spoons of bacon grease per muffin. My mother, sister, and I took some comfort that night in our own low-fat, high-fiber diets; but I still figure that the three of us will end up just like that—taking our place in a long line of scrawny, stub-born old women dying by inches.

My mother and I had run home to get pajamas for my grandfather and other supplies for the night, when we got a call to come quickly. Just before we got back to the room, she died with her husband and other family at her side. My mother and I were sad to have missed her death, and in the grand tradition of the Vickery women, we have borne guilt and regret about it ever since.

After Grandmother's death, my mother, sister, and I washed her body, singing old hymns and talking about her and her sisters. I couldn't stop thinking that they all looked something like this in death and that my mother, sister, and I wouldn't look much different. The closest I can come to describing my experi-ence tending her body is that it was sacramental. Generations of women have washed the bodies of their dead parents and grandparents and then have been washed by their own daughters, sisters, and granddaughters, all participating in something much larger than themselves and all of those lives and deaths put together. Years later, when I first washed the bodies of our newborn daughters, I thought, "Good Lord, the cycle is starting all over again."

After the washing was over and the men had joined us for one last round of prayers and hymns, my sister and I decided that we were going to do this thing the old way, staying with the body and seeing her home. For eighty-four years, she had managed never to spend the night alone; we figured we could keep her company one last night. We watched as the nurses wrapped her up and put her on a gurney to be taken to the mortuary van. We followed the van to a mortuary that prepared the dead for transfer to smaller towns, and the late-shift mortician reluctantly let us stay the night in the mortuary office where we could see her body through the open door. At dawn the next morning—a Sunday—we drove behind the hearse for Grandmother's last trip home. We sped past rice and cotton fields, past winter soybeans and silage, and past state highway 17, which led north to the land where her family had sharecropped and the cemetery where the Vickerys were buried.

With my sister keeping watch at the funeral home in Grandmother's town, I went by the house to make coffee for family and friends who would be arriving soon. A few of Grandmother's used tissues were scattered on the floor. (She could not see well enough to know they were there.) Inside the refrigerator, I found two stale muffins from her last batch of cornbread. I would never have guessed that I could grieve so, over used tissues and stale cornbread.

Back at the funeral home, my sister, having been ousted from the room where they kept the body, was napping in the office. The old tradition of sitting watch with the body does not work so well out of sight of the body, so we gave up and walked to church to visit Grandmother's Sunday school class, a dwindling group of women in their eighties. The class leader mistook us for a delegation from the youth group, perhaps because we were not properly groomed for church, having spent the last thirty hours traveling and keeping vigil. They were distressed to hear of Grandmother's death, but were clearly more practiced than we were at the art of grieving for the dead and then going on with the next thing—in this case, the Sunday school lesson.

The next few days are a blur—a stream of sweet ladies who loved my grandmother and indiscriminately hugged anyone connected to her; a procession of gladiolas, carnations, and white lilies; and an unending supply of ham, fried chicken, macaroni and cheese casseroles, and pies—including at least one mincemeat. Daffodils and crocuses from Grandmother's yard filled vases around the house. The afternoon of the visitation at the funeral home, my mother, sister, and I dressed her body. Putting on panty hose is never an easy task, but putting them on someone who has been dead for several days is particularly challenging. It was also maddeningly pointless, but none of us had the nerve to send Grandmother to the visitation—her last party—with bare legs. By the day of the funeral, all of the family had gathered. Most of her grandchildren participated in the funeral service and burial, and some of us stayed to fill in her grave. That afternoon when the women divided her jewelry and a few personal items, I received, among other things, a flower catalogue with glorious pictures of daffodils! Crocus! Tulips! Iris!

I know these details because I wrote it all down at the time, in the grand tradition of the Vickery women. One week after my grandmother's death, I wrote, "I am dead-tired . . . and overwhelmed by the beauty of her death and burial and by the way I still miss her." Over the next weeks, I was working through my grief in a rush of activity—just as Grandmother had forty years before. I took long walks with my husband, entertained guests, cleaned out closets, reorganized kitchen cabinets, rearranged our furniture, and cooked—among other things—waffles, grits, biscuits and gravy, red beans and rice, and several pies. Three weeks after Grandmother's death, my mother, who had taken wonderful care of her own mother, called to talk about her grief and deep sense of guilt at not having done more. She concluded, "Well, I need to get out and do something."

Several years later, when my grandparents' house was sold, I picked up a trunk that Grandmother had left to me. It had belonged to her mother and held family treasures saved first by my great-grandmother and later by Grandmother and her sisters. When I got the trunk home, I poked around inside, looking at pictures, flipping through family letters, and reading Grandmother's notebooks describing the first sixty years of her life. A decade passed without a full exploration of the trunk's contents. I was preoccupied with my work as a teacher; the births of our daughters; and the simple daily rush of cooking, cleaning, and living.

While writing this essay, which was at first only about Grandmother's death, I decided to look through the trunk to see if I might find anything about other family deaths. Going through the trunk for the first time, I found family pictures, telegrams from a son fighting in World War I, scores of letters written by my great-grandmother, and a box of letters and records from the time of my great-grandmother's death. The box contained a record book from the funeral home listing the names of the flowers and the pallbearers, a scribbled list of foods brought to the family, and a handful of letters from my grandmother and my aunt describing their grief and the small tasks that followed their mother's death. In one of the letters, my grandmother wrote about their mother's "little trunk" and asked her sister Laura that it be kept "intact," because "the things in it meant so much to her." I also found several things my grandmother had placed in the trunk—including a half dozen notebooks telling about her life and the lives and deaths of her family. Under her notebooks were baby pictures of generations of Vickery children, Sunday school certificates, and an old hymnal. At the very bottom of the trunk was a small cloth book bag with a grammar school reader tucked inside. On the first page of the reader, in clumsy letters, a little boy had written his name in pencil more than ninety years before—Henry Vickery.

This essay began as a simple story about my grandmother's death. If it were not for the trunk, I would never have known how much my grandmother's death story and our experiences of her death were part of a larger family story. The old family stories opened up parts of my own story that I had missed—that grief is so often saturated with guilt and regret; that it so often spawns exhaustion and, at the same time, a manic rush to cook and clean, to plant and write; and that our memories of death and grief are anchored in the smallest, most mundane details such as the flies and summer heat of 1913, mincemeat pies, cornbread muffins, crumpled tissues, a little boy's book bag, a baby's tiny feet, white lilies, sweet williams, Japonica! Daffodils! Crocus!! Dogwoods!! Beautiful!! Amazing!!!

Yesterday I put everything back in the trunk. On top of the old boxes, I placed several accounts of Grandmother's death. Soon, I will add this essay, and I expect to add new stories after other deaths. I do not know what our daughters will someday make of these stories or even what I would want them to make of the stories. I certainly would not want them to repeat the cycle of guilt or to take on their great-grandmother's fear of death. I prefer to think of them climbing, surreptitiously, into their caskets for a quick picture. But, of course, I have no more say in their telling and living of the stories than Grandmother had in mine. All I can do is tell the stories. I pray that as our daughters come of age in a culture that often reduces death to a series of medical failures and judges human lives by their economic productivity, they will have been trained to tell and live another story. I pray that they will be formed by the stories of the saints and continually transformed by the story of a God who made us, who came into the world to redeem and sustain us, and who, in the end, will bring us home.

Endnotes

1. "Account of Caster Garret," *Arminian Magazine: Consisting of Extracts and Original Treatises on Universal Redemption* (London) X:1 (1787): 20-21.

2. Richard Bell, "'Our People die well': Death-bed Scenes in Methodist Magazines in Eighteenth-century Britain," unpublished manuscript, Annual Meeting of the Association of Education in Journalism and Mass Communication, 2003.

Mundane Grief

Bonnie J. Miller-McLemore

My oldest son leaves for college next fall. I am experiencing what psychologists have called "anticipatory grief." Or so an interior voice—my best intellectualizing defense mechanism—tells me. I imagine the absence of his light humor at our dinner table, the emptiness of his room, or the house without his music; and I rehearse my impending loss. Like a tongue searching the raw gum after a lost tooth, I stretch toward it, find the missing spot, and then shy away. Mostly I dart away. I even put off writing this because I did not want to touch it. I do not want to spend much time exploring the edges of this loss. But, truth be told, at midlife, as I gray and wrinkle, as my parents mark with gratefulness their days of good health, and as my three sons surpass me in height and life expectation, I spend more of my time grieving change than I ever anticipated.

Life has graciously spared me many hardships addressed in other chapters. Most accounts of bereavement focus, as they should, on major loss—death, divorce, miscarriage, and serious illness. I have not lost a child, a parent, a sibling, or an intimate friend to death. Few close family members suffer from a chronic, debilitating disease. My marriage remains strong, and none of my pregnancies ended in miscarriage or stillbirth. Although there is little point in judging losses comparatively or claiming some kind of superiority in suffering, an unapproachable difference must be recognized between such major anguish and the kind of minor, daily sorrow that I want to consider here. Nothing compares to the suffering of tragic loss. Any book on grief must look at these most difficult parts of life.

This should not, however, preclude considering the relationship between Christian faith and mundane loss. The topic is remarkably absent from most discussions. I cannot think of many books or articles on it. Most people do not talk much about their struggle to deal with minor loss except during a major life milestone or when horrible tragedy strikes. At such points, people expect tears but are surprised when they come at any other time. Yet, if I were radically honest with myself, I would have to argue that I have been living with loss during most of my parenthood and am closer to crying recently than I would like to admit.

Most people yearn to associate parenthood with its many blessings rather than its innumerable sorrows. But I would venture to say that an elementary aspect of good parenting is learning to live with loss. Frankly, I'm not sure how well I've done. And this book raises an even harder question that I have not asked myself often enough: What does the Christian faith, my own conviction, have to do with chronic, nontragic, mundane daily loss?

My computer thesaurus suggests some interesting substitutes for "mundane": earthly, secular, temporal, and worldly. The Western Christian tradition tends to disassociate the sacred and the mundane, the religious and the ordinary, and has often identified spirituality with extraordinary times of silence, solitude, prayer, joy, and rebirth. Yet, in mundane loss, there is a great deal of room for the sacred. Indeed, if day-to-day parenting is, as I argue elsewhere, a religious practice *par excellence*,[1] and if parenting is filled with loss, then how one learns to grieve within families comprises an important spiritual discipline.

Nontragic Daily Loss and Christian Faith

In the "empty nest syndrome," contemporary society has invented a rather truncated, hackneyed depiction of parental anguish. This oft-used phrase confines loss to the final stage of a child's official departure and obscures the infinitesimal leave-takings that occur daily and at each life stage. Otherwise helpful psychological insight unfortunately renders parental sorrow a "syndrome" or abnormal affliction that one ought to get over, rather than as an inherent, ongoing aspect of all parenting. As a result, many parents experience what other psychologists describe as "disenfranchised grief," or grief over bereavement that is denied social and religious legitimacy.[2] Disenfranchised grievers must do grief work in private without social support.

So a first step in a Christian response to mundane grief is simply faithful recognition and community support. Ironically, clinical language, spouted by popular efforts to put death back on the table, has been used just as easily to control, manage, and evade suffering. Even the Christian tradition itself has had a hard time appreciating the "prayer of lament" as central to its larger corpus.[3]

Parents, as art historian Anne Higonnet remarks, "inevitably begin losing their children as soon as they are born."[4] This is epitomized in the very nature and condition of pregnancy itself. In conception and pregnancy, a mother experiences a tenacious link to another that begins in separation. In the pregnant body, the other is both the self and not the self and is hourly, daily becoming more separate until that which was the mother's becomes irrevocably another. And this initial subversive state of being pregnant—what French feminist Julia Kristeva dubs "a continuous separation, a division of the very flesh"—is only a very tiny piece of the subtle bereavements that fill parenthood. Most parents are not all that different from Mary, the mother of God, who, as biblical theologian

Beverly Gaventa notes, contends with a child who is "profoundly hers and yet not hers at all."[5]

Perhaps this is partly why the author of Luke kept the account of Jesus' parents' discovery that they had left their young twelve-year-old son behind in Jerusalem as a central story (Luke 2:41-52). It is significant that this particular aspect of parenthood is the only account of Jesus' childhood included in all four canonical Gospels.

In her analysis of this pericope, Gaventa argues that the New Revised Standard Version—"your father and I have been searching for you *in great anxiety*"—fails to "capture the poignancy of the word Luke selects *(odynoun)*." A better translation of verse 48*b* is, "Behold, your father and I have been looking for you *in anguish*." The emotional claim that Mary makes here "is the real and present terror of parents who do not know where their child is."[6] I once dropped off my twelve-year-old youngest son at Starbucks to let him walk across the street with his drink to meet me in my office, and he got lost on the university campus and showed up a half-hour later. Mary and Joseph searched for three whole days—an almost unfathomable amount of time for parents who have become hysterical in only minutes when a child did not show up at an appointed time and place.

Not surprising, parents are perhaps most distressed by what many acknowledge as among the hardest tragic losses—the death of a child. "It's so wrong, so profoundly wrong," exclaims Nicholas Wolterstorff, who lost his twenty-five-year-old son in a disastrous mountain climbing accident, "for a child to die before its parents."[7] He, like others in his situation, has to work hard to reconfigure his beliefs about God, suffering, and death. Such parents are irrevocably changed, perhaps by this more than by any other single life event. For Wolterstorff, a chasm opens up between time before the disaster and time after.

Again, any comparison between death of a child, in which the "*neverness . . . is so painful*"[8]—never again to be with the person—and the kind of daily loss I'm considering is ludicrous. Yet all parents stand on a continuum as people vulnerable before the utter precariousness of the created lives most dear to them, whether they live with present loss or forebodingly contemplate impeding loss. In fact, those who have suffered the death of a child are precisely those who are in a good position to remind the rest of us, as pastoral theologian Bruce Vaughn does, that mourning is "an ongoing and fundamental dimension of what it means to be human." It is not a "discrete, diagnosable, and transient clinical entity" to be spotted and cured, but rather a spiritual challenge to be met. People need, Vaughn argues, "not 'grief recovery,' but the recovery of grief" as an ever-present, existential reality.[9] Or, as funeral director and author Thomas Lynch puts it, "the question is not so much whether or not, but rather how well, how completely, how meaningfully we mourn."[10]

The Lukan account of Mary and Joseph's search is a powerful portrayal of parental distress, foreshadowing the ultimate sorrow awaiting them at the death of their son on the cross. Some commentators have criticized Mary in Luke 2:48 for her selfish concern about how Jesus treated them and her failure to recognize the important mission to which he was already drawn. She seems to have forgotten quickly her earlier words magnifying God and rejoicing in God's blessings. Yet all good parents can identify with getting caught up in the complicated tension between hopeful care and overbearing solicitude that interferes with a child's growth. From another perspective, Mary's anguish over young Jesus seems entirely justified and does not contradict her previous proclamation of joy and faith. Nor should parents see their own similar distress as incompatible with committed Christian practice. In this same Gospel, Jesus gives those who mourn special status, alongside the poor and hungry.

Parenting demands a constant giving up and letting go, whether literally at the doorway of the day care, preschool, and college dorm; or figuratively in making a huge array of disciplinary and recreational decisions about a child's everyday life that close off certain possibilities while opening others. Children are gifts in the best Christian sense, given to us on loan, so to speak, by a gracious God as part of God's good creation. At the same time, adults owe them care, nurture, discipline, and guidance. Finding the right balance between holding on and letting go is perhaps one of the most difficult challenges of parenthood over the long haul.[11]

The parental role must be, as Catholic ethicist Christine Gudorf remarks, "a constantly diminishing one in the life of a child."[12] Her claim is accurate in one sense, but it also exaggerates or simplifies a complex process that involves something a bit different than mere parental diminishment. Instead, dealing with mundane loss requires seeking new, creative ways to sustain and deepen intimacy under increasingly distant and more limited circumstances.[13] In the best of all possible worlds, a decreasing role in one sense is balanced by a different, possibly richer, kind of connectivity in another sense.

Many factors inhibit such fine balance. Fear often lures parents to exert excessive control. Parents are also tempted to overidentify with children, as especially prevalent in the middle-class obsession with children's achievement in sports, school, and beyond. I would wager that behind some of this anxiety and preoccupation stands the deeper problem of fear of loss. To let go means to admit one's own limits and mortality.

Mundane Loss as Curse

Faithful recognition of life as a "school in the art of dying," as Henri Nouwen dubs it, comes in part out of a larger twofold Christian proclamation on death as curse and as that over which God has triumphed.[14] In contrast to popular opinion, one stream of the tradition sees death as a curse and not as a natural part of life. Our family just watched *Forrest Gump*, a movie two of our kids had not seen yet. It dawned on me as I held this essay in the back of my mind, that the movie's appeal lies in its willingness to confront daily loss, loss of intimate relationships, loss of dreams, loss of physical and mental potential, and loss of time gone by. At one poignant moment, Gump comments, "My momma always said, 'Death is a part of life.' I sure wish it wasn't." When Gump adds his own twist to his mother's truism, he stands closer to the Christian tradition than he realizes.

Common rhetoric today claims dying as a natural part of life to counter the pervasive repression of death in our modern technological society. Psychology coaches an acceptance by reminding us, as did Elisabeth Kübler-Ross decades ago, that death is as much a part of life as birth. At a fundamental level, the Christian tradition does not agree.

The early tradition, including Paul and then, most definitively, Augustine, declared death a punishment for sin. Seeing loss in this way sounds antiquated to modern ears, but it captures an important facet of Christian faith. Although Paul develops this idea because he wants to draw a sharp theological contrast between Adam—the father of sin and death—and Christ—the source of grace and new life—Augustine grapples with loss on a more personal and spiritual level. He ponders the strangeness of time, recognizes the deep human aversion to dying, and fights back tears at his own mother's deathbed. Such tears flowed as a natural response to the severing of body and soul—a "harsh and unnatural experience as long as it lasts" that mocks the immortal life for which God created humans.[15]

Not much can really be said in the face of this rending, as is most clear in dire situations. Wolterstorff pleads, "Please: Don't say it's not really so bad. Because it is. Death is awful, demonic.... What I need to hear ... is that you recognize how painful it is."[16] There is a decided relentlessness to time and finitude against which even good faithful Christians fight. Pleading rhetorically whether there is "no one who can slow it down, make it stop, turn it back," Wolterstorff asks, "Must we all be swept forever on, away, beyond ... sorrow hard on sorrow, until the measure of our losses has been filled?"[17] The very goodness of creation "makes death all the more difficult to live with." Although Christians do not worship the world or human bodies, doctrines of creation and salvation affirm the inherent worth of embodiment. We are more than our bodies, but "of nothing on earth do we have more intimate possession."[18] Grief involves the real loss of the materiality and minutia of ordinary touch, nurture, and affection. Even as I celebrate my sons' growth, I sometimes grieved the transition, often around four and twelve-years-old, when immediate physical touch began to change to less tangible forms of intimacy. No wonder many parents cling long and hard to their youngest child.

Early theologians labeled death not simply an unnatural evil, but a curse, because loss is made harder by sin and guilt. In caring for one another, people fail or, worse, pervert and damage each other, sometimes despite intent, but sometimes by mean-spirited intention. Guilt intensifies loss because it adds to the anxiety of death that is, in Paul Tillich's words, "an anxiety which it would not have without guilt, namely, the feeling of standing under judgment." People are anxious about the future, not only because of its brevity, but also because of "its impenetrable darkness and the threat that one's whole existence in time will be judged as a failure."[19] Both he and Wolterstorff contrast this Christian view with that of the Stoics and, I would add, with contemporary discourse. Whereas Stoic rhetoric asserts, "Be calm and accept death as a part of life," Jesus says, "Weep with the wounds of the world."[20]

"Bambelela"—*Never Give Up: God Triumphs*

Fortunately, this is not Christianity's final word. There are other steps in grieving mundane loss besides faithful recognition, justified anguish, irate defiance, and remorse. Although Christians lack immediate, concrete, empirical proof, faith in the face of loss is also all about the sometimes uphill battle to trust the whole gospel—that God conquers death and guilt. As Christ was raised, so too are we, however literally or figuratively we understand this promise. Death and mundane loss are not all there is.

Letting go of children goes against the grain of human self-preservation. It requires trust that we are preserved and upheld by a force greater than our own efforts. The Christian tradition has long hoped to sustain such trust. Perhaps the hardest spiritual lesson or the most difficult virtue to acquire in the care of children is entrusting oneself and those most loved to God's care and protection. It is only such trust that finally allows one to stop short of using one's children to build up oneself and to love others genuinely.

Struggle with loss, as I see with the impending departure of my son, is closely aligned with the depth of love. Grief is a testimony to attachment or, as Wolterstorff comments, to the immeasurable "worth of the one loved." In what Lynch calls the "dull math" or illogic of life, we love or are commanded to love one another; therefore, we suffer and God suffers with us.[21]

Loss is made especially difficult because in loving the other we take that other into our own being as part of our self. This past spring, in a course on psychoanalytic self-psychologist Heinz Kohut, one student remarked that Kohut's theory does not deal with grief. I countered that loss stands at the heart of his understanding of how infants and children develop. He argues that self-structure results from "optimal frustrations" or incremental nontraumatic disappointments in parental response to need. When the parent fails to answer the baby's cry for food, the infant must internalize a representation of the remembered parental response as a rudimentary internal self-soothing function.

We usually think of development in terms of the child incorporating aspects of the parent. But it works both ways. After months and years of a parent guarding and supporting a child, the child becomes what Kohut calls an important "self-object" for the parent. A "self-object" is a psychoanalytic term that attempts to describe that aspect of the self, which is neither completely self nor other, but a combination of the two. It is a transformed aspect of the other that a person internalizes to sustain the self. So, at his son's burial, Wolterstorff cries, "I buried myself.... It was me those gardeners lowered.... It was me on whom we shoveled dirt. It was me we left behind."[22]

The good news is that God enters into suffering and triumphs over it, turning pain into sympathy for the world's wounds; anguish into trust; and distress into gratitude, deepened commitment, and expanded love. While writing this essay, I found myself drawn to a South African freedom song I sang at a retreat center a month ago.[23] The repeated lyric urges *bambelela* or "never give up." In times of trouble, when times are hard, or when we are in pain, we should "never give up." The refrain, like good liturgy, allows the singer to moan in lament, and then echo "never, never, never give up." *Bambelela;* God triumphs.

"On Eagle's Wings": Held in the Palm of God

Right after I started writing this essay, I had to go pick up my oldest son at the airport. I waited, as person after person filed past, for him to appear around the corner. When he did, I found myself surprised by tears, and the more I thought I might cry, the more I wept and the more my son looked at me strangely. I figured I'd just spent too much time on this essay, but I really couldn't explain it to him easily. To stare finitude straight in the face seems like something brilliant philosophers such as Søren Kierkegaard can pull off better than I can.

I have come close enough to spark some insights, but who needs to stand mourning at the turn of every corner? No need to become the tragic character in a novel I read recently, *The Secret Life of Bees,* who sees the pain on everyone's sleeve magnified and eventually takes her own life. One cannot live always at the point where Wolterstorff arrives when his bereavement causes him to notice that "we are surrounded by death.... Before, I saw it only here and there." But now "the dead show up.... All around me are the traces and memories of the dead."[24]

It is not that I will move on and leave mundane loss behind. It's just that there is always, as in the words of another hymn, a time to be "raised up on eagle's wings" and to rest "in the palm of God's hand."[25] It isn't just that grief doesn't feel good. Nor is it that grief should be controlled or managed. Ultimately God has promised more abundant life than sorrow. Christians await the day when the old order will pass away; and death, mourning, crying, and pain will be no more (Revelation 21:4).

Endnotes

1. See *Let the Children Come: Reimagining Childhood from a Christian Perspective* (San Francisco: Jossey-Bass, 2003).

2. Kenneth Doka (ed.), *Disenfranchised Grief: Recognizing Hidden Sorrow* (New York: Lexington Books, 1989), cited by Lucy Bregman, *Beyond Silence and Denial: Death and Dying Reconsidered* (Louisville: Westminster John Knox, 1999), 111.

3. Kathleen D. Billman and Daniel L. Migliore, *Rachel's Cry: Prayer of Lament and Rebirth of Hope* (Cleveland: United Church Press, 1999); Walter Brueggemann, "The Costly Loss of Lament," in *The Psalms and the Life of Faith,* ed. Patrick D. Miller (Minneapolis: Fortress, 1994), 98-111; and Denise Ackermann, "On Hearing and Lamenting: Faith and Truth Telling," in *To Remember and to Heal: Theological and Psychological Reflections on Truth and Reconciliation,* ed. H. Russel Botman and Robin M. Petersen (Cape Town: Human and Rousseau, 1996), 47-56.

4. Anne Higonnet, *Pictures of Innocence: The History and Crisis of Ideal Childhood* (New York: Thames and Hudson, 1998), 200.

5. Beverly Roberts Gaventa, "The Challenge of Christmas," *The Christian Century* (15 December 1993): 1270f; see also my essay, "'Pondering All These Things': Mary and Motherhood," in *Blessed One: Protestant Perceptions of Mary,* ed. Cynthia L. Rigby and Beverly Roberts Gaventa (Louisville: Westminster John Knox, 2002), 97-114.

6. Beverly Roberts Gaventa, *Mary: Glimpses of the Mother of Jesus* (Columbia: University of South Carolina, 1995), 68.

7. Nicholas Wolterstorff, *Lament for a Son* (Grand Rapids: Eerdmans, 2002), 16.

8. Ibid., 15.

9. S. Bruce Vaughn, "Recovering Grief in the Age of Grief Recovery," *The Journal of Pastoral Theology, 13:1* (Spring 2003): 36-38; see also David L. Massey, "Theological and Biblical Interpretations of Current Movements and

Emerging Paradigms Within Bereavement Studies," *Pastoral Psychology*, 48:6 (July 2000).

10. Thomas Lynch, "Good Grief: An Undertaker's Reflections," *The Christian Century* (26 July 2003): 20.

11. See Herbert Anderson and Kenneth R. Mitchell, *Leaving Home* (Louisville: Westminster John Knox Press, 1993).

12. Christine Gurdorf, "Dissecting Parenthood: Infertility, in Vitro, and Other Lessons in Why and How We Parent," *Conscience, 15:3* (Autumn 1994): 22.

13. See Pamela D. Couture, "Over the River and Through the Woods: Maintaining Emotional Presence Across Geographical Distance," in *Mutuality Matters: Faith, Family, and Just Love*, ed. Herbert Anderson, Edward Foley, Bonnie J. Miller-McLemore, and Robert Schreiter (Lanham, MD: Sheed and Ward, forthcoming).

14. Henri Nouwen, *A Letter of Consolation* (San Francisco: Harper & Row, 1982), cited by Wolterstorff, *Lament for a Son*, 95.

15. Augustine, *The City of God*, trans. Henry Bettenson (London: Penguin, 1972), 515 (Book XIII.6).

16. Wolterstorff, *Lament for a Son*, 34.

17. Ibid., 23.

18. Ibid., 31, 36.

19. Paul Tillich, *The Meaning of Health: Essays in Existentialism, Psychoanalysis, and Religion*, ed. Perry Lefevre (Chicago: Exploration Press, 1984), 190.

20. Wolterstorff, *Lament for a Son*, 86; and Paul Tillich, *The Courage to Be* (New Haven: Yale University Press, 1952), 17.

21. Wolterstorff, *Lament for a Son*, 5; Lynch, "Good Grief," 20.

22. Wolterstorff, *Lament for a Son*, 42.

23. "Bambelela," adapted and recorded by Marty Haugen on *Turn My Heart: A Sacred Journey from Brokenness to Healing* (GIA Publications, Inc.) (see http://www.giamusic.com/scstore/P-547.html).

24. Wolterstorff, *Lament for a Son*, 79.

25. "On Eagle's Wings," *The United Methodist Hymnal* (Nashville: The United Methodist Publishing House, 1989), 143.

Grieving and Reconnecting in Community

R. Esteban Montilla

In 1970, at the age of seven, I was suddenly and unexpectedly introduced to grief and mourning. My sister Carmen, two years younger than I was, was taken to the hospital and never returned. To this day, the image of Carmen that remains in my mind is of her being carried out of the house in the arms of my mother. She looked so beautiful with her long black hair and yellow dress with a flower embroidered on it.

I have no recollection of being told Carmen had died, of being at her funeral or graveside service; but I instinctively knew she was dead. The week after my sister's death, something very peculiar took place. It was something that for many years I did not understand. One night my mom was called to a neighbor's home; they had found me sleeping under their bed. My mom went to wake me up and take me home. As she was leaving our neighbor's house, she apologized, stating that she could not understand why I was sleepwalking. She thought it was somehow connected with the loss of my sister. The first month after my sister's death was difficult for me. I felt "invisible." No one discussed Carmen's death with me or asked how I was coping with the loss of my sister.

In the months following, my mother took me along to the cemetery when she visited Carmen's tomb. During those visits, she would talk to my dead sister. That was confusing to me. My mother explained to me that, although Carmen was dead, she was still part of our family, and we needed to maintain our connection with her. During those cemetery visits, I began to make sense of my little sister's death. I reconnected with her and from time to time found myself engaging her in conversation by using my memories and imaginative capacities. The sleepwalking stopped and never recurred. Perhaps my mother was right in connecting it with my grief. Today, after more than thirty years, I feel a strong bond with Carmen. She is still a part of our family.

I give thanks to my mother, who introduced me to the process of making sense of my sister's death by learning to connect with her on a different level. This process was completely different from the academic training I received on death and dying many years later. Experts on thanatology taught me about the importance of separating from those I have lost, resolving my loss, and moving on with my life. My mother, on the contrary, taught me the importance of *reconnecting with the deceased, keeping them alive within the family, and continuing the relationship*. From her perspective, grieving was a social experience that strengthens the individual, the family, and the community. Assembling to grieve and mourn reactivates the powers and energies within us, reminding us of our own mortality.

For many years I abandoned my mother's teachings on death, mourning, and grief and embraced the concepts I had learned from my undergraduate and graduate teachers. Therefore, for almost two decades, I understood grief as being intrapsychic, as a very personal and painful process of detachment that ends with the achievement of full resolution of the loss. Ultimately one "gets over" the loss.

But why should we "get over" the loss of one whom we cherished? Reconnection is at the heart of grieving. It is important to keep in mind that *people die, not our relationships with them.* The dialogue and bond continue to be present and alive because we use our living memories to engage in conversations with them, embody their legacies, and experience their symbolic presence.

A New Old Paradigm of Death and Dying

Because of my interest in the topic of thanatology, and because of my internal struggle as I tried to relate my mother's lessons with my academic training, I kept searching and reading on the subject. In the late 1990s, I found some articles by scholars that talked about grief in ways that looked familiar to me.[1] According to these articles, grief was a relational and transformative process and was usually accompanied by an orchestra of emotions and feelings, including sadness, anger, and guilt, as well as joy and pride. Reconstruction of meaning, relearning the world, reconnection, and dialogue with the departed are at the heart of mourning. This new paradigm of grieving and mourning, practiced and embraced by my mother thirty years ago, has given me strength and courage to face the losses of close friends and family members.

Latino families such as ours tend to approach death and grief by focusing on family relationships as primary resources, by appreciating the spiritual and psychological continuity between the living and the dead, by continuing to work on relationships even with the dead person, and by creating a new shared understanding of the family unit in the past, present, and future.[2]

Grief, Mourning, and Celebration

On September 6, 1999, the person who most influenced my life and was always there for me suffered a heart attack and died. I spent five days in deep mourning with all my sisters and brothers. Our regular activities ceased. Day and night we celebrated the life of our heroine and beloved mother. We told one another stories about her, we recommitted ourselves to one another as a family, and we pledged to keep her memory alive and allow her strengths to continue motivating our lives. During those five days we cried, screamed, suffered, laughed, celebrated, and experienced the blessing of her life and death as a community of mourners. We were well aware that our mother was dead. We could no longer enjoy her physical presence, but she would continue to be with us through her memories and teachings.

Six days after my mother's death, I returned to the United States from South America. Two days later, my wife and I welcomed into this world our beautiful daughter, Anisah. Joy filled our grieving hearts, and I could feel my mother joining with us in celebration on the occasion of the birth of our daughter. But our elation was also accompanied by a sense of disappointment and sadness because our daughter could not receive the traditional blessing from her grandmother. The following ten months were characterized by deep pain, happiness, suffering, and a sense of emptiness, as well as moments of joy and celebration.

Four years later, my mother's presence and influence continue to be felt in our family. There are things—voices, songs, smells, people's features and characteristics, foods, sayings, events, and occasions—that make her very much alive in our midst. Her teachings, interests, mysteries, love, care, laughter, sadness, and spirit are still a part of us. We miss her. We cherish her unconditional love, caring, and hope. She is still very much with us. We value her contribution to our lives and her continuous companionship on our life's journey.

My family and I will be responsible for sharing with Anisah the heritage of her paternal grandmother—the story of her life, her dreams for her grandchildren, her determination, her fight for equality and justice, her commitment to serve the outcast and marginalized, her strong character, her faith and dedication to God's reign, her love for people, her healing talents, and her tenacity and stubbornness.

Anisah and I like to watch the movie *Charlotte's Web,* a film based on the characters from the book written by E. B. White[3] that focuses on the friendship developed by Wilbur, a runty pig, and Charlotte, a special and sophisticated spider. In this film I find a great truth about the power of memory to reconnect with loved ones who have died. The spider, Charlotte, is approaching death and shares with Wilbur what it means for her to be dying. Charlotte asks Wilbur to take care of her cocoon and brood.

After Charlotte's death, the eggs hatch and hundreds of spiders come out of the cocoon. They go their separate ways, except for Iranian, Joy, and Nelly, who stay with Wilbur. They ask him to tell them about their mother. Wilbur relates his memories of Charlotte to the little spiders, and thus he experiences the healing power of grief; and Iranian, Joy, and Nelly reconnect with their mother.

This is precisely what I am doing with my daughter, Anisah.

Grief as a Journey of the Heart

We are used to looking at grief and mourning from a negative perspective. The idea is that we need to say good-bye and abandon lost relationships to make space for new ones. But our hearts have a great capacity for multitasking. We can love many people at the same time and with the same intensity. We do not need to make space in our hearts by forsaking our past relationships; instead, we need to reconnect with those from our past, living and dead, at a different level.

Grief as a journey of the heart is characterized by difficult times and moments; it can also present opportunities for new friendships, new hopes to be embraced, and new paths to be commenced. In short, it is a journey into a new life filled with dreams about *mañana* and fueled by the memories of yesterday.

I find Attig's understanding of grieving very encouraging, especially when he presents it as a "journey of the heart." He goes on to say that grief

> brings us to the fullness of life of the flesh and blood, here and now, and into the future with those who still share the earth with us. In this life, we still have places in our hearts for our families, friends, and communities. We can and often do make places for others who enter our lives later. And we have room in our hearts for self-love and the many cares that make us unique and distinct individuals.[4]

This view of grief gives us the permission to love others without forsaking, separating, or ceasing to love those who are no longer physically with us.

Four years have passed since our mother's death. We continue to grieve and grow. I believe it is impossible for us to visualize, imagine, or contemplate a day when the relationship with our mother would cease to exist. It has been an ongoing process of accommodating and adjusting to her loss. This has been a transformative process; the entire family is redefining itself. New leaders and directions are emerging. We are embracing a new family identity. Many of our traditions and family rituals go on to this day, but we are also creating new traditions that give our family a sense of well-being. We continue to make sense of our loss and continue to justify our existence as a family.

Life Is but a Breath

We cannot escape death. We are not the only ones who mourn. I think of a legend from India that tells of a woman who lost her only child, a three-year-old son. This young mother, in her love for him, carried the dead child clasped to her bosom. She went from house to house, asking if anyone would give her some medicine that would cure her dead son. The neighbors began to question this mother's sanity. They said, "What is happening with this woman who carries on her breast the dead body of her son?"

With much anguish and desperation, she visited a holy man and asked him to cure her son. The man responded, "I can do so. What I will need is a handful of mustard seed." The woman immediately said, "Yes, I will find what you are asking for." The man continued with the request saying, "I require some mustard seed taken from a house where no one has experienced sorrow." "Very good," she said, and still carrying her dead son, she went to ask for the mustard seed at the different houses. Yet she could not find a single house that had not suffered loss.

"The living are few, but the dead are many," she was told. One said, "I have lost a son"; another, "I have lost my parents"; another, "I have lost my husband." At last, not being able to find a house where no one had died, she began to think, "This is a heavy and difficult task. Indeed, I am not the only one whose son is dead." With these thoughts, she continued with her grieving process by cremating her son and learning to relate with him at a different level. As the woman followed the wise man's recommendation, she was able to experience the healing power of sadness and sorrow. In that process, she also received help from a community of mourners that exists and endures despite its grief. (The origin of this parable is not clearly known; many attribute it to the teaching of Siddhartha Gautama on the mortal nature of all humans.)

The Hebrew psalmist sings, "You have made my days a mere handbreadth; the span of my years is as nothing before you. Each man's life is but a breath. . . . He springs up like a flower and withers away; like a fleeting shadow, he does not endure. . . . What is your life? You are a mist that appears for a little while and then vanishes" (Psalm 39:5; Job 14:2; James 4:14 NIV).

Death, as the cessation of our existence, is our common and natural destiny. Even if we make the healthiest lifestyle choices, our genes and our environment converge to bring us to the end of our days. We all face it. As the psalmist wrote, "The length of our days is seventy years—or eighty, if we have the strength; yet their span is but trouble and sorrow, for they quickly pass, and we fly away" (Psalm 90:10 NIV).

Grief is a complex and holistic experience. It comes with a myriad of reactions and multiple ways of coping with it. It escapes our simplistic attempts to systematize how to relate and connect with those who precede us in death. It would be arrogant to pretend to suggest a one-way approach to grief.

A Community of Mourners

Yes, death as a natural part of the cycle of life is common to all of us. The difference is how we face the process of dying.

As social beings, we are relationship-oriented. We exist in order to be in community. We are born, reproduce, grow, mature, and die in community. Because of our gregarious nature, we need the community in order to receive the healing power of grief, and we need it to experience a good death. Our human interactions do not take place in isolation; rather they occur in connection with others and with the rest of creation.

This natural need for being with others was clearly expressed by Solomon: "Two are better than one because they have a good return for their labor. For if either of them falls, the one will lift up his companion. But woe to the one who falls when there is not another to lift him up. Furthermore, if two lie down together they keep warm, but how can one be warm alone? And if one can over-power him who is alone, two can resist him" (Ecclesiastes 4:9-12 NASB). If in my grieving I should stumble, there is someone there to help me—a sister, a brother, a wife, a child, a friend. In community, sorrow cannot overpower me.

Throughout history, we humans (in particular, Western, urban humans) have experienced a tension between the individual and the community. This is due in part to our lack of ways to honor our need for self-determination at the same time that we embrace our need for one another. I believe that a healthy and balanced approach calls for valuing each person's uniqueness and freedom, while recognizing that the maximum human potential is experienced only in relationships. Indeed, it is in relationship and community we discover the real meaning of being human.

My mother modeled for us a healthy way to manage this tension. She was a midwife for more than fifty years and raised not only her own children, but also six others who were not hers. She taught us the importance of coming together, caring for one another, and recognizing our interdependence. She exemplified the reciprocal connection between the individual and community in which principles of equality and freedom are mutually respected. The idea always was to be together and work together for the common good.

It would be cruel to expect human beings to face the gradual process of death alone. In this time, as children of God, we desperately need to join our neighbors in mutual cooperation, dialogue, and harmonious relationship, and walk together with them through the "valley of the shadow of death." Accompanying one another and walking together, we can empower the dying person, the bereaved, and the community because as we enhance the life of others, our own lives are refreshed.

I was struck by a sense of the power of community in Felix Lope de Vega's play *Fuenteovejuna*. The story is about a small town named Fuenteovejuna, under the tyrannical rule of Don Fernan Gomez, Knight Commander of the Order of Calatrava. After much suffering, the townspeople finally rebel and kill the commander, placing his head on a pike as the banner of their freedom. Their battle cry is *"Fuenteovejuna, todos a una"* (Fuenteovejuna, all are one). When the Grand Master of the Order hears of this, he appeals to Ferdinand and Isabella, who appoint a judge-inquisitor to find the guilty parties and punish them.

The judge, however, finds that he can make little progress in his inquiry, for whenever he asks, *"¿Quién mató al comandante?"* (Who killed the commander?), the answer is always the same, *"Fuenteovejuna, señor."* Finally the judge asks for instructions from Isabella and Ferdinand, who respond that, given such unanimity, there must have been just cause for the commander's death. If one member of the town was hurt under the commander's rule, all felt the pain. It was the community, and not any individual in it, that killed him.[5]

Likewise, if one member of a community grieves, the entire community joins in the mourning. "If one member suffers, all suffer together with it; if one member is honored, all rejoice together with it" (1 Corinthians 12:26). Indeed, we are all a community of mourners. This may explain why sometimes, without being aware of the reason, we find ourselves weeping at the death of one we have never met. When Princess Diana and Mother Teresa died, I remember crying in my car while driving from work and listening to musical tributes celebrating their lives. My friends and colleagues have also reported similar responses to the deaths of good, renowned people.

Grief, Mourning, and Celebration Redux

Still, it is death within our immediate community that affects us most deeply. While working on this chapter, I received a phone call from my family in South America to inform me that my sister, Maria Uben, had died. It took me about two hours to absorb it. She was only fifty-four years of age; I could not believe that my sister was dead.

After my mother's death, Maria Uben became the matriarch of our family. Her wisdom, great sense of humor, life experience, wise counsel, and culinary gifts were often sought by each of us. She cared about the well-being of the entire family (nuclear and extended, although we Venezuelans do not subscribe to that kind of division of the family), and she would take the initiative to ensure that we were lacking nothing.

I am just now beginning to grasp how central Maria Uben was to our family. Once again we came together to face another extremely sad and painful loss. Maria Uben's children have been robbed of the most important human being of their lives. They find almost no consolation. My nephews' and nieces' lives are altered in ways they could never have predicted. How can we survive the death of our mother? How can we keep the unity of the family? How can we live without her?

I hear what a wonderful person Maria Uben was and what a key role she played in her children's lives. At this moment it is impossible for them to visualize their existence without her. Our family does not try to answer these existential questions. In love and togetherness, we simply experience the pain and the sense of emptiness that comes with the loss of such a powerful woman.

We come together as a community of mourners to silently, or noisily, celebrate our sister's life. In our midst there are no right or wrong questions, there are no right or wrong answers, there are no right or wrong ways to grieve and mourn our sister. We suspend all kinds of judgments, love each other, and embrace the mutual care that empowers us. This is what our loving mother taught us.

Hope and Mañana

My mother used to say that hope is the most wonderful gift our Creator has bestowed on us. Unfortunately, we tend to misuse or underuse it. Hope is the motivating energy that invites us to embrace the past, to live in the present, and to dream into the future. Hope reminds us of our temporal and perishable nature. It tells us that few things in life are permanent.

More important, hope tells us that there is a *mañana*.

Hope tells us that God "makes all things new." This promise helps us face our present pains and hurts with the certainty that we have the power to transform them and, with God's strength, can construct a better world. Hope encourages us to be honest about the way grief shapes us. Hope allows us to take advantage of that opportunity for growth.

Hope is at the center of our faith and religious beliefs. The apostle Paul, giving a blessing to the church in Rome, refers to the Creator as the God of hope: "May the God of hope fill you with all joy and peace as you trust in him, so that you may overflow with hope by the power of the Holy Spirit" (Romans 15:13 NIV). This hope, which implies a living relationship, provides us with the means to endure and grow out of our losses. This hope reminds us that "in all things God works for the good of those who love [God]" (Romans 8:28 NIV).

Indeed, a life without hope is a solitary, chaotic, and senseless one. What has motivated me to persevere in this journey of life amid many losses is this living hope that keeps me connected with those who precede me in death. It is this hope that maintains me as I touch what is transcendent. It carries me into a *mañana* filled with healing and growth opportunities. This hope produces in me a sense of self-worth and efficacy that enables me to make something out of my loss and be actively responsible for the life I still have to lead.

Endnotes

1. See R. A. Neimeyer, *Lesson of Loss: A Guide to Coping* (New York: McGraw, 1998); T. A. Attig, *How We Grieve: Relearning the World* (New York: Oxford University Press, 1996); and G. Hagman, "The Role of the Other in Mourning," *Psychoanalytic Quarterly, 65:2* (1996): 327-352.

2. E. R. Shapiro, "Grief in Family and Cultural Context: Learning from Latino Families," *Cultural Diversity and Mental Health, 1:2* (1995): 313-332.

3. E. B. White, *Charlotte's Web* (New York: HarperTrophy, 1952, 1999).

4. T. A. Attig, "Relearning the World: Making and Finding Meaning," in *Meaning Reconstruction and the Experience of Loss,* ed. R. Neimeyer (Washington, DC: American Psychological Association, 2002).

5. J. L. González, *Mañana: Christian Theology from a Hispanic Perspective* (Nashville: Abingdon Press, 1990).

References

Attig, T. A. (2002). Relearning the world: Making and finding meaning. In R. Neimeyer (ed.), *Meaning Reconstruction and the Experience of Loss.* Washington, DC: American Psychological Association.

————. (1996). *How We Grieve: Relearning the World.* New York: Oxford University Press.

Hagman, G. (1996). The role of the other in mourning. *Psychoanalytic Quarterly, 65(2),* 327-352.

Gonzalez, J. L. (1990). *Mañana: Christian Theology from a Hispanic Perspective.* Nashville: Abingdon Press.

Neimeyer, R. A. (1998). *Lesson of Loss: A Guide to Coping.* New York: McGraw Hill.

Shapiro, E. R. (1995). Grief in family and cultural context: Learning from Latino families. *Cultural Diversity and Mental Health, 1(2),* 159-176.

————. (1996). Family bereavement and cultural diversity: A social developmental perspective. *Family Process, 35,* 313-332.

————. (2001). Grief in interpersonal perspective: Theories and their implications. In M. S. Stroebe, R. O. Hansson, W. Stroebe, and H. Schut (eds.), *Handbook of Bereavement Research: Consequences, Coping and Care.* Washington, DC: American Psychological Association.

White, E. B. (1952, 1999). *Charlotte's Web.* New York: HarperTrophy.

65—Now What?

M. Basil Pennington

There is "a time to weep, and a time to laugh" and sometimes they come together (Ecclesiastes 3:4). Recently I had the happy experience of attending the birthday party of a good friend. He was celebrating his sixty-fifth, although it wasn't pure celebration. He was surrounded by his large family and a wonderful selection of friends, representing some of the varied facets of his rich and fruitful life. Nonetheless, he expressed a certain poignancy about arriving at this age, which in his younger years he had looked upon as representing an almost unbelievable antiquity. My friend felt anything but old. He would perforce be stepping down from some of the powerful positions that had been allowed him and had enabled him to do much good. As he looked out over the sea of faces, he realized that some of these he would be seeing less as he let go of certain reins and entered into new pursuits. He had his new sailboat, his retreat in Nova Scotia, a small company he had recently bought, and invitations to serve on the boards of different ventures.

Not many who arrive at this age of transition have such possibilities. When I reached retirement, I sought out a bishop who had retired the previous year and asked his advice. "Plan it," was his emphatic counsel. And that is what this article is about.

But again, not everyone gets an opportunity to do that. Retirement can come upon one quite suddenly by reason of health, commitments, or the politics of an organization. One can be abruptly torn from that which had filled one's life, from one's plans and hopes, and from many of the people who filled each day with engagement and friendship.

Another person whom I consulted was an abbot, well into his eighties and still full of life. His advice was to give more time to *lectio divina* and Centering Prayer. Such a program does not mean forgoing activity—this man's own retirement has been filled with ministry, including a three-year stint in East Africa.

We men often fill our lives with activities to the point that we do not leave time for family and friends. Confronted by a new situation, when suddenly our accustomed activities are no longer there, we can experience an immense void in our lives. If most of our associates are business and professional connections, we will see them quickly disappear. If retirement means a change of location, most of our personal friends will become distant geographically and ideologically.

As we face all this, and new and perhaps unfamiliar feelings begin to churn within us, we may feel like the paralyzed man in the portico at the pool of Bethzatha who told Jesus that he had no one to help him (John 5:7).

There is one friend who has always been with us (even if we have not always been very much aware of his presence) and always will be. This is what is at the bottom of the abbot's counsel. *Lectio* is a personal meeting with God, with Jesus, in God's inspired and inspiring Word. Here the ground for a growing, evermore meaningful friendship is found—a friendship that will surely last as long as life here on this planet. And Jesus is the friend who will be there with us as we pass beyond and enter into the fullness of eternal life. Moreover, Jesus is more than a friend; he is our master and teacher. Jesus has wisdom to impart that will speak to us and serve us in our new situation. Jesus literally has it all and it is ours for the seeking.

For *lectio* we do not have to figure out the Scriptures or read commentaries—though they can enrich us. We need just to listen to what God has to say to us. Through story and poetry, myth and image, as well as through straight talk, God will tell us how much we are loved, how much God is with us. God's friendship can become an ever fuller presence in our more spacious life.

For some of us it may seem that our significant activities are now over as far as we are concerned. What remains? It is here where *lectio* is apt to unlock perhaps the most meaningful dimension of life: the vocation or call, common to us all, to move ahead to become a leaven of peace and unity for the whole human family—"may all be one. As you, Father, are in me and I am in you ... that the world may know that you have sent me and have loved them even as you have loved me" (John 17:21-23).

Lectio Divina

Let me speak a bit more about *lectio*[1] because, for me, it has had such a profound and important role to play as I moved through the grief of retirement. *Lectio* is a Latin word, but it has become one of those words that pass over into other languages and find their home in many of them. There is an old Latin saying, *traductor traditor est* ("every translator is a traitor"). When we translate a word, we leave behind its native nuances—not to speak of its contextual richness—and in the process it takes on many new ones. *Lectio* is literally translated as "reading," but in the context of the spirit-filled tradition of the Christian community, its meaning is very rich. It is not just collecting ideas or even exploring them with the mind. Rather *lectio* is an opening to the inspired Word that lets it open us to new realizations and to the experience of the Divine.

In this regard I think of the annunciation of the angel Gabriel to the Virgin Mary (see Luke 1:26-38). This young woman, formed by the Jewish tradition, knew that there is but one God, the transcendent God of Sinai. Then the angel told her that God has a Son, and she is asked to bear that Son. This revealed to her two basic mysteries of Christian faith: the Trinity and the Incarnation. By the grace of the Holy Spirit, Mary was able to receive this astounding word. When we come to listen to the divine revelation in Scripture, we want to have the same openness as this humble woman of Nazareth. We want to be profoundly aware that God is present in the Word, speaking to us. Enshrining the Bible, as our Jewish brothers and sisters do in synagogues, can help us remember this. And we need the Holy Spirit to help us hear, to let the Word come alive to us and lead us into that experience of God that we call contemplation. Jesus promised at the Last Supper: "The Holy Spirit, whom the Father will send in my name, will teach you everything" (John 14:26).

The important thing in *lectio* is listening. We all hear with parameters formed by our life experience. We are not inclined to notice anything that falls outside of those borders, which can be both confining and impoverishing. In *lectio* we let those boundaries fall away as best we can with the help of the Holy Spirit, so that God can expand our listening and bring us increasingly into the presence of divine reality. We need to give some spacious time to *lectio* for this to happen. Not necessarily a lot of time, but a spaciousness that allows the Word to resonate within us, albeit but a single sentence or phrase that is given. Taking with us a word that has spoken to us in *lectio*, letting it rest and repeat itself in our mind and heart as we move through the day, allows God to be present with us in a way that can be consoling as well as transforming and enlightening.

It is appropriate that before we finish this time of conversation with God, we take a moment to thank God. Can we imagine what our life would be like if we had never heard the name "Jesus," if we had never been formed in any way by God's covenant of love? I find such a thought frighteningly impoverishing. No, *impoverishing* is not a strong enough word. It leaves me devastated.

I have enjoyed *lectio*—though it has not always been a joyous experience— through many, many years. And I found that when I was engulfed in the grief of retirement, *lectio* had a powerful role in my life. Jesus speaks to us in action as well as in word. I go to the garden of Gethsemane. There I see a young man in the prime of life, having just experienced a triumphal welcome into the capital city, crowning years of wonderful, life-giving ministry. But now it is to come to an abrupt and totally unjust end because of the jealousy and spite of far lesser men. This beautiful and great person is sweating blood and crying to be let off as he faces public humiliation, horrible physical degradation, and death (see Mark 14:32-42; Luke 23:39-46). He surely can commiserate with the grief of retirement.

For reasons that are not altogether clear to me, it sometimes takes years for the message of the Gospels really to get to me. In this respect, there comes to mind the experience of my friend Henri Nouwen, one of the great spiritual masters of our time. Though he attained what few immigrants have ever hoped for—professorships at both Yale and Harvard—he nevertheless did not find peace and went to seek it living among the disadvantaged. Finally, in what proved to be the last days of his life, one of Jesus' stories that he had heard many times especially spoke to him. He not only heard how the prodigal son squandered the rich inheritance his father had given him. He also came to understand that the prodigal son had a prodigal father, who ever awaited his son's return (see Luke 15:11-24). Nouwen experienced the Father's totally unconditional love and surrendered to it and died fulfilled and at peace.[2]

I never like to miss my daily meeting with God in *lectio*. For anyone for whom challenge is the spice of life, these daily encounters keep life full of flavor. I never know when I am going to experience what Bernard of Clairvaux liked to call "the visit of the Word," those moments when the text opens up and we are brought into the immediate, immensely consoling, transforming, enlightening, and empowering experience of love.[3] This is the Love that Teilhard de Chardin saw as "the most fundamental form of all passion,"[4] which brings us to "the heart and summit of the world."[5]

Abbot Emeritus

I was surprised when I became an "abbot emeritus" by how difficult the transition was. Confessedly, I had not prepared for it. As abbot, all my time and attention had been given to God in love and service of my community. I let many other activities go. I had little time for other friendships. The fifty-one monks rated all I had to give. When suddenly my service was complete and wisdom dictated I step away to leave ample space for my successor, I felt as if almost every friend had been torn from me. There were immense voids in activity, communication, affection, and intimacy. To make the experience more agonizing, backward looks seemed to make me painfully aware of all the ways I had fallen short in my service, as we say "in all that I have done and in all that I have failed to do."[6] A bit of realism was called for here: none of us is perfect. As I moved on, I needed to distinguish between what actually happened and the story I tell about what occurred. These tend to collapse into one, for better or worse—more likely for worse—limiting what is possible as we move on.

It was time to turn more fully to the one abiding friendship, to use some of the new time and space to listen to God speaking to me through the Gospels, and to accept the invitation: "Come to me...and I will refresh you" (Matthew 11:28). It was the moment to enjoy more of the disciple Mary's "best part" and sit quietly at Jesus' feet, letting others care about the serving (see Luke 10:38-42). I found the practice of Centering Prayer especially helpful here.[7] I also learned rather quickly that it is necessary to schedule time for this. It is surprising how quickly the spaces of retirement fill, but often not with things that satisfy our deepest needs. We can succumb to the numbness of the passive spectator, to ever-longer naps, to rehearsing memories (we are prone to stay with the darker ones, and these can begin to color our whole outlook), and to other more dangerous and debilitating escapes.

With retirement we inevitably find ourselves in a new community. Even when we do not move geographically, the persons who surround us and fill our days are different. I did move to another place where, happily, I had some old-time friends. But years and events had intervened. These friendships have had to be revived so that they can be meaningful again and satisfyingly intimate. A whole new set of concerns have had to be appropriated so that I can truly become a member of my new community. To make room for this, I have had to let go of the issues that so filled my life before. Not easy!

Love is eternal—all true love. I still love deeply every member of the community I had served. We do not just simply drop out of our lives the people we love. The challenge is to continue to express our love for them appropriately, allowing us to have the time and energy we need to bring the caring love we want and need to our new community. A lot of patience and some good advice are required while this is worked out.

Counselors

"No one is a good judge in his own case." Saint Bernard of Clairvaux expressed this sage advice more colorfully: "The man who is his own master is the disciple of a fool." These aphorisms can be pushed too far, but there is truth in them. A certain amount of objectivity from the outside can be a real help. Though what I think is of greater value is the accompaniment and sense of care and concern that a counselor brings. No matter how a retirement came about, even if it is just the ticking of the clock, we have been wounded. And like an injured animal, at least a part of us wants to withdraw and lick our wounds in solitude. Regardless of what testimonials we received, what accolades, we feel in some way unappreciated and unloved. Regardless of how long the list of accomplishments we can cite or how impressive our resume, we tend to see in flashing lights our real and supposed failures. The grace of this time of transition can be a growth in humility, a truer picture of self in the acceptance of this. But to face the pain and depression of this time, we most basically need to know and experience God's totally unconditional love, the love of the prodigal father. Hence, the importance of *lectio*, meditation, and prayer. But we also need an understanding and compassionate friend and companion to whom we can reveal all and still receive the love, respect, and care we need. We may have to turn to a psychologist or clergyperson to find the climate of confidentiality we need to begin to be so open. Shame and a certain humiliation may beset us as we find looming up within ourselves thoughts and feelings of anger and resentment, of self-pity and vindictiveness. It may take time to get it all out, to come to the openness that can allow the reassuring response we need. Again, be patient. It is a project worthy of some of the new time and space we now have.

The Future

Whether we planned or not, as the personal matters fold into place, it is time to begin to create a future for ourselves. How am I going to respond to God's love today? How am I going to bring God's love to others? Maybe it is time just to sit in this love.[8] Then I will be ready to respond to each one who walks into my life. Or maybe it is time to take some initiative to enter gently into the lives of others. We may be fortunate enough to have friends pressing in with ideas, suggestions, and invitations. Somewhat daringly we may want to try some new things we never considered before or perhaps dreamed of years ago.

We all have a tendency to project for ourselves a future that is created out of our past, imposing on it all sorts of limitations. Why do we do this? Well, we know we have survived; we got through the past, no matter the cost. With that assurance, it seems safer to continue to follow the known course. I would not want to take this away from anyone. But let me suggest that the familiar can be set aside for the moment. It is still there. We can get it any time we want. But for the moment, forget it. Now, what is the future we would really like? Give that really wonderful faculty we humans enjoy—the imagination—a chance to play a bit. Yes, there needs to be some realism here. We would love to have a few million dollars, a private jet, homes in Hawaii and Maine and a number of places in between, and so forth. I am not talking about pie-in-the-sky dreaming, but realistically asking ourselves what are some of the things we would really like to do with our time and talents and the resources we can tap into that would be courageously different and satisfying? It will certainly add vitality to our life and maybe enrich others if we play around with some of these dreams for a bit. Maybe it is time to live in the realm of possibilities.

The future—whether chronologically encompassing a week, a month, a year, or decades—is, in fact, something that does not yet exist. We only live in the "now," even if the task of the "now" is to plan the future. We only have the grace for now. The past is gone. The future is not yet, so why burden ourselves with it? We can enjoy the present project of planning, but we do not need to do any of the worrying. When the time arrives, we can handle what comes.

Yes, there is grief when the curtain descends on one era of life, no matter how loud the applause. It is over. We have died to it. Or it has died to us. But in each now, there is a great love in our life, an infinite love, a love we want to make time and space for, to enjoy, to establish as the unfailing, solid ground for all the successive "nows."

I find that retirement is not the event of a day—or a week or a year. It is a new chapter of life. It can be as full and as meaningful as we want to make it. The spaces and the time are ours. The love is ours—an infinite love that can ever expand our hearts and our lives to embrace more fully and satisfyingly not only God, but also each of our loved ones and every stranger who comes into our lives. And with that love there is nothing we cannot be a part of, such as making this a better world for us all or making a contribution that is eminently satisfying. With the help of regular *lectio*, by the grace of the Holy Spirit, we can remain at this level of consciousness and, leaving our grief behind, live a life that is full of love, joy, and peace.

* * * * *

The Method of Lectio Divina

- It is well to keep the sacred Scriptures in our home in a place of honor as a Real Presence of the Word in our midst.
- Take the sacred text with reverence, and call upon the Holy Spirit.
- For ten minutes (or longer, if you are so inclined), listen to God speaking to you through the text, and respond to God.
- At the end of the time, choose a word or phrase (perhaps one will have been "given" to you) to take with you, and thank God for being with you and speaking to you.
- More briefly, we might put it this way:
  Come into the Presence and call upon the Holy Spirit.
  Listen for ten minutes.
  Thank God and take a "word."

The Method of Centering Prayer

- Sit relaxed and quiet.
- Be in faith and love to God who dwells in the center of your being.
- Take up a love word and let it be gently present, supporting your being to

God in faith-filled love.

- Whenever you become aware of anything, simply gently return to God with the use of your prayer word.
- After twenty minutes, let the Our Father (or some other prayer) pray itself.

Endnotes

1. For a fuller, practical treatment of *lectio divina,* see M. Basil Pennington, *Lectio Divina: Renewing the Ancient Practice of Praying the Scriptures* (New York: Crossroad, 1998).

2. See Henri Nouwen, *Return of the Prodigal Son: A Story of Homecoming* (New York: Continuum, 1996). A book that helped me to open more fully to this experience is David Benner, *Surrender to Love: Discovering the Heart of Christian Spirituality* (Downers Grove, IL: Intervarsity Press, 2003).

3. See Bernard of Clairvaux, *On the Song of Songs*, 4 vols. (Kalamazoo, MI: Cistercian Publications, 1971–80).

4. Teilhard de Chardin, *The Phenomenon of Man* (New York: Harper and Brothers, 1939), 267.

5. Teilhard de Chardin, *The Future of Man* (New York: Harper & Row, 1964), 235. A very helpful study for understanding de Chardin's teaching on "the centric power of love" is Henri de Lubac's *The Eternal Feminine* (New York: Harper & Row, 1971).

6. From the public confession used at the beginning of the Eucharistic liturgy in the Roman Catholic church.

7. See M. Basil Pennington, *An Invitation to Centering Prayer* (Liguori, MO: Liguori, 2001), and *Centering Prayer: Renewing an Ancient Christian Prayer Form* (New York: Doubleday, 1980).

8. The simple, ancient method of Centering Prayer is one way for us to begin to do this. In case the reader is not familiar with this type of prayer, I have included a very brief outline of the method at the end of this article.

"My Lord, What a Mourning": How Faith Is an Asset in Grief

Donna Schaper

Faith is an asset in grief in at least three ways. Faith gives us "flow," the ability to cope while our heart is still broken, to put one foot in front of the other even though we do not feel like it. Faith gives us the normal life of "yesterday" even though everything has changed. Faith also gives us resilience; at best, a capacity to come back tomorrow, or minimally, to believe there is a tomorrow coming. And it leads us to gratitude, the best healer for the broken and lost heart. Gratitude, flow, and resilience are what we call blessings: they come from God as gifts. We do not earn them so much as receive them.

By "faith," we mean that trust that many people have in God's existence, even when circumstances make cognitive belief difficult or impossible. Trust is the foundation of faith, and it is the asset that heals us in grief. When we speak of faith, we are not talking about certainty. In fact, faith may be the opposite of certainty. It is instead a trust that allows us to keep going when we do not think we can. Faith has the three faces of flow and resilience and gratitude—even in the face of hard things—and at its bottom and base is trust.

When we lose a loved one, many of us think that our life is also over. We are filled with fear and its cold emptiness. We join thousands of people who have stared at their future with the dread of perpetual loneliness and sadness. What faith does is attack these fears. It does not ignore them or stop them so much as create a simultaneous set of happenings. We flow into trust. We find ourselves enjoying breakfast and cannot imagine how. We wake up one morning no longer mourning.

A woman lost her husband about two months after he retired. They had bought a condo in Florida, moved into it, sold their house in New Jersey, and were experiencing real excitement about long days of golf and fresh air. But he suffered a sudden stroke and died. She went into a major depression, marked by anger and a feeling of being gypped. Two years later, she volunteers in my office and drives cross-country with friends. She wonders how she found her way forward. She need not wonder. She trusted in a higher power, whom she called God and whom others might call Spirit or Force or Font or Foundation. At the same time that she was feeling angry and hurt and lost, bouncing around in real estate blues and "not knowing what to do," trust was growing in her. She was being healed by a mysterious presence that was forcing her to flow back into her own life river. She thought she had been pushed off into an estuary. She thought she was at the end of the road. Instead, she was watching the river bend into a new direction, which had a place for her. She could still play golf. She could still enjoy the fresh air. She could still make a contribution to life. The Spirit knew that even when she did not. Simultaneously, she was lost and found. Even as she was angry and teary and acting out and up with anyone who would listen, she was flowing in a new direction. This flow is a spiritual fact: it is God working in us when we are unaware of it. It comes from faith's sister, hope, that "thing with feathers that perches in the soul," as Emily Dickinson put it.[1] The resilient part of the flow was the way she stayed available to her river.

She could have moved back to New Jersey. She could have convinced herself that her life was over. Instead, she stayed put, endured the nights of anguish and pain, and found the truth of the psalm, "weeping may linger for the night, but joy comes with the morning" (Psalm 30:5). We might even say that joy can come in the mourning. She had to go through the hurt. She also needed not be afraid of the hurt and the fear. Simultaneously, she was healing. God was working in the flow to make her resilient, to bring her back to life. One day last month she said to me, "I am so grateful that I knew John all those years. We had forty-seven good years together. Now I can remember them without crying. Now I can open the photo books and be warmed by them. It took me two years, but I am back to the forward of my life." I loved her saying that she was "back" to the "forward." That showed how grief and pain ride alongside flow and resilience and healing. They are all a part of the days of early grief.

Folk wisdom says that we should not make any major decisions about the rest of our days until a year after our loved one has died. This wisdom applies to a lost mother or father, sister or brother, husband, wife, or partner. Their passing will change our lives, especially if we are close. (Their passing may change our lives even if we were not close!) This recipe for grief is dangerous. It took my friend two full years. I have also seen people flow into their new river in six months. The former is not sick, nor is the latter cold. People's rivers merely are different. Some of us have prepared for grief by knowing what we would do or not do if left bereft. We have replaced our mother with a good friend. Or we have plans we cannot do while taking care of our father—plans all ready in the "drawer" for the next stage of our life. Or we may have talked things through with our life partner early and often, making grief less of a surprise and more of an expectation. These preparations can help us through grief, but they do not have anything to do with the length of the time of the pain. Pain has its own calendar.

Not all grief arrives at thanksgiving easily. Flowing with, rather than against, our own personal river and calendar gives us the resilience we need for the long, hard, early days. Gratitude is what we get after the flow and resilience are in place. Gratitude is a spiritual gift in the same way that flow and resilience and "keeping on keeping on" are gifts. Sometimes the person we have loved and lost also drove us crazy. We may have spiritual work in the form of forgiveness to do. My friend only had to forgive her husband for leaving her too soon. Others have to forgive their partners for hurting them and disappointing them. Still others will be glad their so-called loved one is gone.

Forgiveness is our destination in this kind of grief, lest we turn lost blessing into genuine curse. Lost blessing is when time runs out on the gifts we might give each other. Lost blessing is different from genuine curse, which is active, such as when parent and child are no longer speaking or connecting at all. When grief comes inside a broken relationship, we still enjoy the spiritual gifts of flow and resilience. But gratitude is hard to achieve. When the lived relationship has been very complex, the grief will also be very complex.

Complex grief is either lost blessing or genuine curse. Blessing and curse should be understood on a continuum: in blessing, we have some relationship and connection—if not good relationship and connection. In curse, we have either nothing or genuine disapproval of the other. Where there is no relationship, people have just given up. They have decided not to try to connect any more. Too many efforts have failed. We have had one difficult Thanksgiving too many, one angry phone call too much. In disapproval, the continuum continues from the neutral absence of relationship to an actively negative one. Many homosexual people know this curse far too well: their parents have said they are no good because of their sexual orientation. Thus, the child has been cursed by the parents' disapproval. When the cursing parent dies, things get complex. We do flow back to life. We do have the resilience to go on. But we do not end our own life with words of thanksgiving on our lips. We go silent, and we hurt "empty," rather than "full."

We must move to forgiveness—another spiritual asset—if we want to be free of the cursing or distancing ghost of our parents. The actress Whoopi Goldberg speaks of coming to terms with the ghosts of her ancestors. Although most of us would not be so intimate with the thoughts of more ancient peoples, we still know about the past and its seeping and creeping into the present.

If we cannot forgive our lost loved one for not being what we wanted and needed, we can at least neutralize his or her curse. The way forward is not to return hate for hate or disrespect for disrespect. Often in complex grief, we come to the hard rock at the bottom, the realization that our parents or partners did not know how to love us. We ourselves may also have inherited their incapacity in the area of love.

Both curse and lost blessing involve the rejection of us. That curse survives death and will carry on if we do not deal with it. Loved ones may have cursed us with neglect or with controlling attention. They may have done only what their parents did to them. As children, we often do not understand why one parent can abandon another. Later, we may be able to comprehend.

The first thing we need to know is that complex grief is as normal and ordinary as simple grief. Flow and resilience are the simultaneity of both loving grief and distanced grief. We are being restored even while we are experiencing the sadness and anger and lostness of grief. Like a wound that is healing over, we are scabbing. We are building new flesh. The time will come when we look the way we did before we were wounded.

When it comes to the loss of a life partner, we often experience a rich pain. Gratitude and anger and disappointment mingle. We find ourselves experiencing "everything at once." When it comes to parents' death, the more realism we can mount, the better. Many will get to gratitude quickly because they enjoyed a positive life relationship with their parent. The parent is a positive legacy, and grief has a destination in gratitude.

However, life for many, many Americans is not as Norman Rockwell pictured; June Cleaver was not everyone's mother. How do we forgive our past for not being all it could be? We let it go. We put it in a cage and lose the key. We "compartmentalize" until we are ready, slowly, and with help, to let the bad memories out. Where does the present get the power it needs to finish with the past? By the grace of God and an active patience, many are able to substitute God's more excellent parenting love and acceptance for the injury done by biological parents. Many are also able to find mentors, friends, clergy, teachers, new families, and other relations to substitute and to parent them. Finally, at maturity, we are able to become our own parents and to give ourselves the acceptance we needed earlier. We mend. We do remedial work. We go back through the stages of love and acceptance that we missed. We let others help us, both professionals and nonprofessionals. The larger question is whence hope, given the pervasive nature of the injury? Remember hope, as Emily Dickinson told us, is the thing with feathers. We find it when we find it, where we find it—often in the serendipity of looking for something else. We come to terms with the fact that our parents, who were supposed to love us, failed to do so, and we move on. We do so when we realize that not moving on will only reproduce "them" in "us," and we decide not to let them have that legacy as victory. A spouse who insulted us was simply making a bad error in judgment: we are not that bad.

We become tough-minded and tough-hearted enough to love ourselves, even though we have not been well loved. We join the great crowd of other under- or over-parented people—and carry on with every hope of keeping our parents' failures out of the spiritual gene pool.

A parent can leave behind more hate than love, more fear than comfort, and more despair than hope. These are burning legacies: the parent probably did not want to leave such a legacy but lost the power to do otherwise. We can still take what was good from his or her life; we can still do the rituals that mark simple grief. We can read letters and go through papers and photographs, but we may have to do so afraid of what we will find. Our task will not be unmitigated joy, but rather mitigated joy.

Mitigations are blends; they are discriminations. They refuse to lump all that our parents or partners did wrong in one big pile and to whine about it the rest of our lives. Instead, they pick the good out of the trash and let the rest go. Think of complex grief as a gorgeous flower arrangement that has seen better days. Even at the end, there are a few roses left worth saving. Pick them out. Put them in a new vase. Add fresh water. And carry on. Toss the rest of the bouquet into the compost pile and turn it over into soil and learning.

Our task will be getting free of curse—and that is not always simple. Curse is the forecast of trouble far into the future; blessing is the opposite. Blessing is the forecast of good: "Surely goodness and mercy shall follow me all the days of my life, and I shall dwell in the house of the Lord my whole life long," as Psalm 23:6 concludes. That is deep blessing. Doubt that we have a worthy house or that love is real is potentially a deep curse as well. We may fear that we will become like our father, unable to make and keep real covenant. We may fear that we will become a double person, one who has no place to tell the truth of her.

Fears that we will reproduce our parents' weaknesses are a real curse. They predict trouble, and they prohibit hope. What we want, even in complex grief, is to wrestle our parent for a blessing. We look clearly at the curse that is present. We do not ignore it. But then we look deeper for the blessing.

My own mother was saved by my aunt when her mother tried to drown her in a bathtub at an early age. My grandmother was put into a mental institution. It is amazing that my mother can love as well as she can—and also hard on me that she did not love better. My life task is to improve my capacity to love, not to let the curse of my grandmother continue.

As we go through the grief and the memorabilia, the funeral and the cards, we can prepare ourselves for mixtures of gladness and sadness. A picture of our father at our softball game, cheering us on, need not dismay us. We can enjoy the blessing he tried to give; we can even treasure it. We do not have to throw the baby out with the bathwater. Blending is possible. We "have to take the good with the bad," as the very wise and not really trite folk saying so well says it.

One parishioner of mine found love letters that her father had received from his lover. They were in his bottom drawer, under new packages of socks he had never opened. Lorraine remembered the Christmas packages of socks and smiled ruefully that he had not opened them. She found the letters under the ton of socks, knew they were written in a woman's handwriting other than her mother's, and did not open them for several weeks. She just left them on her dresser, wondering what to do. When we discussed the question of whether or not she should open them, she said, "Hasn't he hurt me enough already with his constant criticism of me and Mom? Why do I want to know more?"

She had known for years that her mother, his wife, was unloved in certain very obvious, deep ways. There was a lack of attention, a lack of consideration, and forgotten birthdays and anniversaries. But she had not known of her father's divided attention. This discovery sent her grief process into high gear: she was able to dislike certain parts of her father. She had been sufficiently intimidated by him that she had not been able to reciprocate his criticism of her and her mother with her own criticism of him. She thought he was right about her and her mother. As she saw the real "crime" in the love letters, she let go of the burden of her grief being all sorrow. She let a fierce anger burn off some of the confusion and chaos she had known so long. She experienced some relief—and she noticed the same in her elderly mother. Her mother was also experiencing, unacknowledged, some renewed spirit in her own step. She was free of a man who had not fully loved her while pretending so to do. Lorraine never let her mother read the letters, but she did change the way she talked about her father's death with her mother. Lorraine showed her mother that though she was an old woman, she might yet have some new life left in her. She could be both grieving for someone loved and also glad that someone she loved was gone. Her love might not have been so much pure and romantic as practical and wounded. The truth can be healing. It can make sense of realities. Spiritual reality is the flow and resilience of grief. We need not fear it; we may welcome it. It is our river, and it is moving our way, toward our truth, bending toward gratitude and forgiveness.

The truth can also hurt a lot. The comparison in complex grief is often a difficult one. What will hurt more? Knowing the truth about our relationship with our parents, or not knowing it? Lorraine never showed her mother the letters. She made a choice to keep a secret. Sometimes secret-keeping is just a way of protecting ourselves from the hurt. Lorraine would often say that the letters would have destroyed her mother. I often wondered whether they would "destroy" Lorraine. They did not. Lorraine made peace with the truth of her life and the truth about her father. His death, and the mature way she dealt with it, brought renewed life to her and to her mother.

My own grief for my father is complex. I was glad, at first, that he was gone. My mother had left my father in June of the year of his death—this time, for good. She had left him before but had always gone back. He was the kind of guy who could not insure a car, so rich was his driver's rage and his penchant for attacking the state police. Once he threw a recliner into a forest on the side of a rural road in North Carolina. He just got tired of carrying it around. When the state policeman driving behind him arrested him for littering, he slugged the state policeman. That was not the first time. My mother was the kind of woman who stuck with her man, for fifty-three years; through richer and poorer; and always making excuses about what a terrible, impoverished childhood he had. He responded to her generosity with a mental and physical abuse that does not win records in most prisons, but was nonetheless pretty hard to see. Simultaneously, with a few highballs and a dance at the Moose Club, they would appear to be the happiest couple around.

One June, when he toyed with a trip she was planning to see her grandchildren—which he did with great regularity—she had had enough and drove her car out of the driveway, not to return.

Three months later, her ex-husband was dead. He died alone, with the body not found for four days. My brother, whose grief is even more complex than mine, discovered him by odor. My father's mental illness had been fairly low-key during my childhood; it increased when my brother was born seven years after me. Jesse, my brother, suffered nearly his whole life from my father's angry disapproval of him, often violently expressed at sports events. "Take that kid out, he's been up twice and hasn't hit a thing," he'd yell. The death was so bad that it made the separation and divorce look easy. We were all recovering when the matter of the gravestone surfaced.

My father had not been able to keep a job. His anger was often the cause. So we moved every year from the time I was eleven until I was eighteen. My mother would hold things together, sort of, economically and otherwise. Daddy was often legitimately angry at things that happened to him in the garment business, such as losing his pension at age fifty-nine after being fired when he would have been vested three months later. He was moved by the same company; they did him wrong in a hundred ways. We never could tell whether he was responsible for his anger or if "they" had done it.

Thus, we became a family with an up-and-down history—up and down the East Coast, New York to the Carolinas, West Virginia, and back. We three kids blamed Daddy for the lack of a physical home, and my mother really blamed him. She never let him forget his failures for a minute.

That is why the gravestone was such an issue. It involved locating a home.

We had buried my father last year with his own father in Kingston, New York, without a stone or marker. Just incoherent grief. No one spoke the obvious question, which is whether my mother would choose to be buried with her parents, up the stony hill, or with him and his father.

It took her a year to decide. When she decided, I drove south to pick up the stone that had both of their names on it. (They had purchased the stone years ago as an act of preparation for their deaths.) They had lived in South Carolina for many years by then and had assumed they would be buried there. They also had a plot in New York with their families of origin. It turned out that the best thing to do was to bury them in New York, together, and use the stone with both names on it. We experienced an utter paralysis once that decision was made. No one could figure out what to do next. The decision to bury them together rang false—as false as the decision to bury them separately might have done. We were in a double bind. Ritual did not make sense. Not having ritual did not make sense either. We had complex grief.

A part of me was furious that my mother would make the choice to be buried next to him. Another part of me was delighted. A third part of me drove the stone north from its location in the south where they had hoped to be happy together.

What saved me was a series of narrow doors. Those resiliencies that opened my closed heart can only be considered miracles. They were God's action on God's side of the door, not mine. I was lost in a kind of pickle jar, inside a deep closet, back on a shelf. A vat of vinegar. I could not get out of my jar, much less open my door.

On the positive side, I was able to remember being close to a family, even if it was a troubled family. I was able to receive the grace of God, which is what had always comforted me when my biological family failed me. Children always want their parents to be together because it makes it easier on us. On the negative side, I felt that my mother had agreed to be a carpet, both in life and in death. She had so many chances for so long to leave him: why did she wait until three months before he died?

Finally I felt that I did not have to have lifelong grief for my parents' inability to form a marriage that included joy. I could stop grieving that now. That story was over. She was free of him. He was free of her. There was no doubt that God had taken my father home.

Indeed, I would never have the reconciliation with him that I had so longed for and had spent years in therapy coveting. Whatever I had done to make him so disdainful of me, I could no longer undo. My part in our curse would remain my bent-out-of-shapeness—or my particular shape, take your pick.

Instead of having those happy endings, I stood at his grave tearless. My own daughter asked me why I did not cry. She was fourteen. She will remember that I was tearless there. I know I disappointed her. I was just using the same cold side of the resilience I had known so long. I was in my normal flow, even at his grave. Both resilience and flow have cold, hard sides, and it is important to name that. My daughter wants to imagine a blessing, way back, of simple grief, simply expressed, in normal ways. She does not want to imagine the possibility of a curse in her own family. I do not blame her. She already has the desire for a textbook grief.

When we stand at complex graves, we are rarely capable of faking grief. Loss is still there, even if we are secretly glad the parent is gone. Good grief in complex situations does not fake emotions. It lets them be what they are, attractive or not, good models or not, pretty or ugly, and cold or hot. The spiritual gifts of flow and resilience come inside spiritual reality, well perceived, not outside of it.

Death closes the doors on chapters; it does not close the door on maturity or development. Although some things can never happen once a loved one is gone, other things can happen. I often notice that the difference between "old" people and "young" people is that young people talk about the future; old people talk about the past.

One of the tricks in complex grief is not to get buried in the parent's tomb. Although some do. We end up chewing the old bones. We sometimes even come to enjoy our resentments.

As Dick Sparrow, in a recent devotional message, put it,

> Some of us fume, God … slowly burning over a resentment from a moment or decade ago and in the fuming give the "incident" extraordinary power over every aspect of our lives. It's not like we choose to fume, but more like the fume-bug infects our core, feeding on our peace and leaving us diminished. We want to be healed. But we have acquired a love of our resentments.

No matter how complex the grief, the comfort is equally complex. Like a river that flows in the direction it must, our grief takes its path, resolutely and resiliently, toward home. Once hurt, we can hurt ourselves again and again, over and over, by refusing to turn the page on the next chapter. Many can and do get stuck in complex grief, with no door out. But still more flow in with the river and go where they must.

Strange and healing things happen along the way. Narrow doors open. The sour turns sweet. Joy comes in the mourning, and in the morning.

Endnotes

1. Emily Dickinson, "Hope Is a Thing with Feathers," *The Complete Poems of Emily Dickinson* (Boston: Little, Brown, 1924).

A Soul-Size Exploration

Donald J. Shelby

Do you remember the first time you encountered the pain, chaos, and emptiness of grief at some catastrophic loss or at the death of someone you loved? I was seven when my maternal grandfather died and I had my first experience of grief. Although I could not completely understand what was happening, I remember sitting between my mother and father at his funeral, sitting as close to each of them as I could and hanging on to their arms for fear that they might also die and be taken away from me.

Two years later, my father did die—when I was nine—and my world was changed forever. The void in my life created by his death remains still, many decades later. In the days immediately after he died, several well-meaning relatives tried to fill the void with words and gestures of comfort. I say they *tried* to fill the void because the indelible memory of those dark days is the terror and immense loneliness I felt. One of my relatives told me, "God has taken your daddy because God needed him in heaven." I inwardly railed against that idea. If God loved us, I thought, God knew that we needed our daddy on earth more than God needed him in heaven. If God had indeed taken him away, then I decided in my young mind that I might never be able to trust God again.

Thus did I discover early in my life that when grief overcomes us, when our world is turned upside down and life hangs in the balance, people can turn *from* God as well as turn *to* God. Life's pivotal crises (the word "crisis" is cognate of the Greek word *krisis,* which is most often translated in the New Testament as "judgment") do not necessarily bring us closer to God; they can also separate us from God. A crisis is a spiritual boundary in which God's presence may become clear and steady for us, as our faith deepens and life is filled with hope and excitement. A crisis can also be a border moment when faith in God disintegrates, when darkness descends, and when we give up on believing in anything and trusting anyone.

The Bible narrates the experiences of countless people who have stood at the boundaries of life and found their faith ebbing away. This is a recurring cry in the lines of the psalmist and from more than one Hebrew prophet. Moses stood at such a border moment, and so did Job. The disciples of Jesus were plunged into such dereliction after Jesus was crucified, and the apostle Paul reveals how he struggled more than once in such an abyss. Most stalwarts of the faith across the centuries have walked through a shadowed valley of suffering with its awful sense of distance and disconnection from God. Saint John of the Cross called it "the dark night of the soul."

In the first congregation that I served as pastor, I was called one day to the home of a young father, whose wife and four children had been killed when a train struck their automobile at a grade crossing in the community. The family was actively involved in the life of the church, and the father was a committed Christian. I shall never forget the traumatic moments I spent with him. His over-whelming grief became intense hostility. He almost shouted to me that as far as he was concerned, God, in killing his family, had killed him—along with killing the man's soul, turning his desire to keep on living into dust. He wanted noth-ing to do with a religious funeral, but his extended family insisted that there be one. He did not want to pray. He would not listen to anything I tried to say to him.

The man sat defiantly through the funeral and spurned any gestures of com-fort from friends and family. At the cemetery, he stood apart from the assembled group before the five white caskets lined up on the grass before five open graves. When I spoke the words of committal and final blessing, his anger and enormous loss became a primal scream as he fell to his knees, lifted his face to the sky, and raged at God. For several months following the funeral, I regularly called on him and continued to pray for him, despite the fact that he remained unreceptive and inaccessible. No one could reach him. He began drinking heav-ily and literally destroyed his own life.

No matter how deep our faith may be, no matter how mature our spiritual per-spective is, the crisis of loss can test and undermine our faith. It can distort our perspective until a sense of God's presence can only be inferred from a haunt-ing sense of God's absence. Some people share the experience of a woman from Rwanda, who, after the massacres in that troubled land in 1994, said simply, "The angels have left us."

Yet there are those who struggle through the pain and desolation of their grief and, in that process, maintain or reclaim their faith in God. They pick up the pieces, let life take precedence over their sorrow, and in so doing discover a deeper dimension of meaning in life and a greater understanding of love. These people are drawn to a new appreciation of and response to the Bible; and with heightened awareness in their praying, they resonate with God's near presence. If they are Christians, their commitment to Christ becomes more vibrant and centers their life. They do not downplay either the struggle through which they have come, or the pain and moments of despair with which they have coped. They confess that although they endured many episodes of doubt, fear, desper-ation, and anger, their faith in God remained intact. They discovered that although they might have temporarily given up on God, God never gave up on them. Gradually their faith, which had ebbed away, began to flow again and grew stronger. Moreover, they report that an increased eagerness for life returned, and they realized that love is all we have and is all we ever keep.

How do we account for the difference between people who turn from God and people who turn to God in the crisis of grief? Why is it that some grieving people lose their faith and become embittered about life and detached from others? In contrast, why do some others in their grief turn to other persons for help and encouragement, never stop praying, continue to worship God, pick up their shattered lives, and return to those activities that added excitement and meaning to them? While never "getting over" the loss of the loved one, they nonetheless accept the reality of it and choose to consecrate that loss by "living each day in eternity's sunrise," as William Blake put it.

Out of my own experiences of grief, along with those I have shared with people across forty-five years of pastoral ministry, there have emerged three compelling insights into the contrasted differences in responses to loss. The first is that every person handles grief in his or her unique way, according to his or her individual timetable. This is because grief grows out of our deeply held individual emotional responses and perceptions, the makeup of our personality, the family matrix out of which we have emerged, the strategies we have developed for handling reality, the patterns of our personal relationships, the fundamental attitudes we have toward life and death, and the shape and strength of our faith.

This is why there is no "standardized" way of handling grief, no "officially sanctioned" religious way to grieve, no predetermined timetable for grief, no packaged program that people can follow to move through their loss and grow in faith and spirituality. This also means that there is no "right" or "wrong" method to grieve, despite the plethora of books suggesting the "right" way. Such publications (including this volume you hold) can be helpful, but they are never definitive.

Although there is no "right" or "wrong" method to deal with grief, there are "productive" and "nonproductive" methods. The productive ways are those through which we find understanding, impetus, and resources for further personal and spiritual development. Such growth enables us to let life take precedence over our sorrow, renders us reachable and teachable, prompts us to seek and accept the support of others, moves us closer to God as we claim again the promises of scripture and faith, and opens us to divine power that can make grief a transforming experience.

The second insight involves clarifying the expectations we hold about our religious faith, so that they are realistic and focused instead of illusory and distorted. By this I mean what we expect from God and God's revelation of love and purpose in the life, teachings, death, and resurrection of Jesus Christ; and what this implies for us when we face crises and contradictions in life. It also refers to what we expect from God's involvement in our world, in human history, and in our personal lives and relationships. It further includes clarifying what God expects from us when we commit ourselves to a life of discipleship, what we expect from prayer, what we expect from living from the Bible as God's Word, and what we expect from "loving one another" and "[being] of the same mind, having the same love, being in full accord and of one mind" (Philippians 2:2).

More than we tend to realize, our expectations determine our perceptions. They help shape the level of our belief and determine the responses we make to the enigmas and challenges of life. To clarify the expectations that we hold about God, about Jesus and God's salvation promise in Christ, about what living our lives in commitment to God and God's promises means, as well as understanding what God expects of us, are crucial dimensions of a vital faith. Such effort and spiritual discipline are underscored in the words of the apostle Paul to the church in Philippi: "Work out your own salvation with fear and trembling" (Philippians 2:12). There is a sense of urgency in his exhortation, calling us immediately to this task so we will be prepared when crises break upon us.

To clarify our expectations is a vigorous spiritual, mental, and emotional exercise. It demands honest and persistent examination of what we believe not only cognitively, but also at the deepest levels of our being. It consists of spending time in thought, prayer, and reflection; and it is helpful if we can join other people in a study group in which we can check one another on the integrity of the conclusions we reach.

The following questions are suggestive of those we will face and ponder, along with those that other people will raise for us to consider:

- Does faith in God and God's love in Christ guarantee that we will be spared the loss of our loved ones too soon or in violent ways? Does belief in God provide us with immunity from dangers, disease, suffering, and calamity? Does it mean we will never have to raise the questions, "Why us, me, him, or her? Why now?"
- Does faith in God and a personal relationship with Jesus Christ endow us with spiritual ecstasy and power that will prevent or alleviate the pain of grief and any experience of despair, emptiness, and doubt? In responding to our prayers, can we expect God to send us a cure and postpone death for us and our loved ones? Does faith in Jesus' resurrection mean our grief will be short and that we will cope easily with our losses?
- For a person of faith, is death an intrusion into life or an integral and accepted part of God's plan for life? Can we experience the beauty, joy,

constancy, and fulfillment of loving and being loved without the risk of emptiness, suffering, and drastic changes that death and loss bring? Does everyone have to walk shadowed valleys alone? In such valleys are we really alone, or does God in Christ walk with us?

● Does faith in God translate into a rational understanding of why things happen to us in life? Or is faith instead accepting the reality that there is much that we do not understand about the little that we do know—that life, truth, beauty, and love are adventures in which we never know enough to spare us the adventure, but the little that we do know is enough to prompt the venture?

For experiences of loss to be openings for spiritual growth, we must clarify the expectations of the faith we hold, our expectations of God who holds us. This truth is underscored by John Claypool in *Footsteps of a Fellow Struggler,* a book written after the death of his eight-year-old daughter from leukemia:

I was not disappointed then—at the bottom of the darkness my religion truly did make a difference. Why? Partly because I did not erect false expectations. I let God be God and give me what [God] willed to give and what was appropriate. And also because long before, I had come to see [God] as a Shepherd-God—the One whose nature is to give power to the faint.[1]

The third insight into the difference in people who cope with grief in positive and productive ways is derivative and a corollary of the second. It focuses on the intentional choices people make that shape their response to and attitudes about their loss. Like clarifying our expectations, it is also a rigorous exercise. For when we are numb with grief and the pain we feel is our only reality, it can be a challenge to summon the energy and find the motivation to make choices, to sort out and then decide what we are going to do and when.

It seems so much easier to let the chaos control us instead of controlling the chaos ourselves. It is so tempting to choose to respond as a victim, to allow self-pity and helplessness to overcome us, to resent loss as unfair and undeserved, and to yield to despair and abdicate responsibility. Because the experience of grief is such an emotional shock when everything on which we have depended suddenly changes, life and the future are fraught with uncertainty. Little wonder that C. S. Lewis suggested that "grief feels like fear." That is why we want to imagine the reality of it away, to hide until it somehow disappears.

Not knowing how to handle the enormousness of the events erupting around us, we seek to blame someone else for them (especially God), or we look around for someone to resolve them for us. No longer able to control our emotions, we withdraw from other people. Or we may find ourselves projecting on other people the hostility and resentment that fester within us. The last thing we want to do is make decisions, to face what has happened and cannot be changed.

The point is, however, that although we cannot undo what has happened, we can change our attitudes about what has occurred. We can choose to pick up the pieces and begin again; we can decide to stop feeling sorry for ourselves and begin thinking of others. Instead of asking "Why me?" we can ask "Why not me?" or "How shall I make it through?" We can pay the bills, clean the house, mow the lawn, and, instead of putting them off, engage the myriad other tasks that follow in the wake of someone's death, despite the feeling of only going through the motions. We can return to church and worship God with friends in the congregation. We can also pray as we can and keep on praying, living into the healing and help we seek and need.

We can refuse to be bitter at our loss and can acknowledge how much remains with us of all that we have shared and been through with our loved one across the years. We can choose to thank God for blessing us with amazing grace—and for continuing to bless us. The reason we can make these movements is because we choose to do so. As we decide to be open and hopeful, courageous and caring, affirming life and saying yes to God, we will find ourselves moving and growing on.

Because all human crises involve or evolve into a story, I conclude with the story of a young man and woman, Mark and Leslie, who began worshiping with the congregation in the church I served before I retired. They were studying for their Ph.D. degrees at a nearby university. They had been nurtured in the Christian faith, were strong believers, avid students of the Bible, and lived out their faith in a response to others in need. I had the privilege of presiding at their wedding. Soon after that event, they relocated to Memphis, where the wife had received a faculty appointment. In their frequent correspondence with me, they described how ecstatically happy they were. Their fulfilling life was made even more so when they became the grateful parents of a son, Aidan.

Later still came the exciting news that Leslie was pregnant again. However, in the sixth month of her pregnancy, she began hemorrhaging and was hospitalized. While every effort was made to save her and the unborn child, a miscarriage occurred and the baby died. Moreover, because her hemorrhaging could not be stopped, Leslie also died. Mark was understandably overwhelmed with grief in a world that had collapsed for him. And something else occurred—he found his faith in God collapsing as well. When people tried to talk about religion or to comfort him with the promises of biblical faith, he found them to be mere words expressing a loving sentiment that nevertheless fell far short of reassurance. It was a lonely, empty, and chaotic world through which he stumbled as he tried to adjust to the fact that he was a single parent with a young son and without the wife to whom he was devoted and whom he loved very much. He wondered where Leslie was and what she was doing. He turned in various ways for help and answers—to religion, spiritualism, and psychology. He prayed, he read book after book, he talked to professionals in each of those areas, but to no avail. He said, "I grew up as someone who believed in God, heaven, eternal life, and all that stuff; and I would have sworn without a doubt that is what I believed. Now I needed something more." He said he felt like C. S. Lewis, who, after his wife died, likened his religious faith to a house of cards that had collapsed.[2]

As Mark made his way through his grief, he began examining and clarifying his expectations of faith, his belief in God, and his commitment to Christ. He realized that he had choices to make and a life to live in a world that had changed dramatically for him. So he made hard and exacting decisions, even when his heart was heavy and his eyes were filled with tears. He kept saying to himself, "There is a lot I can do, a lot that I want to do, and there might not be much time to do it." He knew he must stay steady for his son, Aidan, an energetic boy who also had a new world to explore. So they explored together. In a speech he gave to a Grief Recovery Group, Mark concluded by saying, "I am trying to work through my problems, resolve my issues with people. I try not to be mean to other people and try to help out wherever I can." Despite his faith in God taking on a tentative feel, he never stopped worshiping with his congregation and stayed involved in the life of the church.

Today, my friend is still exploring his new world, which now includes a woman he hopes to marry. His son provides much joy, life has taken precedence over his sorrow, and the grief through which he has come has been transformed. His faith in God through Christ is stronger, life for him is alive, and the future beckons.

Mark discovered how we can grow spiritually as we cope with and move through grief in—what the British playwright, Christopher Fry, in a telling encapsulation called—"soul-size exploration." May it be so for you.

Endnotes

1. John Claypool, *Tracks of a Fellow Struggler: Living and Growing Through Grief* (New Orleans: Insight Press, 1995).
2. C. S. Lewis, *A Grief Observed* (San Francisco: Harper & Row, 1989), 48-49.

Underneath Are the Everlasting Arms

Karen Stone

When my grandmother Gjelten died, my father was at her side. Later he told us her last words: "Underneath are the everlasting arms." The image of the everlasting arms was so potent to me, a fifteen-year-old, that I carry it with me today. Those arms carried me at the end of Thelma Marie Rue Gjelten's life.

My mother taught me to nest. Thelma kept a cozy home. She sewed curtains, made pillows, put pictures on the wall. The house was tidy (not spotless, just always nice). Often we came home to the fragrance of fresh-baked cookies or homemade cinnamon rolls. In season, a muslin bag hung from a wooden spoon stuck through two cupboard pulls, dripping grape or chokecherry juice into a bowl for jelly. She painted, decorated, and moved furniture.

So I nest. Every summer I devote the first week at our cabin to arranging and reclaiming the house from mice and dust mites. A short stay at a flat in Cambridge wouldn't seem worth the trouble—but no, I have to move the furniture around and shop for a salad spinner, flower vase, or poster for the wall. Even on overnight motel stays, I fiddle with the room until it suits us.

There I was, nesting, that mid-August in 1999. My husband, Howard, and I were on research leave. We had moved into our friends' handsome town home in the medieval market town of Saffron Walden in England. It is a lovely house, but I am Thelma's child, so I spent three days making it ours. A guest bedroom became a study. Tables were moved from room to room; items we had acquired went on the mantel. I rearranged the kitchen. As I worked, I thought of how easy it was to do these things because of the little tips and tricks my mother had taught me. The joy of launching into a project, doing it right, and admiring the results was pure Thelma.

Nesting accomplished, I cooked a nice stir-fry and sat to enjoy the first proper meal in "our" home. The telephone rang. My sister Elizabeth was on the line, crying. "Mom's had a stroke." An enormous weight thudded onto my chest. She was in the hospital, undergoing surgery for the bleeding in her brain. It sounded as if she was not going to make it.

My head reeled. I couldn't eat the nice dinner.

I remembered the last time I had seen her—May, it was. At eighty-three, she seemed old to me (finally), needed help stepping up a curb, and couldn't remember the right freeway exit when I drove her to the Tacoma Mall to buy shoes. During one of our conversations, Mom told me, "I'm ready to go when the Lord calls me. I just worry about the people I'll leave behind."

She must have sensed that everything wasn't right. Her failing memory distressed her. She'd walk into a room and forget why she had come. She fell a few times—didn't stumble or pass out, just fell down for no reason. We did not want to see the signs. Mother was the healthy, hardy one; she would live forever, or at least well into her nineties.

When Howard and I shared our plans for a sabbatical year abroad, including three weeks in South Africa, she told my father that she was worried about us being so far away. "What if something should happen?" Our travels had never worried her before. We traveled all of the time. How did she know?

A week before we were to leave for Africa, here I was making midnight transatlantic phone calls. What should I do? Go? Wait? The news sounded more hopeful by morning's light. Mom had survived the surgery. She was conscious. She recognized people. Before long she was talking, then sitting up in bed, then taking physical therapy for her sciatica. I talked with her on the phone. She told me about the kitchen shears that my dad had given her for her birthday a few days before the stroke. "They're in the drawer by the stove," she told me. "Like my mother always told me, 'A place for everything, and everything in its place.'"

Filled with hope, we decided to go ahead to Africa. Immediately on our return, I would fly to Olympia and spend time with Mom. She'd be better then and could enjoy the visit more. But the following day—thirty-six hours before we were to leave for Africa—I got a call from my brother, Paul. "You'd better come," he told me. "Her brain is bleeding again."

I got busy. KLM would postpone my flight to Johannesburg for a week if I could produce medical documents. The flight to Seattle from England was trickier. I walked down Gold Street to the first travel agent around the corner. The nice woman patted my hand and found me a flight from London to Seattle the following morning.

August 28 was the day we were to leave for South Africa. At 4 A.M., Howard drove me to the nearest airport where I boarded a coach for Gatwick Airport. He flew to Africa later in the day, committed to a lecture schedule in Pretoria. I got on the airplane not knowing if I would find my mother dead, in a coma, or sitting up and talking. The flight is a fog. Maybe I slept a little. Probably I cried. On the trip from Minneapolis to Seattle, I sat next to a young woman who was feverish and sneezing. Embarrassed and apologetic (that's the Thelma in me, too), I requested another seat because I knew I wouldn't be allowed in intensive care if I appeared to be sick.

My brother met me at the airport. I fell into his arms. As we sped to Olympia, he filled me in on new developments. We talked about letting Mom die. Dad was feeling guilty about signing permission for surgery—second guessing, wondering if he should have allowed her to go that first day. Paul and I agreed to help him understand that the surgeries had given us a chance to be together one more time.

In August, it was already dark at 8:30, Douglas fir trees black against the slate sky, as we drove into the hospital parking lot. Paul knew the ropes by now; I only had to follow as we half ran to the ICU. My father, Elizabeth, and Paul's wife, Kathy, sat in the tiny waiting area, but I only wanted Mom. They were busy doing a procedure on her shunt. That means she's alive, I thought, she's alive, she's alive—I made it in time!

The quarter-hour wait seemed longer than the twenty-three-hour journey. In those minutes, we talked about what was to come. No more heroic measures, my father pleaded.

Finally I sat by Mother's side. My initial feeling was not passion or sorrow, but discomfort. She had a bonnet on her head (they'd shaved her thick, wavy hair). Tubes. Machines. A clear bag collecting the blood that leaked from her brain. Yellow skin. But she looked like Mom, I thought gratefully. Changed, but still Thelma.

I told myself to wait, keep looking at her until I could get used to it. Just wait. After a few minutes, I took her hand. She opened her eyes. "Karen! It's so good to have you here." You can't imagine the joy—she knew me, she could talk, and I could understand her. Right away I launched a litany of thanks, trying to get in everything I loved about her, every reason I had to be grateful, every instance when I was blessed by her teaching, training, and caring over the years. I didn't want to regret later on not saying these things. I squeezed her hand three times, which is our family signal for "I love you." Thelma squeezed back four times: "I love you, too." Then she squeezed about ten more times.

Elizabeth joined us. I wanted her there; this was hard going alone. "I'm sorry," Mom kept saying. "So sorry … mistakes … should have. . . ." It's all forgiven, we told her. All forgiven. All that is left is the love. But she seemed agitated. I taught her the Jesus prayer, and she responded to it eagerly. She was dying, but still learning. "Jesus Christ, Son of God, have mercy on me, a sinner" repeated quietly, like a mantra, was the Jesus prayer. This was a good prayer for a good woman struggling with guilt. It took her a little time, at the end, to rest easy in God's mercy.

Pulling at her tubes, Mom asked, "Why are you letting me go on like this?" "We're not," we told her. "The doctor will be here in the morning."

Her mouth moved, "Jesus loves me." So we sang the old song and then more hymns. She asked for "Kum Ba Yah." We sang verse after verse of it—someone's crying, Lord; praying, Lord; singing, Lord; dying, Lord; kum ba yah. We made up new verses. She joined in the singing. We prayed the Lord's Prayer, and she spoke every word. Then it was time to go. I said the blessing my father had repeated all those years as a parish pastor: "The Lord bless you and keep you, the Lord make his face shine on you and be gracious unto you, the Lord look upon you with favor and grant you peace." Peaceful smile. Kisses. Goodnight. She slept.

The next morning was Sunday, August 29. The neurosurgeon on duty was a young resident. We told him that the family wanted all life support removed. He just said, "Does she have a living will?" We assured him she did. "All right," he said. "You can stay with her if you want." We clearly were in his way, sitting on both sides of Mom's bed as he performed this last little surgery to remove the shunt from her brain, but he worked around us. That simple act of humanity meant more than I can describe. When her eyes opened wide at a moment of pain, it was so good to be there, to reassure her, and to tell her what was happening. "Good!" she said. "Thank you!" The only tube left would be the morphine drip in her left arm.

August 29 was a busy day. They moved Mother to the fourth floor—comfort care, they called it. We settled her into the room, arranged flowers, set out items from home, and installed a rollaway bed for the person on watch. Ah, yes, nesting again.

My cousin Larry, a physician, and my cousin Philip, a Lutheran pastor, came with their wives. Philip celebrated communion with the family and touched Mother's lips with a drop of wine and a crumb of bread. Larry said, "It won't be long—a few hours, maybe." A hospice volunteer came to take Mother's information, but we sent her away. The physical therapist arrived, and we sent her away, too.

We worked out a schedule for the watch. I was still seriously jet-lagged, so the early morning hours were mine. Whenever we were at Mom's side, we sang hymns. The family sang her out of this life. Dad had a tape recorder to play music for her while the singers rested. She responded to each song with wide eyes and moving lips; but when we sang a hymn of praise, she raised her eyes upwards and lifted her good right hand as high as she could. "She's seeing something we can't see," I told my father; "she's already on her journey."

In the afternoon there would be a Mass said in the chapel. Though we had celebrated communion in the morning, I felt a need for the whole liturgy; so I sat in the chapel alone and wondered how many people there were on watch with a dying loved one. The words and cadences of the liturgy swept over me like a healing stream. I went back to Mother's bedside refreshed and nourished, remembering my grandmother's dying words with an almost physical sense of God's arms beneath me.

Soon after sunrise on August 30, my father came in. This was so hard for him. As I perched on the edge of the bed, he sat on the other side—actually got up on the bed—and wrapped his arms around Thelma, saying over and over, "I love you, I love you." Her good arm was pinned underneath him. I asked her, "Do you want to give Dad a hug?" She opened her eyes wide. I held her right arm over his shoulder, and they embraced. Dad said, "This is how we started out, isn't it—you, me, and our first child?" She moved her lips; and then, for the last time, my mother spoke clearly and in an unwavering voice: "The first family." Those three words burn in my memory.

By now we were running on stored-up energy. Fitful sleep back at the house, stolen ZZ's on the rollaway cot, and bowls of hot soup from the hospital cafeteria held off collapse. We also were running out of hymns. I know scores of them by heart from years of playing and singing along but our tired memories were strained. I would catch a line or two from a hymn I wanted to sing for her, but the rest would elude me. "Peace, like a river . . . sorrows like sea billows roll . . . well with my soul." Not enough for a song. In the afternoon, Elizabeth brought my mother's green Lutheran hymnal to the hospital. We sang alone; we sang together; we kept on singing. Still Mother raised her right hand for the hymns of praise. I taught her a new South African hymn, and she took to it, eyes wide open, right hand in motion: "Alleluia, we sing your praises, all our lives are filled with gladness."

On August 31, which was our thirty-sixth wedding anniversary, at 3 A.M., I dressed and went to the hospital. As I walked from the parking lot to the hospital entrance, I looked up through the centuries-old firs. There was an aura around the moon. Clouds scudded by. Stars pierced the dark sky. I looked at a moon circled by a rainbow and cried out loud, "Mom. Mom." I could feel her spirit out there, as if she were taking her leave a little bit at a time.

For our anniversary, Howard and I had planned a festive meal with our South African friends. This was a festivity of a different sort. As I moistened my mother's mouth and sang a familiar hymn in a quiet but increasingly raspy voice, Howard called from Pretoria. I held the phone to her ear. She had asked why Howard wasn't there and seemed to understand when we told her he was lecturing. But she loved him. She needed to hear his voice, at least. When he spoke to her, I could see the recognition on her face. He told her that he had heard a choir of Zulu women singing their gorgeous hymns. Afterwards, he told these women that his mother-in-law was dying. They stopped right there and prayed for her. Tears seeped from the corners of Mother's eyes as he told her about their prayers for her. Those everlasting arms, reaching around the world to uphold her.

The comfort care ward was a place of spiritual healing. Talking with a nurse in the middle of the night, I asked, "How do people get through this without faith?" She said they have a pretty hard time of it. Her husband had died of brain cancer a few years before. She warned me that we should not believe it when people tell us it will get better, that time will heal our wounds. "You'll never get over it," she said. "I grieve for my husband as much today as I did the day he died. But you do start living again. The pain isn't so debilitating. You function; you have happiness. You just never get over it. I don't think I'd want to. I still talk to him. In so many ways, he's still part of my life."

Medicare would not continue paying for Mother's hospital room. She had to move to a nursing home. Someone loaded her into an ambulance for the half-block ride to the nursing home. I walked alongside.

On September 1, two o'clock in the morning, my sister arrived back at the house from her watch. She was sobbing. In the middle of the night, Mother's IV had failed, and she wasn't getting any morphine. The only person who could help was busy with another patient. Liz told them to call the doctor. "We can't; it's the middle of the night," they told her. "Then wake up the doctor," she raged. "My mother is in pain. It's his *job*." Mom got her morphine, but my sister was nearly broken from watching our dear one experience such pain in her final hours.

By now my mother was in a deep coma, or so they told us, and near death. But I had been thinking about her history. She had grown up on the Dakota plains, in a spare and hardscrabble life. She was the sixth of seven children, the towheaded beauty of the family. They burned cow chips for fuel, knocked ice off the washbasin to wash up in the morning, and milked cows before dawn. Thelma adored her brother Orlean, the eldest; and I remember her grief when he died of cancer while still a young man. Now, as I sat by her side for my final watch, I whispered, "Just think, Mom, pretty soon you're going to see Orlean." She didn't open her eyes or speak. She just pursed her lips, then moved them, trying to talk. She had heard. Thelma was going to her absent loved ones. Her Lord was calling her home.

Somehow we got through the day. I was scheduled to fly back to England and then Africa on the second of September. Would the airline allow me to change my plans again? I decided to do nothing. Paul and I wept and hugged. We prayed and kept right on singing to Mom. At suppertime I hated to leave, but my tired body spoke, and I drove back to the house and bed. Sometime after 1 A.M., the telephone rang, and I leaped to answer it. I knew. My sister simply said, "Mom is gone."

My niece Kristin was there, and she ran to tell her grandfather. I pulled on some clothes and followed her. I said, "Did Kristin tell you that Mom has died?" He had heard it but did not get it. Now, he put his head in his hands and cried,

"Oh, I wanted to be there!" I reminded him what the comfort care nurse had told us, that the dying have such a strong attachment to their families that often they cannot let go until their loved ones have left for a few minutes' or hours' rest. The bond holding them to this life is too great. With my arms around him, I sang, hoarsely: "Thank the Lord and sing his praise, tell everyone what he has done; he recalls his promises, and sends his people forth in joy, with shouts of thanksgiving, alleluia, alleluia." Once again the liturgy provided words and images I needed for this beautiful, hard time.

At the nursing home, Elizabeth and the night nurse had washed Mom's body. We left Dad alone with her and walked to the chapel. On the wall we read the words of the *Magnificat* ("My soul magnifies the Lord, and my spirit rejoices in God my Savior") and the *Benedictus* ("Lord, now let your servant depart in peace, according to your word, for my eyes have seen your salvation"). Oh, Mother, you've gone home. I will be the next to go. In ten years, or twenty, or thirty—in the blink of an eye—I will be seeing you.

There was no more sleep that night. We found Mom's Bible, every single page notated and underlined. We found notes for her funeral in the back of her hymnal. "Blessed Assurance, Jesus Is Mine" was the hymn she requested. We added "Kum Ba Yah." I wrote a draft for the newspaper announcement and planned the funeral with my father and siblings. Mom loved her garden, and it was still splendid. We decided to find a florist who would use her own flowers and vegetables—nothing from a greenhouse—for the funeral arrangements. Should I stay? Our friends had planned a trip to Zimbabwe, gotten vacation days at a difficult time, booked a hut, and paid for the jeep. I could hear Thelma's voice in my head: "You go." We had our time together.

Then I was on a plane to Detroit. I sat next to a woman who glanced at a photo of my smiling mother, taken on her birthday, and said, "What a lovely woman." Then to London Gatwick. I missed my bus and booked another one to Stansted Airport. There was smoke in the cockpit, the flight was canceled, and a new airplane put into service. Stansted to Amsterdam, Amsterdam to Johannesburg. In Johannesburg, a young mother from my flight was struggling with suitcases and a baby. I took her rolling bag from her; she thanked me, but I needed to do it more than she needed my help. And there was my love waiting at the gate.

Two hours after we arrived in Pretoria, we were off again to Botswana and Zimbabwe. Since my mother had died, it seemed that all I had done was travel and cry. We arrived that night at a primitive cottage on a ranch near the Botswana border. At the moment of my mother's funeral, I slipped out of my cot and knelt. Back in Olympia, they were burying Thelma. I had helped with the planning; I knew every word they were saying and every hymn they were singing. I was with them.

144

It is odd to say it, but my mother's death was our family's finest hour. People asked me, "Wasn't it hard, not having your husband there?" and I think no, it was not hard. I had my father, my brother, and my sisters. We had the everlasting arms carrying us, holding us up.

This was not a tragedy. Mother's was a good death—too soon, but good. *The Book of Common Prayer* has a line in it somewhere: "If I die, let it not be quick." This is my prayer. Give me a little time to say good-bye. Let me suffer a little at guilt for past sins, so I can come to a simple acceptance of God's grace. Let my loved ones sit by my side. Let my granddaughter Elizabeth play "Amazing Grace" on her saxophone and hug me hard. Let Caitlin sing "Children of the Heavenly Father" as I sang it to her at so many bedtimes, and let her laugh in her breezy way. Let my daughter's cheerful voice fill the room. Let me embrace the love of my life, unless he has gone ahead of me. Let me die as well as my mother died.

Last June, Howard and I hiked in the Andes. It was hard work, but oh my! On the second day we woke up in a hermit's mountain hut at 13,000 feet and walked about, waiting for breakfast and mules to be loaded, taking in the beauty. Howard saw the tears in my eyes. "It's your mom, isn't it?" Oh, yeah. She would have loved this. Mom, I still miss you. I can't believe you are gone.

God, let me work, play, pray, and sing with these people I cherish. Let me rest, in the end, on the everlasting arms that grant me life, sustain me, and will uphold me on my last day.

My Own Experiences of Grief: A Slow Discovery

David K. Switzer

More than forty years ago, I was sitting in a graduate course entitled "Psychology of Religion." I had stopped trying to follow the lecture. My mind was wandering—not daydreaming, just wandering. The day's class topic was anxiety. I had previously taken two classes that dealt with the subject: one on Freud and a few of his disciples, another dealing with anxiety from the point of view of several behavioral theorists.

The lecture was going over old ground for me. I had been struggling to discover what the professor might be offering that was new. The material was disorganized and dull, so my thoughts went somewhere else. Suddenly, a clear thought popped into my mind—grief as anxiety: separation anxiety, moral anxiety (guilt), and existential anxiety.

Anxiety, yes. But where in my mind had the word *grief* come from? I had no awareness that the professor had mentioned it; I wasn't aware of feeling any grief at that time. Hello unconscious. But why grief? I did not know. Anyway, the elaboration of that idea became the basis of my doctoral dissertation—some four hundred (mostly ponderous) pages dealing with grief as anxiety.

During my oral examination on the dissertation, I remember Howard Clinebell asking me if there was not more to it than I had written. I could not think what that would be. He persisted. They passed me anyway.

Howard never told me what he had in mind. Why did I not get it? Why had I not asked him? Why had I resisted? It would be revealed later.

At that time, like so many others my age, I had an intact circle of family and friends. My father and mother were very loving people. They were fair with me, though I doubted it on a few occasions of strict discipline as a result of my disobedience. I was happy and secure.

I was seven or eight when my mother's father died. For several years, he had suffered from a stroke, which resulted from a severe automobile accident. I did not see her cry when she received the news. She and I drove to the city where he lived; but during the funeral, I was left with a cousin at my aunt's home. No obvious mourning of any kind took place in my presence either before or after the funeral—not by my mother or even her sister, with whom my grandparents had been living. (I can understand now: the mourning had all been done earlier, as he languished from his stroke.)

When I was fifteen, one of my best friends walked over to our house. He was weeping. I had never seen a friend cry before. My family was sitting on our front porch, and he came up to us and said they had just gotten word that his older brother had drowned. I had known and liked his brother who played with us from time to time.

I could not think of a word to say. My mother talked with my friend for a few minutes. He told her he just needed to walk, and he left. I sat there. My mother told me to go walk with him. It was such an awkward moment for me—I did not know what to say or ask. My friend just cried; I did not.

I went to the funeral. It was a jam of people, and we had to stand at the back. I could not hear anything the minister said. I did not feel any real sense of loss; I was just "dulled out."

This uncomprehending response and absence of noticeable emotion seemed to be a pattern. In January 1943, at the age of seventeen and after only one semester in college, I joined the Marine Corps—in spite of the fact that I had already promised myself and God that I was going into the ministry. During three years of active duty, it was "face everything, take what's handed out, just do your duty." During World War II, several of my friends, including one to whom I was especially close, were killed. I was sad, but there was no opportunity to go to a funeral. We just carried on.

Discharged at the age of twenty, I finished college and went to seminary. They did not offer any courses in pastoral care, which was par for the course in those days—nothing to encourage self-reflection.

Upon graduation, I served a rural circuit and then a congregation in Houston. While I was at that church, my father had a severe heart attack—his third—at age fifty-five. I drove to my boyhood home feeling anxious and went to see him at the hospital.

As I walked into the room, my father turned his head toward me and murmured, "Son, I was so afraid." Those words cut through me as nothing had ever done before. My dad, afraid? I felt frightened, too. I was scared that he would die. I felt weak. All I could say was, "Dad, I love you." Maybe that was enough.

About eight years later, he died. I not only loved and respected him, but also liked him. It was the most significant loss and the most powerful grief that I had ever known. I was deeply sad. At the funeral there were tears in my eyes, but they never rolled down my cheeks. Why?

Two or three years later, the wonderful man who had been my pastor in high school died. He was my role model, then a close friend, and the man under whose preaching I had made the decision to enter ordained ministry. His son and I were good friends, and I had been in their home frequently. I had spent the summer after high school graduation on their farm, living with them and helping to work crops.

I drove the two hours or so to the funeral feeling the loss keenly. That emotion intensified after the service began. The preacher (also a friend) choked up after only a few minutes. He put his elbows on the pulpit, rested his face in his hands, and wept. A couple of minutes went by. I wept.

That moment was life-changing for me. I learned that as a human being and as a clergyperson, *I did not have to be in control of myself all of the time.* I learned that "myself" included my grief.

I thought of the many funerals I had conducted—sometimes not consciously aware of feelings, other times exerting considerable effort to control them. What a tragedy!

A number of years later, my mother died at the age of eighty-seven. The funeral was held in the small West Texas town that was my parents' last home. At the graveside service, I felt the severe pain of it, the loss, the sense of being alone in the world. I knew that I was not alone, of course, but it was my *feeling*.

As the casket slowly descended into the earth, I began to sob—increasingly, uncontrollably, so that I could no longer hold myself up in my chair, crumpling forward, held from falling off by my wife's arms. We sat there after the service concluded. The other mourners left, and we looked across the sandy soil—the grass burned away by the blistering sun, now lonely, with the bare prairie extending beyond. But I could feel the arm of my wife still around me, and gradually I became aware that God was there as always.

I did not realize it until much later, but all of the losses in my life had found expression at that graveside: mother, father, friends who died in their late teens and early twenties, and family and lifelong friends who had died later.

Since then, at the funerals I have led and preached—almost always the funerals of close friends or their family members—I have not felt at all self-conscious when I choked up for a couple of minutes, tears running down my face, not speaking for a moment, then continuing, often with a quavering voice. It has been such a relief and empowerment to have grieved profoundly.

Now as an elderly man I have begun to mourn my own losses: the diminished strength, vigor, endurance, and health. I grieve over those physical activities that once meant so much to me—team sports, competitive tennis, pick-up basketball games, and more. They contributed to my friendships and to my definition of myself. Now, losing health and strength, living at a distance from lifelong friends and colleagues of many decades, less able to drive long distances, I feel cut off. I have lost something of myself along with them, and I am mourning that.

Howard Clinebell was right. There is more to grief than anxiety. It is the empty place in one's life when a person who has sustained, nourished, and helped us become who we are is no longer present as before. This expression of emptiness and pain, this loss of control, has led to a new sense of myself and new meaning of my present family and of God in my life.

I will admit that when I first saw the proposed title of this book, my mind read *spirituality* instead of *spiritual growth*. I began to complain about the loose use of the word *spirituality to* mean whatever someone wants it to mean, even apart from any response to God. I wanted to argue against what I consider an abuse of the word. Then I reread the title accurately. It stated what God has meant to me, and it led me to explore what God is *going* to mean to me and for me.

A grief I now experience is a projection ahead. I had my seventy-eighth birthday yesterday, August 28. We have a fifteen-year-old daughter. I mourn, perhaps unnecessarily, when I consider her reaction to my death before she becomes more mature.

So in grieving for the past and into the future, my prayer life has become more intense. I reflect on Scripture. I pray for clarity about what my future will be, at the same time I remain grateful for the present.

Doing Our Grief Work with Companions of the Shelf

James M. Wall

The poet Emily Dickinson referred to the many books she had read and reread as "my companions of the shelf." Books, with their wisdom, insight, and shared emotional experiences, become our companions—friends to whom we may turn in moments of need. Dickinson lived before the advent of films, but my guess is that she would have also added certain movies to her shelf from which she would have been able to draw emotional sustenance.

One of our finest film artists is John Ford, a man who made many movies that on the surface were often dismissed as mere "westerns." Ford said that about his own work in a burst of inappropriate modesty, but his films transcended the usual commercial fare. As Andrew Sarris wrote in *The John Ford Movie Mystery*, Ford's visual style offered "the double vision (through classical editing) of an event in all its vital immediacy, and yet also in its ultimate memory image on the horizon of history."[1] Film, as well as television and theater, provides us with an avenue into the ways that humans interact with God by uniting us with our memories, which can sustain us through our darkest moments.

Faced with the death of a loved one or with other losses in our lives, we turn to God and to others to sustain us. Or so we would hope. But grief work is not an easy task, which is why far too often we deny the reality of a loss, refuse to confront the pain and guilt that loss brings, and choose instead to escape down other avenues of unreality. Because we choose to run away from reality with escapism, it may sound like a contradiction to suggest that we may turn to movies, television, drama, or novels to assist us in facing a time of grief. But we think this way only because we look on these forms of communication as means of escape, rather than as companions of the self.

It is true that some fictional narratives do serve merely as escapist entertainment, but many others have the ability to invite us to share our suffering with shelf companions. In doing so, we find that the loss we have experienced, although it brings us overwhelming pain, is nevertheless a pain that has been experienced by others before us. These companions can help us in addressing our grief.

When confronted with great loss, our first instinct is to avoid doing our grief work, which is the task of confronting a loss and reaching out for support from others and from God so that we can continue to live "in spite of" the death of a loved one or another devastating loss. Rather than go through the pain of admitting that what was once ours is no more—a spouse, a child, a job, a parent—it is often easier to dull our senses with various avenues of emotional escape.

So painful is the reality of loss that it is a natural reaction to want to lose ourselves in the "narcotic" of escapism, anything that will remove the pain of the moment. Some of these "narcotics" are destructive avenues, such as drugs, alcohol, anger, or guilt. Others may be constructive, though not liberating, such as intense concentration on our career, hobbies, or various forms of human achievement. Either way, without dealing with the guilt and sadness that accompanies loss, we fail to achieve our fullest potential, which is to live and not just escape or lose ourselves in work.

Ethan Edwards, as portrayed by John Wayne in John Ford's *The Searchers,* confronts the loss of the woman he loved by seeking revenge against those who caused her death. The entire film is a search for Debbie, a young girl who has been kidnapped, driven by Ethan's anger against her abductors and Debbie's mother's killers. Blinded by his grief and anger, Edwards determines that he will also kill the young girl because in his bigoted view, she has been "spoiled" by her Native American kidnappers.

At the close of the film, when Edwards finds Debbie, the narrative suggests he intends to kill her. In one of the great moments of reconciliation in film history, Edwards looms over her and discovers that it is not her death he seeks, but rather her life. He lifts her high over his head, as he had done with her as a child, cradles her in his arms, and says, "Let's go home, Debbie." Ethan Edwards finds that anger and revenge go only so far; neither are as powerful as the love he feels for this girl and her dead mother.

Edwards's grief journey was destructive until he found Debbie. In the narrative of *The Searchers,* considered by critics and historians as the greatest of western films, that destructive journey concludes with a redemptive moment. Such dramatic presentations offer insight into addressing grief. And, at their best, they do more than suggest answers. They take us into the lives of those who face loss and invite us to share the pain and the progress that come through grief work.

We do not often find such experiences on television—a medium that has to operate with the burdens of reaching audiences at home who are distracted by family chores as well as the frequent interruptions of commercials. But some television dramas do manage to look more deeply than others at the human condition. One example is the acclaimed long-running series *The West Wing.*

In an early episode ("The Crackpots and These Women"), Josh Lyman (played by Bradley Whitford), the deputy chief of staff to the president of the

United States, was plunged into an emotional crisis when he was chosen by the National Security staff to be a designated "saved" individual in case of a nuclear attack. He was given a card that would allow him to fly in Air Force One or escape into an underground bunker as part of a small team that would continue to serve the president after an attack.

When Josh discovered that he was the only White House staff member at his level with this special card, he became emotionally paralyzed. He felt that he could not accept this special treatment because it would mean he would be running away from his friends in a time of crisis. Realizing that he was slipping into a paralyzing depression, Josh visited his therapist. In doing so, he began for the first time, the long overdue grief work that had plagued him since the death of an older sister when he was a child.

The therapist patiently waited for Josh to look back on his life. As they talked, he noted that when Josh talked about his new White House card, he included his dead sister's name, Joanie, in the list of friends he could not abandon. At first Josh brushed aside this insight ("We were just talking about her," which was why he mentioned her name). But the therapist knew better. So he asked Josh to tell him how his sister died.

Josh said Joanie was killed while she was baby-sitting him and the house caught on fire. The therapist asked Josh why he wasn't killed. He responded: "I ran out of the house." To which the therapist answered: "You were just a little boy, Josh. That's what you were supposed to do."

Josh said out loud what he had no doubt often told himself in remembering this traumatic moment: "I ran out of the house." He did not stay behind to save his sister. He examined that act of a small child from an adult perspective. As a result, he continued to berate himself for failing to "save" his sister. This dated emotion of guilt would not be easily given up, because it had been the way Josh had learned to adjust to his sister's death. Neither did he overcome the guilt in this narrative. He still asked the president to relieve him of his role as a designated "saved" staff member. But at least Josh began to address his grief, and if he worked at it, he would come to see that there is a connection between his unresolved sense of failure and his need never to abandon his friends. That belief in supporting one's friends is positive, but it can be destructive if it is driven by a negative and unjustified sense of childhood guilt.

Under the Sand, starring Charlotte Rampling, is a French film in which the character Marie is a rather bored woman in her late fifties who has settled into a comfortable marriage with her husband, Jean. The film opens as the couple drives to the coast for their annual vacation. After unloading their luggage, they go for a swim. While Marie lies in the sun on the beach, Jean disappears. When she wakes up, he is gone.

How Marie copes with this loss is the focus of the film. *Under the Sand* is not a mystery story about what has happened to Jean, though on the surface this is an interesting narrative question. But *Under the Sand* does much more than explore Jean's disappearance. It invites us to experience Marie's shock, her self-denial, and then her slowly coming to terms with her loss. How the story is resolved is not nearly as important as the manner in which the director, François Ozon, takes us into Marie's life and invites us to share in her grief work.

It is important that we see films like *Under the Sand* at a level beyond the surface. Some years ago, I developed my own theory of film criticism in which I suggested that we should look at film on two planes, a method I learned from the art historian Susannah Langer. She notes that in viewing art we have to see a work in both its discursive and the presentational levels—what it is about and what it is.

I call these the "aboutness" and the "isness" aspects of film viewing, the obvious surface data and information beneath the surface. Langer refers to the presentational level of looking at art as viewing a work "between the facts." The vast majority of movies do not want us to look between the facts; they prefer to lay them out in appealing special effects or dramatic tales or shallow emotional tricks that dull our need to ask the big questions.

But Ozon's examination of Marie's crisis invites us to think in terms of what the film is, not just what it is about. And the "isness" is not just what we do when confronted with a major loss, but how we respond to the death of a loved one. Seeing this movie offers a viewer the opportunity to experience Marie's loss and then travel with her through her pain and the ultimate breakthrough to the other side as she accepts a new life enhanced by the past, but not burdened by grief.

Death is the ultimate loss, but there are many other experiences that "prepare" us for that particular moment, times when we are disappointed by failure or by less than ultimate losses. How we deal with the grief work involved prepares us for all the future losses we will face. Among film artists, Krzysztof Kieslowski, the late Polish film director, was an artist who combined sensitivity to loss with a strong awareness that we are never alone as we meet defeats and losses.

When Kieslowski died in his native Poland on March 13, 1996, at the age of fifty-four, he left an enormous void in the world of film art. This was not just because of the loss of his creative genius and cinematic skill, but because he was one of the few contemporary film artists whose work projected a spiritual vision in an industry notoriously tone-deaf to spirituality.

Kieslowski, born into the Catholic Church—he insisted that he was not a practicing Catholic, but the influence of the church is clear in his work—effectively employed music to establish the spirit of his films, all of which carry with them a sense of the transcendent. Kieslowski made a ten-part series for

Warsaw television, *The Decalogue*, each part a fifty-five-minute examination of one of the Ten Commandments, with stories set in and around a Warsaw housing complex. These are not didactic pieces, which argue for the commandments; rather they are revelatory films "inspired," as he put it, by each of the ten statements Moses delivered from Mount Sinai.

In an interview, Kieslowski made the assertion that his movies do not provide answers; they only raise questions. What he does not say, although his films convey it, is that his stories evoke the presence of a transcendent reality, which links us to one another and to a divine creative power. In a very real sense, Kieslowski's career was that of an artist who knew that loss was central to the human condition and that working through it was essential for our ability to keep living "in spite of."

In his 1984 film *No End*, Kieslowski focused on a wife whose lawyer husband, Antek, dies while he is working on a case that involved a Solidarity (the reformist party that helped liberate Poland from Communism) worker. The husband's "presence" remains with the wife, a presence she senses but cannot actually see. The scenes in which husband and wife are together, Kieslowski invites us to consider that the dead do not leave us; rather, they become a vivid and inspiring presence.

No End begins with a visual introduction to the lawyer who has died four days earlier. We find out a great deal about him and his family in a few short scenes. We discover that the important case he was working on will have to be confronted during the course of the movie. The transcendent hand that hovers over Kieslowski's films wants this case handled through to the end. And so it is.

In 1993, after the fall of the Berlin Wall and the end of Communism, Kieslowski moved to France, where he made the first film in his trilogy, *Three Colors: Blue*, followed by *White*, and the last picture he made before he died, *Red*. He said in interviews that he meant these to represent the three colors of the French flag, which stand for liberty (blue), equality (white), and fraternity (red).

In the final film of the trilogy, *Red*, we encounter one of the three biblical definitions of love—fraternity. In *White*, the absence or presence of *eros* dominates. In the first film of the trilogy, *Blue*, there is strong evidence of *caritas*, the love that is the search for what is best for the other.

Kieslowski was never quoted as saying that he had these biblical notions of love in mind, but there may be a clue that this is precisely what he was thinking in that when he died, he had already begun writing a second trilogy, tentatively called *Heaven*, *Hell*, and *Purgatory*. Clearly Kieslowski was a filmmaker with a theological hunger and the ability to confront theological questions.

In *Red*, the concept of love as fraternity emerges primarily through the relationship of the central character, a young Swiss model named Valentine, played by Irene Jacob, who meets a retired judge when her car accidentally hits the judge's dog, Rita. The judge, played by Jean-Louis Trintignant, has reached a point in his life at which he is emotionally and spiritually dead. He spends his retirement alone in his house, listening in on the telephone conversations of his neighbors. In an interesting parallel to real life, Trintignant had retired from acting when his daughter persuaded him to take this role, which will no doubt be remembered as one of his best performances.

When Valentine enters his life, she challenges him to live again. How he does this involves self-sacrifice, which includes not only turning himself in to the authorities for his illegal wiretapping, but also his desire to help Valentine deal with her own life crisis. We learn that the judge suffers from the burden of having lost an earlier love, not through death but through the woman's unfaithfulness. His solution to that loss was to retreat to his darkened home and cut off normal relations with others.

Kieslowski's cinematic vision is consistent through all of his films. He believed that the human community is linked to one another in ways fulfilled or, if we so choose, unfulfilled. Chance encounters or meetings were depicted as taking place in ways that suggest, but do not argue for, the presence of a divine hand in our existence. We are linked and are therefore not alone, unless we choose to ignore our human family, which, in turn, is related to a divine creator. It is in this sense that Kieslowski echoed the metaphor that Professor Joseph Sittler employed in his book *The Ecology of Faith,* describing our connections with one another and with God as a spiderweb. Touch one part of the web and every part is affected.

This is unless we deny that intricate connection. Denial stands in the way of connection, and the judge continued to deny until Valentine confronted him with the assertion that he might as well be dead as remain physically alive in such a dark, retreating state. When Valentine returns Rita to her owner and offers to take the dog to a veterinarian, the judge says it makes no difference to him what she does with the dog. Valentine, with the wisdom of youth, blurts out, "Would you say that if it was your daughter who was hurt?" To which the judge responds, "I have no daughter." It is really his way of saying, "I have no human connections of any kind."

Tender Mercies, directed by an Australian, Bruce Beresford, and written by Texas-born Horton Foote, features Robert Duvall as a country music singer and writer who has reached a point in his life at which he is literally on the floor of despair and failure. When the film opens, Duvall, as Mac Sledge, is having a drunken argument with an unseen colleague. They fight and Sledge is left lying on the floor of a small motel by a highway somewhere in Texas. When he wakes up, he finds that his friend has gone and that he is left with a bill he cannot pay. So he offers to work for the motel owner, a widow with a small boy, until he has paid what he owes. She agrees to let him do so, but says, "Remember, no drinking."

In the course of this movie, a relationship develops between Sledge and the young widow (Tess Harper). It soon becomes apparent that the film is "about" this relationship, but it is far more than that in terms of its "isness." *Tender Mercies* addresses loss, grief, and unresolved confrontations with the reality that follows loss. The setting, or the "aboutness" of the movie, is an isolated motel in the middle of Texas. The "isness" of the film is growth and the ability of the human spirit to rise above the darkest of moments, to embrace life, and to surge forward.

Sledge and the young widow get married, and a teenage daughter whom Sledge has not seen since she was a child reenters his life. At one point, his daughter comes to see him and, before leaving, asks if he remembers the song he once sang to her as a child. He mutters something about not remembering.

As she drives away, he stands at the window and begins to sing quietly the song she had wanted to hear, "On the wings of a snow white dove, he sends his pure white love." The past in which Sledge had left his wife and the young daughter to escape into his own alcohol-driven career as a singer is still too painful for him to confront. But gradually, by embracing her presence in his life and his new married life and sobriety, Sledge begins to live again. That is, until he suffers another loss of a loved one. Darkness descends, and after the funeral, he joins his wife in the garden, poking at weeds with a hoe.

He laments the circumstances of his life, in which he is spared to live and others are taken from him. Then with a deep sigh, he says, "I never trusted happiness. I never have and I never will." Yet in the very next scene, the film draws to a close as Mac and his stepson go out to the field and begin to toss around a football. Without saying it in dialogue, the film tells us that Mac Sledge will also rise above this latest loss. His grief work has been done.

Endnote

1. Andrew Sarris, *The John Ford Movie Mystery* (Bloomington: Indiana University Press, 1975), 173.

Useful Grief Observed

Halbert Weidner

On Good Friday, 1969, after formal church services, I went to a Catholic pentecostal prayer meeting at a local university. Although I was only twenty-three and certainly was not suffering what classmates were experiencing in Vietnam, I had had my share of grief already. During the Good Friday service, we all came forward to kiss the large plain cross held by acolytes and guarded by candles. It was an act of thanksgiving and of acceptance. Everyone coming up had her or his story to tell if anyone was interested.

Going to the prayer meeting was in addition to that service. I never became a member of the charismatic or pentecostal movement, but there were two people at the prayer meeting whom I remember well and who helped me very much. They were my age and had just begun in the pentecostal movement. Since I did not "convert," they may have thought of themselves as failures regarding me at this introductory meeting. Yet after all these years, I have not forgotten them, and what they said has helped convert my grief into something I can claim and call my own.

The meeting was among the first charismatic Catholic gatherings on the East Coast. It was meant to explain the charismatic movement and bring more Catholics into the movement. It was held in a classroom in the philosophy building in which I had been incarcerated in a rigorous two-year honors program. In contrast to all the left-brain workouts there, in the prayer meeting we were awash in a naive "chapter and verse" style of talking about the Bible. There was also witnessing about the wonderful, almost miraculous, things God had done for the new folks who had joined up. One man said that his being at the meeting on time had been because the hand of God had "held up" the plane he had been on during a storm. He had been, he promised, ready to die and meet God, but he asked God to hold up the plane for the sake of all the others on it who were not so ready.

Besides all the talk, there was hymn singing and singing in tongues. I had never before heard singing in tongues, and I found it beautiful. If anything attracted me about the style of worship, this was it. (Maybe for the same reasons, I have always found Gregorian chant seductive in the best possible sense of that word.)

Most of the witnessing of the leaders left me cold. They were apologetic because they were just getting started and there had been no miracles. But, they quickly added, they did love one another! I had been in a religious community for five years already, and I thought that if these people are apologizing for "only" being able to love one another, then they did not know they had their miracle and certainly knew nothing about spirituality.

After the poor start with the leaders, we were divided into groups. There I met the two young people who were asked to witness as beginners. We sat in a circle of school desks. The young man who spoke first had tussled hair, a plaid shirt, and was in his stocking feet, which he curled into the bars of the bookshelf under the seat. He did not look up much, but he spoke clearly and very, very slowly. He said that since he had come into the movement a good friend had killed himself. He said that most of the world spent its existence like Mary at the foot of the cross. But standing at the foot of the cross with the rest of the world, he could see the suffering Christ and believe in God. Without the Spirit, he said, he would not be able to do this. I cannot convey the starkness and depth of the tone of his voice nor the distant look in his eyes as he looked at something I could not see. His voice and his eyes said more than his words. I cannot imagine him now as cheerful in any sense of the word, but I can see him as loving and compassionate.

The other new member who spoke was a nursing student at the university. She said that since joining no miracles had happened to her, but that every day was now full of an appreciation of life. What she was learning in nursing classes about the human body seemed miracle enough and that just being able to move and breathe was overwhelmingly miraculous for her. She said all this simply, but in a very radiant way. She obviously paid attention to her health and had an attractive face, full of light. Her words, though, sounded like an older person who wanted to tell us young people something before it was too late. I can imagine her older and still radiant, though maybe more secretive now about the wisdom that energizes the everyday.

Obviously, I remember these two people and their words because time has tested them. I had not experienced three decades when they spoke to me. Now their words are measured against more than three added decades of living. I am the oldest male in my family, and in the past thirty years, I have finished burying all the men in the generations before me. A male cousin, an athlete and six months older than me, died before I turned fifty. One of my nephews died that same year. So I suffer these deaths intertwined with realistic assessments of my own mortality. In 1994, coming back from an overseas meeting, I went past the scene of the 1964 World's Fair. I had been at that fair on my way to seminary. I realized then and there that I did not have another thirty years and must be especially serious about my choices. I chose three projects for the last part of my life.

Knowing that there is an end to my life helped me. And by an "end," I mean not only a finish, but also something to be finished. Of the three projects, I have nearly finished with one—owning a dog; and I have almost finished another—starting a house of my religious community; and I have made some progress with the third—leading a broken parish back to something like health. Actually, the dog may outlive me, and the other two projects may not get finished—at least not by me. But it was satisfying to pick something I valued, and I could die trying to do worse.

Counting up the grief that I experienced during these added thirty years, I see my time came to experience the suicide of a friend. I have also buried a parishioner's teenage son who committed suicide. I have counseled people who point-blank asked me for a reason to keep on living. As for the dying, I cannot count the deathbeds I have attended. I have buried babies, children, teenagers, and young adults. They have died in hospitals, in accidents, and at home in bed. In one poor parish, I had only one parishioner die in the hospital. The rest died at home. One had only a little painkiller and an IV. But all of the poor died surrounded by a loving family. I cannot say that of all the affluent deaths I attended.

Among the deaths of the past two years was that of a beloved staff member. I was one of the first to reach the hospital once her body was taken out of a van after a hit-and-run accident. I had staff members with me, also her friends, and met the family there. We said the prayers for her as she lay on a gurney wrapped in sheets. I could not, of course, keep the sobs back. There was an intern Clinical Pastoral Education student there doing her seminary training. The regular chaplain does not usually take the weekends. She tried to console me and said how hard it must be to have two "roles" to play. I was angry at such a stupid remark. My love for our staff member and my ministry are not roles. I am a person and this was someone I loved who was killed on her way to church. After nearly two years, we are still waiting for the city to prosecute. She was a real servant of the Word, and it was wonderful to know her. But she had had her grief, and now she is part of mine.

Her death was followed in a few months by that of another staff member. This time it was our Korean-born, married deacon. He had survived the Japanese occupation of his homeland and the Korean War. He was a man of radiant faith. We had a chance for some short talks as the disease had its way with his body. The sharing was brief because he was a man of not many words when it came to important things. But his words were both few and crystal clear. One of the moments ended with watery eyes and a struggle to breathe. That I received from him something special is undeniable, but I still grieve for him and would give back the gift to have him alive again.

But there has been wider suffering than just the local deaths. Terrorism and war, something I experienced while living in Europe and in Israel, are now very American. We are all connected by suffering. We all stand at the foot of the cross. Suffering knows no distance. I live five thousand miles from New York, but a local friend's goddaughter died in the terrorist attacks of September 11. Two sons of friends here were close by. One was a few blocks away and could see the horrors. Another just missed getting out at the World Trade Center subway station. These are not coincidences. They are signs of a human community that is always in some way personal in its grief.

In this list, I have not mentioned the divorces of my parents or my friends or in my family. When I say grief does not go away, I mean it and cannot talk about the continuing suffering that living people have experienced in the betrayal of their deepest feelings. Living in our divorce-tolerant society did not make it any easier. My losses and their losses are as big a challenge to hope as death is. In fact, at funerals I can be more hopeful than I can be at many weddings. And there seems no solution for marriages in contemporary society. Avoiding the likelihood of pain by going with prolonged premarital sex often results in what is justly called premarital divorce. The personal devastation is no less even without the lawyers. One of the hardest times I ever had was counseling a "divorcing" nonmarried couple, splitting up after three years of sex that started when they were high school sophomores.

The hymn says that peace can flow like a river, but if there is anything that can do that, it leaves the one grieving adrift in a void that has no up or down, no left or right. Grief sounds and looks like depression, and depression must be cured. But grief is not depression, and it cannot be cured. Grief is a realistic human reaction to an unrecoverable loss. The only cure possible is the recovery of the lost, and this impossibility guarantees the permanence of grief.

Because the world of the grieving has been destroyed, only blind imperatives and amazing grace can help. One blind imperative advocated by the culture says to keep going. Whatever of the day is left to the grieving can be saved by obeying the imperative, though some cannot and are carried away by the river. To keep going is a mechanical reaction protected by routine. Here the emptiness of gesture opens a possibility for new gestures and compassion growing out of the empty. The nursing student understood that the body knows how to live if we let it. It is a miracle that the body functions in the first place. It is another miracle that the body continues to function when the soul is withered by grief. Discounting ritual and routine in the spiritual life is to lose something that can see us through on raw nerves when all else fails. And we know there will be enough times when all else will fail.

What finally can prevail is one simple fact: grief is not useless and does not finally destroy us the way depression can. A new world can be entered (let us not say "must" to anyone grieving). This world is not like the lost one. False hopes cannot grab anyone living in this new world. The illusion called permanency cannot cover anything in the world that emerges in grief. All that remains of the old world are the many people who do not notice we are no longer alive in a world we once shared with them. The people around us might think we have "reentered" into the old world we had together. We can let them think that. Who can communicate from the other side of grief?

I have a friend, an Israeli from Poland, who is the only member of his family to survive Auschwitz. I cannot remember talking to him directly about that. I certainly never argue about God with him. He is glad to be a Jew, but he has no Jewish religious practices that I can see. On a trip back to his native town of Krakow, he visited the Jewish cemetery to look at the graves. His mother had died before Auschwitz and was buried there. His wife told me that she went looking all over for her mother-in-law's grave. But her husband just sat in the middle of the cemetery with his thoughts. She asked him if he didn't want to help her find the grave. He just replied, "She knows we're here." From his side of grief, I think his statement communicated more than one great mystery.

This Israeli friend continues to be a passionate lover of people. His specialty is foreign students coming to Israel. He and his wife took me in as a much-beloved member of their family. They made great room in their lives for a Roman Catholic priest. I trust my friend in his sufferings. What I have suffered compares little to his, but I must say that my belief in such human things as dialogue has been battered, if not shattered. I asked him once about the Jewish philosopher Martin Buber, author of *I and Thou,* the great hopeful classic on the possibilities of dialogue and its special wisdom. My friend still not only believed it, but also thrived on the hope for those possibilities every day. It was part of the energy behind his teaching. I have not learned yet to recover that kind of energy.

So compassion marks the gate to this new world opened by suffering. We stand under our grief and understand the grief of others. Grief shocks sufferers into equality if it does not kill them. After grief, we realize how theoretical we were about a common humanity. We did not want to be especially elitist, but before our suffering we were. All aristocrats share one idea: public grief is bad taste. The real aristocrat will never share suffering, show suffering, or talk about suffering. To do so destroys a hierarchy that the very definition of self must maintain. We imagine that, if necessary, we could stand before the firing squad or on the scaffold and deliver well thought-out speeches. We not only are ready to die with dignity, we insist on it—even if we have to stage it ourselves. The aristocrat in us believes that suffering destroys human dignity rather than enhances it. *Shame* is another word for *suffering.*

The luxury of private grief so valued by aristocracy is not allowed for most of the world. Suffering in public makes all equal, and all suffering there has a public effect. The number of persons who are suffering at any one time can overwhelm anyone paying attention. But for those of us who are economically secure, seeing such suffering can drive us to inattention, to isolation. We want to feel spared and deserving like aristocrats when we see even a little of what the rest of the world endures. But the illusion of privilege can last only so long, and then our time comes. We then learn who we really are and how little difference there is between ourselves and those who are not, and never were, high or mighty. If suffering is a shame, it is a shame like nakedness: common to all who are born because all are born like this and will die like this.

The prevalence of a crucifix, often bloody and artistically tasteless and traditional in some churches, captures something of the blatant insistence of the poor that their suffering is not degrading and is not shameful; or, if it is, then it is shared with Jesus. In some cultures, there is a statue of a corpse laid out, lacerated, and cruelly stiff. The poor flock to the churches with a dead Jesus. Good Friday often rivals Easter because the suffering is closer to reality. Easter is something to be hoped for and not experienced yet. Once, while walking around in a major art gallery of medieval paintings, I was asked why Jesus was always pictured so bloody and battered in Roman Catholic paintings. I answered, "It's in the Bible."

For a Christian like myself writing this essay during Easter, all such emphasis on pain may seem a denial of the founding experience of hope brought by Jesus. But all of these wounds are part of the Easter proclamation. The resurrection stories have a lot of strange aspects, but none stranger than the picture of a risen Lord who still bears the wounds of dying on the cross. The doubter is invited to touch the wounds to see if Jesus is real. So if Jesus is resurrected, real and wounded, so will we be. We, too, will always bear our wounds, even after our own resurrection. They are part of who we are, and we do not lose them because of who we are. In fact, we could not be recognized without them. So the wounds are transformed, but never done away with. Anyway, why would we want them to be taken away? They opened a new world to us and united us with most of the rest of the human race, whom we knew before only from a distance—on television and in the newspapers. We discovered a world that we did not want to find even though it was our true home. As another old hymn says: "*O Crux, ave, spes unica.* . . . Hail Cross, our only hope."

Rituals Lost and Found

Susan J. White

In the months following September 11, 2001, the *New York Times* published a series entitled "Portraits of Grief," mini-eulogies gathered from the families and friends of those who lost their lives in the World Trade Center, at the Pentagon, and on the planes that were deliberately crashed on that brilliant fall morning. The portrait of Robert Andrew Spencer, a securities broker at Cantor Fitzgerald, appeared exactly four months after the day of his death and poignantly described his love for his wife, Christine, their two young daughters and newborn baby boy, and the life they shared. But in a single paragraph at the end of the tribute to her husband, Christine Spencer reveals not only her private grief, made so intensely public by the nature of the event, but also the place of ritual in the journey of mourning. In what she called a "celebration of life," the "Portrait" concludes, "Mrs. Spencer decided to have the baby's baptism and her husband's memorial service on the same day."[1] These conjoined rites, like all good ritual, allowed Christine Spencer to hold together the seemingly irreconcilable realities of her life: a future imagined in the birth of a baby; a future lost in the death of a husband. Baptism and memorial rites served to give her grieving shape and form, allowing it to be expressed, contained, and reflected upon.

In most instances, mapping the landscape of grief is seen to be the task of geographers of the human spirit: poets, pastoral theologians and counselors, and students of spirituality. This is because grief is so often regarded as primarily an interior reality, an experience belonging to individual persons, although perhaps with various social and behavioral manifestations. But what happens when we look at the process of grieving from the outside, as essentially a *ritual* process, a process that is principally public, external, and shaped by particular sets of social conventions? Do we discover anything new about the nature of grief by attending to the constellations of religious symbol and ritual that have been claimed and directed by those who grieve, even as they themselves are claimed and directed by the ritual action? Are we *called* to anything new in our own processes of mourning by approaching them in this way?

The ritualization of grief is one of the most ancient of all recorded human activities. Rites that enable lamentation, that help the living separate from the dead, and that structure comfort and community support are found in every culture throughout history. The power of such religious rituals is undeniable, and although many deeply secularized societies have begun to abandon the rites that have traditionally marked adolescent maturity, marriage, and the birth of children, alternatives to religious funerals are few and weakly rooted. As one student of Christian worship says, religious ritual serves to place private grief on a wider canvas, one that stretches beyond "the circumscribed needs of the individual."[2] At the same time, the ritualization of grief reaches and gives voice to the emotional complexities so often experienced in loss, serving as "a kind of expanded thought capable of bearing an emotional load that would otherwise remain inexpressible, precisely because it is unthinkable. The symbol enables us to come to terms on an intuitive level with facts whose literal meaning we cannot yet deal with."[3]

These attributes of religious ritual—its ability to hold together multiple and often mutually contradictory meanings, to express what is essentially inexpressible, and to place the "local" and "interior" onto a wider context—give ritual its persistence and power in the human experience of grieving.

It is in recognition of this power that I often admonish my students preparing for ordained ministry to resist, if at all possible, the temptation to preside at the funerals of close family members and friends. In times of deep grief, I tell them, it is important to lean back and let the rituals of lamentation do their work; I tell them that to focus their attention on orchestrating the liturgical proceedings is the most effective way of short-circuiting their own processes of mourning a loss. The funeral may be the only setting in which it is deemed safe and permissible to cry, and to do so in the company of others, to touch, and to be touched. The funeral may be the sole place where we are encouraged to speak of the dead honestly and in the context of the wider Christian hope. It would be expected and desired, of course, that all those who grieve, including clergy, will be part of an open, emotionally healthy support community, that they will be able to lament their loss freely and in their own way, without the constraints of what "ought" to be done or how they "should" be handling things. But this is unfortunately not always the case, and busy pastors need to learn when to let go of their ecclesiastical role as worship leader and to embrace the role of a mourner.

There came a time, however, when this rule was tested in my own family. In the summer of 2000, my aunt died following a cerebral hemorrhage and a long period during which she had experienced only a fragmentary recovery of function. Although those she left behind strongly desired to "have a funeral," none of them, including my aunt, had any church affiliation whatsoever. As the sole representative of institutional religion, I was suddenly cast in the role of the "ritual technologist," the one who knew the proper things to do at this time of grief and loss. To put it most succinctly: they asked me to conduct a funeral for my aunt, and I agreed.

In the days that followed, I put my personal grief over the loss of my beloved aunt on hold while I made arrangements with the cemetery for the use of their chapel, negotiated the loan of vestments and a prayer book from a local church, and wrote a sermon. On the day of the funeral itself, I donned my professional persona, separating myself from my mourning relatives, while at the same time doing all that was necessary to ensure that they were able to enter the rituals of loss meaningfully and well. The day was just as my family wished it would be: they wept and smiled, remembered, and were comforted. I, on the other hand, did not weep, nor did I smile (except in the way that worship leaders do, as they seek to create a sense of warmth and intimacy); the power of memories invoked was lost for me. And although I worked to ensure that comfort was offered, I did not, myself, experience it.

Remembering my admonition to students, I had nonetheless made one decision that I thought, at the time, was wise. My aunt had continued to give an annual donation to the church she had attended as a small child, and I asked the minister of that church to preside at the interment. This, I had assured myself, would enable me to do some measure of the work of mourning as I participated in the rites of burial. But although I had removed my vestments and set down my books, my ministerial distance was not as easily cast off; although I had stepped into the physical space my family occupied around the grave, I had not managed to step into their emotional and spiritual space. I was still their minister, but now utterly dislocated. As a consequence, from the first word he spoke at the gravesite, the hapless visiting minister was subject to my harshest professional critique: Why did he greet people in such a clumsy way? Didn't he have sense enough not to wear brown shoes? Whatever possessed him to choose to read *that* lesson? Wasn't he edging awfully close to a fund-raising appeal? I was annoyed that this man had not known or cared about my aunt; I was irritated that he conducted the burial service in such a folksy, joking way; I was angry that I had allowed myself to pass off my duty to my family onto this particularly dim-witted and ill-equipped person. In the end, not only did I fail to allow the rites of death to do their work, but also I had ensured that any *future* ritualization of my grief would have to override my resistance to the rituals that had actually taken place at the grave on the day of the burial.

One of the difficulties for me in this case, as for others who grieve the loss of a close friend or member of the family in the early twenty-first century, is that the funeral and the burial of the dead have assumed almost the entire burden of the ritualization of sorrow. Our Christian forebears could rely upon an extensive complex of symbolic and ritual elements to guide them through the course of grief: the washing, dressing, and laying out of the body; wakes and other domestic rituals; the wearing of special clothes during the grieving period and the use of black-bordered stationery; the public marking of anniversaries of the death; and periodic rites at the gravesite. Even the process of dying and death itself was a ritual event. Historian Philipe Ariés has described the premodern deathbed ritual as "a public ceremony organized and presided over by the dying individual and following a standard protocol."[4] We can see this in St. Jerome's description of the scene that attended the death of St. Melania the Younger (c. 385–439):

> When the distinguished women of the city learned of her imminent death, they all came, and she, having seen them for a short while, at last said: "Lo, the heavens are opening, and I see an ineffable light and a suspended crown." And she departed with these words. Then there broke forth great weeping and wailing, raised by both her husband and the women. When the lament quieted down, they prepared the funeral bath.[5]

This close juxtaposition of the intensely affective and the intensely practical ("there broke forth great weeping ... when the lament had quieted down, they prepared the funeral bath") becomes the ground for the spiritual nurture of those who participated in the dying of their friend. There are things to be *felt* and things to be *done*; both are necessary, and both are included in the narrative, which is, indeed, acknowledged as a classic in the literature of spirituality rather than as an example of historiography.

For Christian believers, this kind of spiritual nurture afforded by communal participation in the various rituals of dying and death was routinely available for the next seventeen centuries, and was only removed from the life of faith in the post-industrial West with the increasing medicalization of death.

In the long Victorian era, the bereaved family steadily lost the help of relatives, neighbors, and clergy, and accepted the proffered and additional service of other entrepreneurial groups, including funeral directors, drapers, memorial masons, cemetery staff, and, later, medical professionals.[6]

The transfer of the rituals of death and dying from the hands of the bereaved family into the hands of "death experts" (morticians and their staff) marks a significant deterioration in the ability to integrate death and dying into the ongoing spiritual lives of mourners. Glennys Howard says, "The desire of undertakers to utilize their newly acquired 'scientific' techniques, combined with the realization that the body was fast becoming the key to funeral rituals, meant that they were keen to take custody of the corpse."[7] And once the corpse was handed over to undertakers, and later when the body of the dying person was handed over to the hospitals, the rituals of death and dying largely passed away from the control of those who cared the most and who could benefit most from performing them.

Women, especially, have spoken of the power of this process in the shaping of their spirituality. On the American, Australian, and Canadian frontiers, where many families buried child after child and some buried all of their children, women often found themselves without clergy to oversee the rites of death and had to rely on their own ritual resources. In a letter written home dated 1874, one settler on the Western frontier of the United States poignantly describes the death and burial of her young son. Holding her baby as he takes his last breath, Elinore Stewart details the process of dressing his body and preparing it for interment. She then arranges for the making of the coffin:

> Clyde is a carpenter, so I wanted him to make the little coffin. He did it every bit, and I lined and padded it. Not that we couldn't afford to buy one or that our neighbors were not all that was kind and willing; but because it was a sad pleasure to do everything for our little first-born boy. As there had been no physician to help, so there was no minister to comfort, and I could not bear to let our baby leave the world without leaving any message to a community that sadly needed it. His little message to us had been love, so I selected a chapter from John and we had a funeral service, at which all our neighbors for thirty miles around were present.[8]

Indeed, this may perhaps be the most common kind of experience Christians have had in the burial of their dead: tending to the sick person until the end, washing and dressing the body, arranging for a suitable box and burial dress, and seeing to it that the proper words are said over the body as it is put into the ground.

Others have lived in fear of the long-term effects of failing to perform the proper rituals, believing that their behavior at a burial and attention to the rituals of mourning had serious spiritual consequences. At the turn of the twentieth century, former slave Jesse Collins was proud to report that when her husband died, she had given him a "fine funeral," after which she went into deep mourning. She wore continually a "long widow's veil" and went every day to visit the cemetery "and cry all day by his grave." But this seems not to have been sufficient honor for the deceased. Collins continues on to say, "But his spirit started to haunt me somethin' terrible. I had chickens and every night he'd come back wearin' a white apron and shoo my chickens. Every mornin' some of 'em would be dead. . . . Then I got mad and I quit goin' to the cemetery and I took off my widow's veil. I put black pepper 'round the sills of all my doors. That stopped him."[9]

Sometimes the church itself has interfered with what would seem to be the most natural ritual responses to grief. This is certainly true of the desire on the part of those left behind to continue to pray for their departed loved ones; trusting that the living and the dead are one communion in faith, hope, and love;

and that even death cannot separate us from the love of God. Rooted in the fear of idolatry and of the excesses of the cultus of the dead in late-medieval spirituality, the doctrinal and canonical condemnation of prayer for the dead in many of the churches that arose out of the sixteenth-century Reformation has had profound implications for the spirituality of grieving. One man reports the feelings he experienced upon being deprived of the ability to pray for his late father:

> I was a little child when the news came of my father's death, far away. That night, as usual, I prayed for him. But my aunt stopped me. "Darling," she said, "you must not pray for Father now; it is wrong." And I can remember still now how I shrank back, feeling as if someone had slammed the door and shut Father outside.[10]

This becomes a kind of double loss: the loss of both a physical connection and a spiritual connection to a loved parent. When I was teaching in an English seminary, a similar thing happened to one of the students. On a Thursday afternoon, Gareth, a student, was notified that his father had suffered a heart attack and had died. The funeral was held the following Sunday, and Gareth returned to college on Monday morning in time to lead prayers, as he had been scheduled to do, in the college chapel. Spontaneously, he included a prayer for his father in his intercessions, asking that God might continue to surround his father with the same loving-kindness and mercy that he had known in life. As soon as the service ended, Gareth was called to the principal's office and was sternly and severely reprimanded for the serious doctrinal error implied in such a form of prayer. He said to me later, "I felt as if my dad had died all over again right there in that room."

But all is not lost. Many churches, recognizing the importance of ritual in the processes of grief, have begun to reconsider these kinds of prohibitions on prayers for the dead. Some read out the names of those who have died in the previous year on All Saints Day (November 1), calling the whole congregation to remember that although part of the community is no longer seen on earth, fellowship in Christ is not broken. Celebrations of the Lord's Supper at funerals are increasingly common, allowing the bereaved to experience a community that remains whole and hopeful even in the face of death. Other congregations are including columbaria in their building plans, where the ashes of the dead are interred and the names of the dead remembered, often placing the niches in the entryway where each time the members enter the church, they pass by the remains of those who have gone on before. Domestic rituals are marking the anniversaries of a death; memory gardens are being planted, allowing the seasons of nature to mirror the seasons of bereavement; and shrouds and funeral palls are being crafted by members of the congregation to be used for their own burials or the burials of members of the family. It is suggested, too, that Christians understand the church's public worship as a primary resource for the vocation that is our own dying, and in so doing, that we allow it to shape our grieving for those who precede us in death:

> If we were to learn from the celebration of the paschal mystery to surrender our lives totally to God in Christ, the death of the Christian would be but the further and final rehearsal of a pattern learned in life and practiced over and over again in a lifetime of liturgical participation. For those who have learned from the prayers and rituals of the Christian liturgy to let go of all that we cling to in order to save ourselves from the void, the final surrender to death will be a familiar and joyous sacrifice.[11]

It is imagined and implied throughout this book that our deepest grief can be an opportunity for our profoundest spiritual growth, for a movement toward an intensified knowledge of God, of ourselves, and of the breadth of the God-human relationship. But, of course, the operative words here are *can be*. We all know that grief can just as easily crush us; disable us; turn us in on ourselves; and obsess us with guilt, remorse, and sorrow. And we know that the difference between those who are immobilized by loss and those who are ennobled by it is neither the degree of our innate goodness, nor our strength of character, nor even the intensity of our faith in the God of love and mercy—although all of these have important parts to play. But what part is played by our ability to ritualize effectively the journey of grieving? To what extent can we allow the symbols and rituals provided to us by others—the church past and present, for example—to help us hold together the multiple facets of our loss? Can we create signifi-cant rituals that will open us to the meaning life holds for us, even (or perhaps *especially*) in the face of bereavement? It was the keen and persistent spiritual intuition of our Christian forebears that to provide for the most basic needs of the dead and the dying is to open ourselves to mystery of death and thus to nur-ture our relationship with the God who is revealed in death. Have the profes-sionals—the doctors, the nursing homes and hospitals, or the funeral industry—taken away so many of the most basic of our ritual responses to death and dying that we cannot now partake of this indispensable opportunity for spir-itual growth?

Once again, there are glimmers of hope. The hospice movement, begun in England and carried to the United States in the mid-twentieth century, is one example. Although the founders of hospice believed that to enter into death in a nonclinical setting—with good palliative care and an attention to anxieties and aspirations—is to maximize the spiritual experience of the person who is approaching death; this strategy also allows those who are closest to the terminally ill person to participate in the dying process in a meaningful way. The growth of the hospice movement is eloquent testimony to its ability to touch these deepest needs for an attention to the spirituality of dying, for all parties involved.

But even the most basic rituals of dying, death, and grieving take time; and time is perhaps the one commodity that we are least able or willing to sacrifice at this stage in our common social history. Might we consider, however, even for a moment, the possibility that our spiritual destiny, both individual and corporate, may depend upon finding the time to ritualize our mourning well? Might it be that to commit ourselves to the rituals of grief is to place ourselves in the hands of an accumulated wisdom about our essential needs? Might we recognize that learning to grieve well may be the best preparation for meaningful engagement with the inevitable process of our own dying? If we do, a new set of priorities will surely emerge, and a host of teachers, encouragers, and guides from the Christian past will be available to lead us into our spiritual future.

Endnotes

1. *New York Times,* January 11, 2002, 15, col. 2-3.

2. Roger Grainger, *The Message of the Rite* (Cambridge: Lutterworth Press, 1988), 30.

3. Ibid.

4. Philipe Ariés, *Essais sur de la Mort en Occident du Moyen age a nos Jours* (Paris: Seuil, 1975), 19.

5. Cited in S. Gerstel, "Painted Sources," *Dumbarton Oaks Papers, 11:3* (1998): 101.

6. P. Jupp, "Enon Chapel: No Way for the Dead," in *The Changing Face of Death,* ed. P. Jupp and G. Howarth (New York: St. Martins, 1979), 102.

7. Glennys Howarth, "Professionalising the Funeral Industry in England, 1700–1900," in *Changing Face of Death,* 124.

8. E. Stewart, *Letters of a Woman Homesteader* (Lincoln: University of Nebraska Press, 1979 [1915]), 190-191.

9. Cited in Mechal Sobel, *Trabelin' On: The Slave Journey to an Afro-Baptist Faith* (Princeton: Princeton University Press, 1988), 47.

10. J. Patterson Smyth, *The Gospel of the Hereafter* (London: J. Smythe, 1913), 24.

11. Mark Searle, *Assembly, 3:*5 (March 1979): 49.

Recommended Readings on Grief and Loss

Heinz, Donald (1999). *The Last Passage: Recovering a Death of Our Own*. New York: Oxford University Press.

Mitchell, Kenneth R., and Herbert Anderson (1983). *All our Losses, All Our Griefs: Resources for Pastoral Care*. Philadelphia: Westminister Press.

Oates, Wayne E. (1997). *Grief, Transition, and Loss: A Pastor's Practical Guide*. Minneapolis: Fortress Press.

Rando, Therese A. (1984). *Grief, Dying, and Death: Clinical Interventions for Caregivers*. Champaign, IL: Research Press.

Rosen, Elliott J. (1998). *Families Facing Death: A Guide for Healthcare Professionals and Volunteers*. Revised. San Francisco: Jossey-Bass Publishers.

Stone, Howard W. (1972). *Suicide and Grief*. Philadelphia: Fortress Press.

———. (1993). *Crisis Counseling*. Revised. Minneapolis: Fortress Press.

Sullender, R. Scott (1960). *Grief and Growth: Pastoral Resources for Emotional and Spiritual Growth*. New York/Mahwah, NY: Paulist Press.

———. (1989). *Losses in Later Life: A New Way of Walking with God*. New York/Mahwah, NY: Paulist Press.

Weaver, Andrew J., Laura T. Flannelly, and John D. Preston (2003). *Counseling Survivors of Traumatic Events: A Handbook for Pastors and Other Helping Professionals*. Nashville: Abingdon Press.

Study Guide

John Schroeder

Suggestions for leading a study of this book

Reflections on Grief and Spiritual Growth contains seventeen essays by writers who consider grief and loss in the context of their own personal experiences as well as in the context of Christian faith. As a discussion leader, you have the opportunity to help others obtain the answers they are seeking on their spiritual journey. The conversations in your group may cover a variety of topics as together you ask questions and seek answers. Here are some thoughts on how best to facilitate this process.

1. Read the entire book before your first group meeting. This will provide you with an overview of the material and will better equip you as a leader. You may want to use a highlighter to designate important points.

2. Be aware that you are about to tackle a difficult subject. Many of your participants are at various points in the process of grieving a loss. There will be sadness within the group along with happy memories of good times. Your participants may at times be at a loss for words. Death of a loved one is tough to talk about. Feelings can be hard to express. Your objective as a discussion leader is to guide the group gently along this journey by being compassionate and sensitive to the feelings of individuals and listening attentively to the group.

3. On some occasions, people will be emotional. They may cry or become unable to talk. You may want to have a box of tissues on hand. If things become particularly uncomfortable, it might be appropriate to pause the discussion and take a break. The touch of a hand by the person next to the emotional person is a good gesture of comfort. As a leader, a brief word of comfort or just an acknowledgment of the sadness may help in these situations. Then, attempt to continue the discussion. Moving ahead can help the grieving person and the group not to dwell on the sadness.

4. As a leader, you want to guide the group without controlling the group. One of the most common mistakes a leader makes is to try to control what happens in the group. The group as a whole is responsi-

ble for what takes place in the session itself. Your job is to keep the discussion moving and to encourage participation.

5. For the first couple of sessions, you may want to begin by reminding participants that not everyone may feel comfortable reading aloud, answering questions, or participating in group activities. Encourage them to participate as they feel comfortable in doing so.

6. At the first meeting, it is important to acknowledge that grief is a difficult and emotional subject. Give the group members permission to shed a tear or be unable to talk. Tell them tissues are available. Remind them that everyone has experienced loss and knows how it feels. No one is alone, and the group is in this journey together with God.

7. Begin each session by reading aloud the scripture and the session objective. Select your discussion questions in advance. Feel free to change the order of the listed questions and to create your own questions. Allow a set amount of time for the questions and for the personal reflection time.

8. The discussion questions refer to specific essays in the book but are also general in nature. Participants are encouraged to read the essays of the authors that relate to the weekly questions and discussion. The essays can be read out of order. Answers to questions may come from various essays, as well as from the knowledge and experience of participants. Also, let the group know that any ventured answer or guess is welcome.

9. Some questions may be more difficult to answer than others. If you ask a question to which no one responds, begin the discussion by venturing an answer yourself. Then ask for comments and other answers. Remember that some questions have multiple answers. As a leader, you do not have to know all the answers. Some answers may come from group members.

10. Ask leading questions such as "Why?" or "Why do you believe that?" to help continue a discussion and give it greater depth, but be careful how you ask such probing questions. You do not want persons to feel as if they are being challenged to defend their position. Give everyone a chance to talk. Keep the conversation moving. If the conversation

gets off track, move ahead by asking the next question. When you have completed the discussion questions, ask if there are any other questions before moving on to the personal reflection time.

Group Guidelines

Explain that this group is a family and has some ground rules for the benefit of the entire family. These rules include:

1. *Confidentiality.* What is said within the group, stays within the group. Do not share personal information from this group with friends or your family. This is a safe place to talk.

2. *Respect.* Listen attentively and receive what others in the group have to say, even if you disagree. Do not interrupt others when they are talking.

3. *Purpose.* This is not a therapy group, a sensitivity group, or an encounter group. We are here to grow in faith and closer to God. We can offer Christian love and support to one another.

4. *Schedule.* Each session will start on time and end on time. Please be prompt. Let someone know if you will be unable to attend.

5. *Equality.* We are all equals. No one is expected to be an expert on a topic.

6. *Acceptance.* It is important that each person be accepted by the rest of the group just as he or she is. We are all members of the family of God.

Session One: Sharing Our Stories

Scripture: For everything there is a season, and a time for every matter under heaven: a time to be born, and a time to die; a time to plant, and a time to pluck up what is planted; a time to kill, and a time to heal; a time to break down, and a time to build up; a time to weep, and a time to laugh; a time to mourn, and a time to dance (Ecclesiastes 3:1-4).

Objective: To better understand how grief has touched us all.

Discussion Questions

1. Share a personal experience with grief. How were you and your life changed by the death of a loved one? What do you hope to gain from participating in this discussion?

2. In your own words, explain grief and how it feels to grieve. Does the passage of time affect grief? If so, in what way? What have you learned so far about grief that has helped ease your pain?

3. How old were you the first time someone you knew died? Share how you felt. Have your feelings about loss and death changed over the years? If so, in what way? Is it getting easier or harder to cope with death? Why?

4. Herbert Anderson tells us how he had to unlearn lessons about grief taught by relatives. Has that been your experience? How have your family members generally coped with their grief? Have their actions helped or hindered your grieving process?

5. Paschal Baumstein reminds us that dealing with death is an ongoing process. It continues to be with us long after the death of a loved one. Our feelings and how we deal with loss change over time. Share your thoughts and experience with processing loss.

6. What factors make some losses more difficult to bear than others? List some reasons why we react differently to every loss we experience. What makes acceptance of a death easier? What makes it extremely painful to accept?

7. Duane R. Bidwell writes about his grief after the death of his friend, Kent. In what ways can you relate to his feelings of loss? How was he affected by Kent's death? How was he changed? How did his essay make you feel? What did you learn from it?

8. The popular hymn "Precious Lord, Take My Hand" was written by Thomas A. Dorsey, who wrote more than four hundred rhythm and blues songs and became a publisher of black gospel music. His best-known hymn was written days after his wife died in childbirth. It is one example of how hymns help us grieve. In her essay, Mary Louise Bringle

shares how hymns can be a resource in dealing with grief and loss. What hymns have been a comfort to you in difficult times? How have they strengthened your faith? Discuss the healing power of hymns.

9. David K. Switzer shares his slow discovery that it is a relief and an empowerment to have grieved profoundly. He writes that at funerals, "I have not felt at all self-conscious when I choked up for a couple of minutes, tears running down my face, not speaking for a moment, then continuing, often with a quavering voice." What has been your experience in trying to hold back grief? In what way is it healthy and normal to show emotion?

Personal Reflection Time

It seems that the older you get, the longer the list is of people you know who have died. Childhood playmates may be gone. Former coworkers and neighbors may have passed away. Acquaintances, people who were briefly a part of your life, may no longer be alive. Friends may no longer be around, and others, still alive, live far away. Chances are some relatives and family members have died but still live in your memories. And there may even be family pets whose deaths may still be painful.

Spend some thoughtful moments now writing down the names of the departed. Search your memories. Some names will come to you quickly. Others may be people you haven't thought about for a while. Include former family pets if you want. Just write the names of those you know who have died.

Next to each name, write in a few words or a special memory of each individual. Think of a happy time you spent together. Recall a special interest you shared or what bound you together. It might even be how you met.

Continue your journey back in time by reflecting upon, or by putting down in a few brief words, how that person is still a part of you. What keeps you connected?

And finally, for each person listed, complete the following sentence: I miss (him or her) because ...

Consider visiting the grave of one or more of those on your list this week.

Closing Prayer

Gracious God, we thank you for the memories of those who are no longer with us. Thank you for the times we spent together with them and how they touched our lives. We confess it is difficult to let go. Our grief continues to come and go like the waves upon the shore. May we find peace in your love. Remind us that our loved ones are with you and that you are present with us in life, in death, and in our sorrow. Be with us as we continue to cherish your gift of life. Amen.

Session Two: A Focus on Grief and the Grieving Process

Scripture: Even though I walk through the valley of the shadow of death, I will fear no evil, for you are with me; your rod and your staff, they comfort me (Psalm 23:4 NIV).

Objective: To explore the many aspects of loss and the feelings that linger.

Discussion Questions

1. We all handle grief differently. How did Joseph R. Jeter, Jr. cope with the death of his parents? What feelings did he have? Discuss the circumstances that dictate how we handle our grief and deal with a loss.

2. Sometimes death takes its time. Doctors, technology, and medicine can often prolong life. This can also prolong the grieving process. Share your thoughts of watching a loved one die slowly.

3. In her essay, Bonnie J. Miller-McLemore explores the relationship between Christian faith and what she calls "mundane loss." How would you describe mundane grief? Give an example from your own life experience. Discuss some of the aspects and steps of grieving mundane loss. Is the process of mundane grief different from that of grief over a more significant loss? How is it different? How is it similar?

4. Grief is not limited to the death of a family member or a friend. In what ways is the death of a beloved pet the same as the death of a person? How is it different? What does this tell us about grief? Do we remember pets the same way we remember people? Explain.

5. R. Esteban Montilla reminds us that people die, but not our relationships with them. Discuss the importance of reconnecting with the deceased, keeping them alive in memory within the family, and continuing to have a relationship with them. Explain how reconnection is at the heart of grieving. Do we ever "get over" the loss of someone we love?

6. M. Basil Pennington writes that grief often occurs when the curtain descends on one era of life. In his essay, he discusses *lectio divina* and how it helped him move through the grief of retirement. Share your thoughts about *lectio* and coping with grief caused by retirement. How is retirement like a death?

7. Share what you have learned about the importance of ritual in the grief process from Susan J. White's essay, "Rituals Lost and Found." What rituals have been important to you and your family in coping with death?

8. In his essay, "Useful Grief Observed," Halbert Weidner defines grief as a realistic human reaction to an unrecoverable loss. How is grief similar to and also different from depression? List some ways in which grief is useful. What new insights did you learn about grief?

Personal Reflection Time

Reflect on your own grief process and how you have handled your grief in the past. Can you identify some of your own stages of grief? How has this discussion helped you better understand grief? If you desire, put your new insights about grief in writing.

Closing Prayer

Loving God, thank you for being with us in our grief. Your love always surrounds us and helps us through troubled times. Open our eyes to the beauty of your creation when there seems to be darkness all around us. Let us see the love and kindness of others and be receptive to their ministry. Help us remember that death is not the end. Jesus conquered death and offers us eternal life. May our grief draw us closer to you. Amen.

Session Three: Death and Funerals Go Together

Scripture: For now we see in a mirror, dimly, but then we will see face to face. Now I know only in part; then I will know fully, even as I have been fully known (1 Corinthians 13:12).

Objective: To explore the emotions that are often associated with death and how funerals help with the grieving process.

Discussion Questions

1. In his essay, "I Would Do It All Again," Charles Merrick discusses the way we treat death in our society from his viewpoint as a funeral director. Comment on his insights concerning the changes over the years in the way death is dealt with (and not dealt with) in America. What did you learn about funerals and the funeral business?

2. Consider how death contributes meaning to our lives. How can good come from a loss? List and discuss some of the positive outcomes. What factors can determine whether a death contributes meaning or devastates the lives of survivors?

3. Charles Merrick reflected on the loss of his son. Discuss the difficulty of parents losing a child. Does the age of the child really matter? What can some of the effects be of such a loss? How do you cope with a child's death?

4. Discuss the ways that survivors gain closure after a death. Do you think that grief diminishes over time? List some of the "triggers" that can cause grief to return. Share how memories can be both good and painful.

5. After the September 11 terrorist attacks, only a few intact bodies were recovered. In some murder cases or disappearances at sea, bodies are never recovered. When a body is not present at a funeral or memorial service, what effect does that have on survivors? Discuss the difficulty of grieving a death when the body cannot be located. How does viewing a body help us grieve? What makes it difficult to cope with the reality of death in this circumstance?

6. Rebecca L. Miles talks about deathbed stories. How do they contribute meaning to the death of a loved one? What is the effect on the living? How are people shaped by deathbed stories? How do they train us to die and also to witness death? Share a deathbed story with your group, if you desire.

7. James M. Wall notes how books and movies contribute to our views of grief, death, and dying. What lessons do we learn about death from movies? What deaths or death scenes in books or movies had an effect on you? Why?

8. Why is it important to talk about death? How frightened are you of death? What has contributed to your attitude toward death? How would you hope to die?

Personal Reflection Time

We do not choose when we are born or the time of our death. Death will come to each of us eventually. Take some time now to reflect on your own death and your own funeral or memorial service. How do you envision your funeral? What hymns or words of comfort would be a part of it? What philosophy of life and death would you like to leave as a legacy? How would you like to be remembered? How would you help others cope with your death? If you desire, put some of this information in writing and consider sharing it with a loved one.

Closing Prayer

Eternal God, we were created from dust, and to dust we shall return. Thank you for the gift of life, and help us make the most of our time on this earth. Thank you for being with us in the tough times as well as on the happy occasions. Your love always abides with us. Help us serve you and others as we continue our life journey. Comfort us as we grieve the many losses that come in life, and help us in turn to comfort others in their times of sorrow. Amen.

Session Four: The Spiritual Side of Grief—God, Faith, and Resurrection

Scripture: God is our refuge and strength, an ever-present help in trouble. Therefore we will not fear, though the earth give way and the mountains fall into the heart of the sea, though its waters roar and foam and the mountains quake with their surging (Psalm 46:1-3 NIV).

Objective: To examine the relationship between our faith in God and how we deal with loss.

Discussion Questions

1. Donald E. Messer, in "Patches of Godlight," says how we imagine God makes a difference in how we deal with death and grief. How do you

picture God? What are some of the "patches of Godlight," spiritual bright spots, that he suggests help us in coping with loss? Share other "patches of Godlight" you have experienced that have been helpful in coping with loss.

2. Share your vision of the resurrection and life after death. How does your faith help you cope with grief? If the person who has died has a great deal of faith, how does that help you with your grief?

3. Karen Stone tells the story of her mother's death and remarks that she was able to cope with that loss because "we had the everlasting arms carrying us." In her essay, she writes about asking a nurse how people who do not have faith get through a death of a loved one. If you did not believe in God or an afterlife, how would you deal with the death of someone you loved? Discuss the ways that God helps both the dying person and those who mourn.

4. What passages in the Bible or hymns provide comfort and strength to you in times of sorrow? Share a favorite and how it has helped you.

5. When someone dies, we are also reminded of our own mortality. Why is this? Do you think the grieving process is a preparation for your own death? Why is it healthy to be aware of your own mortality?

6. In his essay, "A Soul-Size Exploration," Donald J. Shelby examines how we feel about God when a loved one dies. There is a point when we have a choice of turning to God or turning away from God in our grief. In what ways can death test us or undermine our faith? What makes some people turn to God for the same reason others turn away? Is it your faith in God or your attitude toward life, or both, that determines your reaction to a death? Can we blame God for a death?

7. Donna Schaper discusses how faith is an asset in grief. What did you learn from her about the relationship between faith and grief? Discuss the role that trust in God plays in recovering from grief. Are trust and faith the same? In what way is faith the opposite of certainty? List some of the spiritual assets mentioned by Schaper that are helpful in the grieving process.